OUR EMPIRE STORY

ALSO AVAILABLE FROM
LIVING BOOK PRESS

The Burgess Animal Book for Children (in color)
The Burgess Bird Book for Children (in color)
The Burgess Flower Book for Children (in color)

Our Island Story - H.E. Marshall (Color or B&W)
This Country of Ours - H.E. Marshall (Color or B&W)

Beautiful Stories of Shakespeare* - E. Nesbit (Color or B&W)
Tales from Shakespeare* - Lamb

Home Geography—C.C. Long
Elementary Geography—Charlotte Mason
Viking Tales—Jeannie
Parables From Nature*—Margaret Gatty
The Blue Fairy Book*
      * in AO reading order

Richard Halliburton's Marvels of the Orient
Richard Halliburton's Marvels of the Occident

Charlotte Mason's Home Education Series
1. Home Education
2. Parents and Children
3. School Education
4. Ourselves
5. Formation of Character
6. A Philosophy of Education

And many, many more!

All Living Book Press titles are complete and unabridged, and presented with the original illustrations, sometimes from several sources, to bring these great books even more to life.

To see a complete list of all our releases or if you wish to leave us any feedback please visit www.livingbookpress.com

Our Empire Story

H.E. MARSHALL

LIVING BOOK
PRESS

This edition published 2019
By Living Book Press
Copyright © Living Book Press, 2019

ISBN: 978-1-925729-81-8 (B&W Edition)
        978-1-925729-80-1 (Color Edition)

A catalogue record for this
book is available from the
National Library of Australia

ABOUT THIS BOOK

'The Empire upon which the sun never sets.' We all know these words, and we say them with a somewhat proud and grand air, for that vast Empire is ours. It belongs to us, and we to it. But although we are proud of our Empire it may be that some of us know little of its history. We only know it as it now is, and we forget perhaps that there was a time when it did not exist. We forget that it has grown to be great out of very small beginnings. We forget that it did not grow great all at once, but that with pluck and patience our fellow-countrymen built it up by little and by little, each leaving behind him a vaster inheritance than he found. So, ' lest we forget,' in this book I have told a few of the most exciting and interesting stories about the building up of this our great heritage and possession.

But we cannot

' Rise with the sun and ride with the same,
Until the next morning he rises again.'

We cannot in one day gird the whole world about, following the sun in his course, visiting with him all the many countries, all the scattered islands of the sea which form the mighty Empire upon which he never ceases to shine. No, it will take us many days to compass the journey, and little eyes would ache, little brains be weary long before the tale ended did I try to tell of all 'the far-away isles of home, where the old speech is native, and the old flag floats.' So in this book you will find stories of the five chief portions of our Empire only, that is of Canada, Australia, New Zealand, South Africa, and India. But perhaps some day, if you greet these stories as kindly as you have greeted those of England and of Scotland, I will tell you in another book more stories of Our Empire.

The stories are not all bright. How should they be? We have made mistakes, we have been checked here, we have stumbled there. We may own it without shame, perhaps almost without sorrow, and still love our Empire and its builders. Still we may say,

'Where shall the watchful sun,
England, my England,
Match the master-work you've done,
England, my own ?
When shall he rejoice agen
Such a breed of mighty men
As come forward, one to ten,
To the song on your bugles blown, England—
Down the years on your bugles blown?'

H. E. MARSHALL.
Oxford, 1908

CONTENTS

NEW ZEALAND

SOUTH AFRICA

INDIA

CANADA

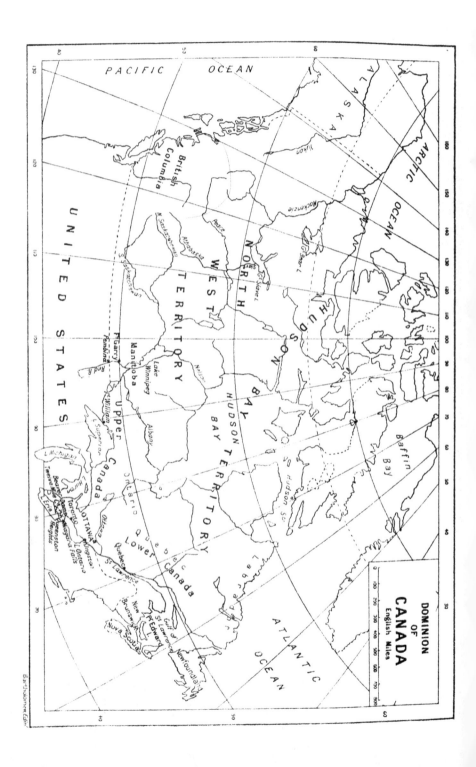

CHAPTER 1

HOW LIEF THE SON OF ERIC THE RED SAILED INTO THE WEST

MANY hundred years ago, Lief, the son of Eric the Red, stood upon the shores of Norway. His hair was fair and long, and his eyes as blue as the sea upon which he looked. And as he watched the sea-horses tossing their foam-manes, his heart longed to be out upon the wild waves.

For Bjarne the Traveller had come home. He had come from sailing far seas, and had brought back with him news of a strange, new land which lay far over the waves towards the setting of the sun. It was a land, he said, full of leafy woods and great tall trees such as had never been seen in Norway. Above a shore of white sand waved golden fields of corn. Beneath the summer breeze vast seas of shimmering grass bowed themselves, and all the air was scented with spice, and joyous with the song of birds.

"I will find this land," cried Lief Ericson, "I will find this land and call it mine."

All day long he paced the shore, thinking and longing, and when the shadows of evening fell he strode into his father's hall.

Eric the Red sat in his great chair, and Lief, his son, stood before him. The firelight gleamed upon the gold bands round his arms and was flashed back from his glittering armour. "Father," he cried, "give me a ship. I would sail beyond the seas to the goodly lands of which Bjarne the Traveller tells."

Then Eric the Red poured shining yellow gold into the hands of Lief, his son. "Go," he cried, "buy the ship of Bjarne and sail to the goodly lands of which he tells."

So Lief bought the ship of Bjarne the Traveller, and to him came four-and-thirty men, tall and strong and eager as he, to sail the seas to the new lands towards the setting sun.

Then Lief bent his knee before his father. "Come, you, O my father," he cried, "and be our leader."

But Eric the Red shook his head. "I am too old," he said. Yet his blue eyes looked wistfully out to sea. His old heart leaped at the thought that once again before he died he might feel his good ship bound beneath him, that once again it would answer to the helm under his hand as his horse to the rein.

"Nay, but come, my father," pleaded Lief, "you will bring good luck to our sailing."

"Ay, I will come," cried Eric the Red. Then rising, the old sea-king threw off his robe of state. Once again, as in days gone by, he clad himself in armour of steel and gold, and mounting upon his horse he rode to the shore.

As Eric neared the ship the warriors set up a shout of welcome. But even as they did so his horse stumbled and fell. The king was thrown to the ground. In vain he tried to rise. He had hurt his foot so badly that he could neither stand nor walk.

"Go, my son," said Eric sadly, "the gods will have it thus. It is not for me to discover new lands. You are young. Go, and bring me tidings of them."

So Lief and his men mounted into his ship and sailed out toward the West. Three weeks they sailed. All around them the blue waves tossed and foamed but no land did they see. At last, one morning, a thin grey line far to the west appeared like a pencil-streak across the blue. Hurrah, land was near! On they sailed, the shore ever growing clearer and clearer. At length there rose before them great snow-covered mountains, and all the land between the sea and the hills was a vast plain of snow.

"It shall not be said that we found no land," said Lief; "I will give this country a name." So they called it Hellaland.

Then on again they sailed. Again they came to land. This time it was covered with trees, and the long, low sloping shore was of pure white sand. They called it Markland, which means Woodland. Again they sailed on, until at length they came to a place where a great river flowed into the sea. There they made up their minds to stay for the winter.

So they cast anchor and left the ship and put up their tents upon the shore. Then they built a house of wood in which to live. In the river they found fish in great plenty, and in the plains grew wild corn. So they suffered neither from cold nor hunger.

When the great house was finished, Lief spoke: "I will divide my men into two bands," he said. "One band shall stay at home and guard the house. The other shall walk abroad and search through the land to discover what they may."

So it was done. Sometimes Lief stayed with the men at home. Sometimes he went abroad with those who explored.

Thus the Northmen passed the winter, finding many wonderful things in this strange new land. And when spring came they sailed homeward to tell the people there of all the marvels they had seen and all that they had done. Then the people wondered greatly. And Lief they called Lief the Fortunate.

Afterwards many people sailed from Greenland and from Norway to the fair new lands in the west. This land we now call North America, and the parts of it which Lief discovered and called Hellaland and Markland we now call Labrador and Nova Scotia. So it was that five hundred years before Columbus lived, America was known to these wild sea-kings of the north.

CHAPTER 2

WESTWARD! WESTWARD! WESTWARD!

MANY hundreds of years passed. Amid strife and warfare the wild Northmen forgot about the strange country far in the West which their forefathers had discovered. They heard of it only in the old, half-forgotten tales which the minstrels sometimes sang. They thought of it only as a fairy country—a land of nowhere.

Then there came a time when all the earth was filled with unrest. The world, men said, was round, not flat, as the learned ones of old had taught. Then, if the world was round, India might be reached by sailing west as easily as by sailing east. So brave and daring men stepped into their ships and sailed away toward the setting sun. They steered out into wide, unknown waters in search of a new way to lands of gold and spice.

Columbus, the great sailor of Genoa, sailed into the west, and returned with many a strange story of the countries which he had seen and claimed for the King of Spain. Then there came to England a sailor of Venice, called John Cabot. If the King of Spain might find and claim new lands, he asked, why not the King of England too?

So one fair May morning the little ship named the *Matthew* sailed out from Bristol harbour. Crowds of people came to see it as it spread its white wings and sped away and away into the unknown. Followed by the wishes and the prayers of many an anxious heart it glided on and on until it was but a speck in the distance, and the sailors turning their eyes backward, saw the land dwindle and fade to a thin grey streak and then vanish away. They were alone on the wide blue waters, steering they knew not whither.

To the West they sped, week by week. A month passed. Still there was no sign of land. Six weeks, seven weeks passed, still no land. Master John Cabot walked apart on the deck, his sailors looked askance at him. Would their faith hold out? he asked himself. How much longer would they sail thus into the unknown? These were days of danger and dread. For Master John well knew that the passion of man's heart and the madness of famine and despair, were more to be feared than the howl of the winds and the anger of the waves.

But at length one bright June morning there came a cry from the sailor on the outlook, "Land a-hoy." Master John Cabot was saved. He had reached at last the port of his golden hopes. They still sailed, the tide running gently and bearing them onward, and so on the 24th of June 1497 A.D., John Cabot landed on "New-found-land."

Where he landed he planted a cross with the arms of England carved upon it. The flag of England fluttered out to the sound of an English cheer as the brave sailor claimed the land for Henry VII., King of England and France, and lord of Ireland.

Cabot called the country St. John's Land, because he first came there on St. John's Day. The exact spot is not known, but it is thought to have been either at Cape Breton or at some point on the coast of Labrador.

After staying a little time, Cabot and his men set sail again, and turned their vessel homeward. The country that they had found seemed fertile and fruitful. But it was not the land of gold and spice, of gems and silken riches which they had hoped to find. So they returned with empty hands, and but little guessing upon what a vast continent they had planted the flag of England. They returned, little knowing that the people of England would carry that flag across the continent to the sea beyond, and that in days to come state should be added to state till the great Dominion of Canada was formed.

But although Cabot returned with empty hands, the King of England received him kindly. He was, however, "a king wise but not lavish." Indeed, he liked but little to spend his gold. So as a reward he gave Cabot £10. It does not seem much, even when we remember that £10 then was worth as much as £120 now. Still, Cabot had a good time with it. He dressed himself in silk and grandeur, and walked about the streets, followed by crowds who came to stare and wonder at the man who had found "a new isle." Later, the king gave Cabot £20 a year. Not much more is known about his life, but it is thought that he, with his son Sebastian, sailed again—perhaps more than once—to the "Isle beyond the Seas."

CABOT

Over the hazy distance,
Beyond the sunset's rim,
For ever and for ever
Those voices called to him,
Westward! westward! westward!
The sea sang in his head,
At morn in the busy harbour,
At nightfall in his bed—
Westward! westward! westward!
Over the line of breakers,
Out of the distance dim,
For ever the foam-white fingers
Beckoning—beckoning him.

All honour to this grand old Pilot,
Whose flag is struck, whose sails are furled,
Whose ship is beached, whose voyage ended;
Who sleeps somewhere in sod unknown,
Without a slab, without a stone,
In that great Island, sea-impearled.
Yea, reverence with honour blended,
For this old seaman of the past,
Who braved the leagues of ocean hurled,
Who out of danger knowledge rended,
And built the bastions, sure and fast,
Of that great bridge-way grand and vast,
Of golden commerce round the world.

Yea, he is dead, this mighty seaman!
Four long centuries ago.
Beating westward, ever westward,
Beating out from old Bristowe,
Far he saw in visions lifted,
Down the golden sunset's glow,
Through the bars of twilight rifted,
All the glories that we know.
Yea, he is dead; but who shall say
That all the splendid deeds he wrought,
That all the lofty truths he taught
(If truth be knowledge nobly sought)
Are dead and vanished quite away?

Greater than shaft or storied fane
Than bronze and marble blent,
Greater than all the honours he could gain
From a nation's high intent,
He sleeps alone, in his great isle, unknown,
With the chalk-cliffs all around him for his
        mighty graveyard stone,
And the league-long sounding roar
Of old ocean, for evermore
Beating, beating, about his rest,
For fane and monument.

                                    WILFRED CAMPBELL.

CHAPTER 3

HOW A BRETON SAILOR CAME TO CANADA

YEARS passed on. England did little more than plant her flag in the New World, as the lands beyond the seas came to be called. Now and again indeed the English tried to found colonies. But the settlers sickened and died, and the attempts failed. Sir Humphrey Gilbert, half-brother of the famous Raleigh, was among the gallant captains who sailed the seas and claimed strange lands in the name of the great Queen Elizabeth. He landed upon the shores of New-found-land—the island which is still called by that name to-day. There he set up the royal arms of England, and, with solemn ceremony, taking a handful of soil in his hand. Sir Humphrey declared the land to be the possession of Elizabeth, Queen by the Grace of God.

So Newfoundland became a British possession, and thus claims to be the oldest of all our colonies.

Meanwhile Spain and Portugal were busy gathering wealth and glory in the New World. But the King of France thought that he too should have a share. He sent a message to the King of Spain asking him if it was true that he and the King of Portugal meant to divide all the world between them without allowing him a share as a brother. "I would fain see in father Adam's will where he made you the sole heirs to so vast an inheritance," he added. "Until I do see that, I shall seize as mine whatever my good ships may happen to find upon the ocean."

So the French King sent men to explore America. And all that they explored he called New France, taking little heed to the fact that the flag of England had already been planted there.

Many daring men sailed forth with the French King's orders, but Jacques Cartier, a Breton sailor, is perhaps the most famous. He made four voyages to the New World, and brought back many wonderful tales of the things he had seen there. He told how he had met with wild and savage folk with dark skins. They painted their bodies in strange fashions, and their only clothes were the skins of beasts. Their black hair was drawn up on the top of the head and tied there like a wisp of hay, and decorated with bright feathers sticking out in all directions.

These men were the Red Indians of North America. They are not really Indians at all. But when the first people found America they thought that they had reached India by sailing west, and they called the natives Indians. We have called them so ever since.

Cartier told too of great beasts like oxen which had two teeth like the tusks of elephants and which went in the sea. Strange fish he saw, "of which it is not in the manner of man to have seen," some with the head of a greyhound and as white as snow, some that had the shape of horses and did go by day on land and by night in the sea.

Besides these tales of strange beasts and men, Cartier told of a fairy city of which he had heard. This city was called Norumbega. The Indians believed that somewhere beyond the rivers and the mountains it lay full of untold wealth and splendid with starry turrets and glittering gem-strewn streets. There the sun shone for ever golden, the air was sweet with the scent of richest spices through which rang, all day long, the song of birds. And when they heard of it, many left their homes and sailed away to seek this city of Delight. Cartier himself sailed many a league. He went where no white man had been before. But he never found the Golden City.

The wild people were not unfriendly. They looked in wonder at the strange men with pale faces who came to their country in winged boats. For although the Indians had canoes made of birch bark, in which they travelled up and down their rivers and great lakes, they had never before seen a boat with sails.

It was while Cartier was exploring that Canada received the name by which we know it.

"Cannata," said the Indians pointing to their village of huts.

Cartier thought that they meant that the country was called Cannata. So he called it Cannata or Canada. But the Indians had only meant to show the pale face their village, and the word in the Indian language really means a village.

Upon the shores of the Bay of Gaspe, where Cartier landed, he raised a great cross of thirty feet in height. To the cross-bar he nailed a shield on which were carved three *fleurs-de-lis*, the emblem of France. Above the shield, in large letters, were carved the words, "Long live the King of France." When the cross was planted in the ground Cartier and his men joined hands, and, kneeling round it in a circle, prayed. About them stood the astonished, wondering Indians. They were a little ill-pleased that these pale strangers should raise this unknown sign upon their land without leave. But they could not guess that in years to come, before the sign of the cross, before the foot of the white man, the red man should vanish away as snow before the sun.

Cartier was kind to the Indians. They grew to love him, and when, upon his second voyage, they heard that he meant to leave them and explore inland they were very sorry. Perhaps, too, they did not want any other Indians to have the beads and ribbons and pretty things which Cartier gave them in exchange for their furs. So they did all they could to prevent him from going. They even tried to frighten him. Three Indians dressed themselves as evil spirits. They painted their faces black, stuck great horns a yard long upon their heads, and covered themselves with black and white dogskins.

Then in a war canoe they came paddling down the river, howling dismally all the time. When they came in sight the other Indians began to shriek and howl too. They ran to Cartier and told him that these were spirits which had been sent by their god to warn him not to go up the river as he intended. "If you go, O Pale Face, fearful things will come upon you," they said. "Wind and storms, ice and snow, will bar your way. None will return alive. Our god will lead you into the spirit land."

But Cartier was not at all afraid. He laughed at the Indians. "Your god is powerless," he said. "My God is all powerful. He Himself has spoken to me, and He has promised to keep me safe through every danger."

So Cartier started on his journey and travelled up the river, now called the St. Lawrence, to an Indian village named Hochelaga. There he climbed a hill and looked around upon the fair country. As far as the eye could reach land rolled before him. Over dark forest and wild prairie, over lake and hill and valley swept his wondering gaze. He followed the grand and shining river, as it wound its way along, until it was lost in the dim distance. It was not indeed the fairy land of which he had heard, but it was very splendid. "It is Mount Royal," he said. And to-day it is still called Mount Royal, for that little Indian village has grown into the great city of Montreal.

When Cartier returned to France after his first voyage to Canada, he took with him two Red Indians, sons of a great Indian chief. This he did so that they might learn French and be able, on their return, to translate for him all that was said.

Many times Cartier sailed to Canada. With him he brought men and women, so that they might settle in the land, and making their homes there, form a New France over the seas. But few people wanted to leave their comfortable homes and go to live in a far and unknown land. So, to get men enough, Cartier was obliged to take them out of the prisons. As might have been expected, people who had been put in prison for their evil deeds did not make good colonists. They met besides with many troubles. They suffered from sickness, cold and hunger. Many of them died, and at last those who were left sailed back again to France. And so Cartier's attempt at making a colony ended.

> Awake, my country, the hour of dreams is done!
> Doubt not, nor dread the greatness of thy fate.
> Tho' faint souls fear the keen confronting sun,
> And fain would bid the morn of splendour wait;
> Tho' dreamers, rapt in starry visions, cry
> "Lo, yon thy future, yon thy faith, thy fame!"
> And stretch vain hands to stars, thy fame is nigh,
> Here in Canadian hearth, and home, and name,
> This name which yet shall grow

Till all the nations know
Us for a patriot people, heart and hand
Loyal to our native earth, our own Canadian land!

O strong hearts, guarding the birthright of our glory,
Worth your best blood the heritage that ye guard!
These mighty streams resplendent with our story,
These iron coasts by rage of seas unjarred,—
What fields of peace these bulwarks well secure!
What vales of plenty those calm floods supply!
Shall not our love this rough, sweet land make sure,
Her bounds preserve inviolate, though we die?
O strong hearts of the North,
Let flame your loyalty forth,
And put the craven and base to an open shame
Till earth shall know the Child of Nations by her name!

C. G. D. ROBERTS.

CHAPTER 4

THE STORY OF HENRY HUDSON

WHEN brave men first sailed across the broad Atlantic they had no thought of finding new lands. What they sought was a new way to the old and known land of India—a new way to the lands of spice and gold. When they reached America, many of those old sailors thought that they had reached India. But when the new land proved not to be India, they said, "These are but islands. Let us sail beyond them and still reach India."

Not until many voyages had been made, not until the white-winged ships had been turned back again and again from the rocky shores of America, were men convinced at last that these were no islands, but a vast continent which barred the way. Then the vision of a new way to India took another shape. Then began the quest for a narrow inlet or passage round or through the great continent. By sailing north-westward it was hoped to find a way which, leading through snow and ice, should at last bring men beneath the glowing sun of India. And thus began the famous quest for the North-West Passage. So it was that Englishmen, instead of making use of the lands which Cabot had found and claimed, almost forgot that claim and gave their lives and spent their gold trying still to find the new way to the land of sunshine.

Among the many brave men who sailed the seas in search of this passage we remember Henry Hudson, because he gave his name to a great inland sea in the north of America, and to the strait leading to it.

Hudson sailed four times to the land of snow. He, too, like Cartier, met with Red Indians. On one voyage he gave them presents of hatchets, spades, and stockings. When he returned next time he was very much amused to find that the Indians had hung the spades and hatchets round their necks as ornaments, and had made tobacco-pouches of the stockings. Amid much laughter the Englishmen put handles on the spades and shafts to the hatchets, and showed the simple savages their proper use by digging the ground and cutting down trees.

One story told about Hudson is interesting, because it is very like a story found in English history. Perhaps Hudson had read that story when he was a little boy.

It is said that once Hudson and his men landed. As usual, the Indians came about them, wondering at the great winged canoes and the pale faces of the men who had come in them. Hudson managed to make himself understood by the savages, and after a time he told them that he wanted some land as he would like to live there. The red men did not wish to give him any land. "Then give me as much as this bullock skin will enclose," said Hudson, throwing it down.

"Yes, you may have that," said the "Redskins grinning and laughing at the white man's jest.

Then Hudson and his men began to cut the skin round and round into a long rope no thicker than a child's finger, being careful always not to break the rope. When it was finished they spread it out in a great circle enclosing a large piece of land.

The Indians were very much astonished when they saw how clever the white men were. They did not know that it was in this same way that the Britons had been cheated by the Saxons, hundreds of years before.

On the 17th of April 1610 A.D., Hudson, in the good ship *Discovery*, sailed out from the Thames. He had started upon his last voyage from which he was never to return. Up to the north of Scotland steered the brave adventurers, then away to Greenland and the land of ice. When June came, and the birds were singing in the sunshine at home, these daring men were sailing a wintry sea where great ice-mountains floated.

These ice-mountains were a terrible danger, for suddenly one would overturn and plunge into the sea. Had the little ship been near, it would have been crushed beneath the falling mass and sunk in the icy waters. So the sailors tried to steer away from them. But ever thicker and faster they gathered around the ship.

With despair in his heart but keeping a brave face Hudson sailed on. But still thicker and thicker the cruel, white ice-mountains gathered. They were like a pack of hungry wolves eager to crush the frail little vessel between their angry jaws. At last the ship was so shut in that it could move no more.

Then there were murmurs loud and angry among the crew. Hudson came to them. In his heart he never expected to see home again. Still he kept a brave face and tried to encourage his men. He brought his map and showed them that they had sailed further into the land of ice and snow than any Englishman had done before. Was that not something of which to be proud?

"Now will ye go on or will ye turn back?" he asked.

"Would that we were at home, ay, anywhere if only out of this ice," they replied.

"Why has the master brought us to die like dogs in this Far North?"

"Had I a hundred pounds I would give ninety of them to be at home."

"But nay," said the carpenter, "had I a hundred pounds I would not give ten in such a cause. Rather would I keep my money, and by God's grace would bring myself and it safe home."

And so there was much useless talk and many angry words. But at length, leaving their grumbling, the men set to work to save the ship from the ice, and after much labour and time they cleared the ice-blocks and steered again into the open sea.

Then once more they sailed onward escaping many dangers, enduring many hardships. Sometimes they saw land, sometimes there was only the sea around them. They suffered from cold and hunger too. In the ship at starting there was only food enough for six months. Now eight months had passed, it was November, and they were far from home. Their hands and feet were frost-bitten. Many of them fell ill and could work no more.

Hudson did all he could. He took great care of the food which was left, and he offered rewards to any of the men who should kill beast, bird, or fish. For they could not hope to live to see home again unless that they found much wild game to help out their scanty store of food. At one time they caught many sea-fowl. At another they could only find moss and such poor plants as grew upon the snowy land. So the winter passed and spring came and their store of food grew less and less.

They were fierce, unruly men, those daring sailors, and now they greeted their master with dark and sullen looks. They were starving, and they believed that he had stores of food which he kept hidden from them. So to quiet them Hudson served out a fortnight's bread at one time. But this made matters no better. They were so hungry that they could not make it last. The terrible gnawing pain was such that one man ate his whole fortnight's allowance in a day.

Louder grew the murmurs, darker the looks with which the master was greeted. Men met and whispered together in dim corners. They would no longer wait, they would no longer suffer, and at last their wicked plans were made. As Hudson stepped on deck early one June morning, two men seized him, while a third pinned his arms behind. In a few minutes he was bound and helpless.

"Men," he cried, "what is this? What do you mean?"

"You will soon see," they replied," when you get into the boat."

Then looking over the side Hudson saw the ship's boat ready launched. He understood. These cruel men meant to turn him adrift on the icy waters.

But all were not against the master. One man who had a sword fought fiercely. But several of the mutineers threw themselves upon him and soon he too was bound. Another, the carpenter, had been kept prisoner below. Now he broke free and rushed on deck.

"Men," he cried, taking his stand beside the captain, "what are you doing? Do you all want to be hanged when you get home?"

"I care not," answered one; "of the two I would rather hang at home than starve abroad."

"Come, let be, you shall stay in the ship," said another.

"I will not stay unless you force me," boldly replied the carpenter as he faced the sullen, angry men. "I will rather take my fortune with my master."

"Go, then," they said, "we will not hinder you."

"THESE CRUEL MEN MEANT TO TURN HUDSON ADRIFT ON THE ICY WATERS."

Then the sick and the lame were dragged out of their cabins and thrust into the boat along with Hudson and his son who was but a boy of about sixteen. Only one of the sick they did not send away. He crawled to the cabin door, and there, on his knees, he prayed the mutineers to repent of what they were doing. "For the love of God," he cried, "do it not"

"Keep quiet," they answered, "get into your cabin. No one is harming you."

At last, nine wretched men were packed into the little boat. Then the ship moved out of the ice dragging it behind. As they sailed slowly along, Hudson and the other poor fellows were not without hope that the mutineers would relent and take them aboard again. But there was no chance of that. Even while Hudson was still upon the ship, some of the sailors had begun to break open the chests and rifle the stores. Now all law and order was at an end. They seized upon the food like hungry wolves. They sacked the ship as if it had been the fortress of an enemy. There was no thought of taking aboard again the master who had held them in check.

As they steered clear of the ice, a sailor leaned over the ship's side. He cut the rope which bound the little boat to the stern. Then they shook out their sails and fled as if from an enemy. Soon they vanished from sight, and the little boat was but a speck upon the cold grey waters.

That little boat was never seen again. What became of brave Hudson and his son, of the gallant carpenter who stood by him, and of all the poor sick men thus cast adrift upon the icy waters, will never be known. Let us hope that death came to them quickly, that the blue waves upon which Hudson had loved to sail were kind to him, and that soon he found a grave beneath them. Where he lies we cannot tell, but the great bay and strait which bear his name are a fitting monument for so gallant a sailor.

Of the mutineers few reached home. Some were killed in a fight with savages. Others died from hunger and cold. The sufferings of those who remained were terrible. They had at length little to eat but candles. One of them, who lived to come home and who told the tale afterwards, said that the bones of a fowl fried in candle-grease and eaten with vinegar made a very good dish.

At length the wretched men became so weak that they could no longer work the sails. Only one had strength to steer. They were but gaunt skeletons, haggard and pale, when their ship drifted to the coast of Ireland, and they at last reached home.

As soon as they arrived in England they were all put in prison. But they were soon set free again. Perhaps the sufferings through which they had passed had been punishment enough even for their ill deeds.

Our fathers died for England at the outposts of the world;
Our mothers toiled for England where the settlers' smoke upcurled;
By packet, steam, and rail,
By portage, trek, and trail,
They bore a thing called Honour in hearts that did not quail,
Till the twelve great winds of heaven saw the scarlet sign unfurled.

And little did they leave us of fame or land or gold;
Yet they gave us great possessions in a heritage untold;
For they said, "Ye shall be clean,
Nor ever false or mean,
For God and for your country and the honour of your queen,
Till ye meet the death that waits you with your plighted faith unsold.

"We have fought the long great battle of the liberty of man,
And only ask a goodly death uncraven in the van;
We have journeyed travel-worn
Through envy and through scorn,
And the faith that was within us we have stubbornly upborne,
For we saw the perfect structure behind the rough-hewn plan.

"We have toiled by land and river, we have laboured on the sea;
If our blindness made us blunder, our courage made us free.
We suffered or we throve,
We delved and fought and strove;
But born to the ideals of order, law, and love,
To our birthright we were loyal, and loyal shall ye be!"

O England, little mother by the sleepless northern tide,
Having bred so many nations to devotion, trust, and pride,
Very tenderly we turn
With willing hearts that yearn
Still to fence you and defend you, let the sons of men discern
Wherein our right and title, might and majesty, reside.

—BLISS CARMAN

CHAPTER 5

THE FATHER OF NEW FRANCE

WHILE Englishmen were seeking the North-West Passage, Frenchmen were working to found New France, for after Cartier, other men tried to found colonies in the lands beyond the seas. Each failed as Cartier had failed. But at last there came a man who was so determined and so brave that he succeeded in doing what others had not been able to do. This man was Samuel de Champlain, often called the Father of New France.

After the discovery of Newfoundland, sailors had been quick to find out what a splendid place it was for fishing. So men from all countries came to fish in the waters there. Others came to trade with the Indians for furs. But they all came and went again. None thought of making their home in that far-off land.

At length a Frenchman, seeing what a lot of money might be made out of furs, asked the King of France to allow him alone to have the fur trade. This is called a monopoly. Monopoly comes from two Greek words, monos, alone, and polein, to sell. So if you yet a monopoly of anything it means that you are the only person who is allowed to sell that thing to others.

The King of France said this Frenchman might have a monopoly of furs if he would found a colony in New France. To this he agreed, and set sail with some friends. All the other fur merchants of France were, however, very angry, because they knew that if only one man was allowed to buy furs from the Indians and sell them to the French, he would become very rich and they poor.

But the colony, which was now founded, did not succeed any better than those before it had done. It was not until Champlain and some other adventurers came to help that things went better. Champlain was a soldier-sailor. He was brave, and wise, and kind too— just the very best sort of man to treat with savages and found a colony.

Champlain did not at first go as a leader, but only to help two gentlemen called Poutrincourt and De Monts. Soon, however, it became plain that he was the real leader, and later he was made Governor of New France.

Champlain and his friends landed first in Acadie. That is the part of the Dominion of Canada which we now call Nova Scotia. On an island at the mouth of the river St. Croix they built their fort, and prepared to spend the winter. But they soon found that they had chosen a very bad place. It was cold and barren. There was neither wood for fires nor fresh water to drink. So after passing a winter of pain and trouble, during which many died, they went over to the mainland, and there built their fort anew. There the city of Annapolis now stands. Then the colonists called it Port Royal.

The new colony had a hard struggle. The second winter was almost as bad as the first. The settlers had eaten all the food which they had brought with them from France, and as the ships which they expected with more did not arrive, they began to starve. Then Champlain made up his mind to take all his people home to France. For he knew that it would be impossible to live through another winter without help. Two brave men offered to remain behind to take care of the fort until the others returned, and a friendly old Indian chief promised too to stay near.

So good-byes were said; the little ship sailed out of the bay, and the two brave men prepared to spend the long autumn and winter alone between the forest and the sea, far from any white man, and with only savages near.

But about nine days after Champlain had sailed, the old chief saw a white sail far out to sea. The two Frenchmen were at dinner and did not notice it. The old chief stood for a little time watching the white sail as it came nearer and nearer. Then, in great excitement, he ran shouting to the fort, "Why do you sit here?" he cried, bursting in upon the two men. "Why do you sit here and amuse yourselves eating, when a great ship with white wings is coming up the river?"

In much astonishment and some dread the two men sprang up. One seized his gun and ran to the shore. The other ran to the cannon of the fort. Both were ready to fight as best they might should the strangers prove to be enemies. Eagerly they watched as the ship came on. Was it friend or was it foe, they asked themselves. At last it was quite near. At last they could see the white flag of France, with its golden fleur-de-lis, floating from the mast. With fingers which trembled with joy, the man at the cannon put a match to the muzzle, and a roar of welcome awoke the echoes of the bay.

Right glad were the newcomers to hear it, for they had been anxiously watching the fort which seemed so silent and deserted, and with thunder of guns and blare of trumpets they joyously replied.

Soon the little fort was full of busy life again, and Champlain, who had not gone far on his journey, hearing that help had come, turned back to join his friends again.

Among the colonists who came in this ship was a lawyer from Paris, called Marc Lescarbot. He was very merry and gay. Always in good spirits himself, he kept others in good spirits too. After the newcomers had settled down, Champlain and some of the men sailed away to explore the country, leaving the others to take care of the fort. They worked hard, felling trees and digging the ground, cutting paths through the forest, and planting barley, wheat, and rye. But when work was done there was plenty of fun, for Lescarbot kept them merry. Among other things he prepared a play with which to greet the travellers when they came back.

Champlain returned somewhat weary and disheartened. He had not succeeded in exploring much further than before. The Indians had proved unfriendly, and several of his men had been killed by them. So with the coming of winter he turned back to Port Royal. They arrived there one gloomy November afternoon. But those who had been left behind were watching for them. As Champlain and his men drew near they saw that the whole fort was a blaze of lights.

Over the gateway hung the arms and motto of the King of France, wreathed with laurels. On either side hung those of De Monts and Poutrincourt, two of the leaders. The gate, as the travellers came near to it, opened, and out came no less a person than old Neptune, sitting upon a chariot drawn by Tritons. His hair and beard were long, a blue veil floated about him, and in his hand he held his trident, and so with music and poetry he welcomed the travellers from the sea.

After Neptune came a canoe, in which were four savages, each with a gift in his hand. These they presented, each in turn making a speech in poetry. Poutrincourt, who entered into the game at once, listened to Lord Neptune, his Tritons and savages with drawn sword in hand. Then after he had made a speech of thanks, the Tritons and savages burst into song, and the returned travellers passed beneath the wreathed gateway to the sound of trumpets and the roar of cannon.

Lescarbot wrote a history of New France in which he tells about all this. He gives there the poetry which was said and sung, not because it is very good poetry, he says, but because it shows that in that unknown country, far from friends and home, they were not sad.

Thus the long, cold winter began, but Lescarbot had many devices for making the dark, dreary days pass merrily. He formed all the chief men of the colony into an order which he called the Order of Good Times. Each member was Grand Master of the order for one day. It was his duty to see to the meals during that day. Each Grand Master tried to manage better than the one before. He would hunt and fish and invent all sorts of dainties, so it came about that there was always enough to eat, and plenty of change, and as a result there was not so much sickness nor so many deaths as there had been during the winters before.

The officers of the Order of Good Times did everything with great ceremony. When dinner-time came the Grand Master marched into the hall wearing his fine chain of office round his neck, a napkin over his shoulder, and a staff in his hand. He was followed by the Brethren, each carrying a dish which he placed upon the table. Then they all sat down to dine. At supper there was much the same ceremony. Then when it was over and the great wood fire burned and roared up the chimney, its flames dancing and flickering and making strange shadows upon the wall, songs were sung and stories were told. And in the circle which gathered round the glowing hearth, many a time a dark-skinned chieftain, gay in paint and feathers, might be seen sitting side by side with the French gentlemen-adventurers, who listened with delight to the quaint tales he told. Then the wine cup and the pipe went round, and when the last pipe was smoked, the last bowl empty, the Grand Master of the day, his duties done, would give up his chain of office to the Brother who should succeed him. And so with laughter and with song the dark days passed and spring came once more.

With spring came bad news. The monopoly had been withdrawn. The colony must be given up. Sad at heart, the colonists left their new home, which they had worked so hard to found, and went back to France.

CHAPTER 6

THE FOUNDING OF QUEBEC

THE little colony at Port Royal had to be given up, but in less than a year Champlain was back again. This time he did not go to Acadie but to the St. Lawrence. Up the great river he sailed, until he reached a place called, in the Indian language, Kebec, which means narrows. There, on 3rd July 1608 A.D., he landed. The first tree was felled upon that wild and unknown river bank, and on the rocky heights above, the foundations of the first house of the town of Quebec were dug. Once again a few brave, white men built their home, and settled down to live far from their friends, among the wild Indians.

The Red Indians were divided roughly into two great tribes, the Iroquois and the Algonquins. These two tribes hated each other bitterly and were nearly always at war. Both the Iroquois and the Algonquins were divided into clans or families, each clan having its own name. But in war they all took sides, either with the Iroquois or with the Algonquins. The Iroquois are sometimes called the Five Nations, from the five chief clans of which they were made up. They are also sometimes called the Long House from the shape of their huts.

The Red Indians were among the most fierce and cruel of all savages. After a battle they held wild orgies, at which the prisoners were tortured with dreadful cruelty, and which often ended with a sickening feast upon the dead bodies of the enemy. One of the horrible things they did was to scalp their enemies, that is, with their stone hatchets, called tomahawks, they would cut off part of the skin of the head with the hair upon it. The more scalps a warrior could gather the greater and braver was he thought. Often a chiefs cloak would be decorated with a fringe of the scalps which he had taken.

Before the Indians went to battle, they would paint their faces and bodies and often shave their heads, but the "scalp lock" was always left as a kind of challenge and defiance to the enemy.

Champlain was filled with two great ideas; to found a colony, by means of which the fur trade might be carried on, and to explore and claim for France the vast unknown regions of Canada. He saw that to do this he must be friendly with one or other of the tribes of Indians. The Algonquins had their homes along the St. Lawrence and around Quebec, so Champlain made friends with them, and promised to help them in their battles against the Iroquois. But Champlain did not know then, as he found out later, that the Iroquois were far stronger and more clever than the Algonquins.

About a year after the founding of Quebec, Champlain set out with the Algonquins to help them against their enemies, as he had promised. They travelled together, Champlain and two or three Frenchmen in a flat-bottomed boat and the Indians in their canoes, far up the River Richlieu and along the lake since called Lake Champlain. All went well for some time. Then one day the Red Men had a quarrel among themselves, and in hot anger more than half of them went home, leaving only about sixty braves to fight the enemy. These however went on, nothing daunted, every day coming nearer and nearer the country of the Iroquois. Then they travelled with great caution, paddling up the river during the night, and hiding in the forests the most of the day. At last one evening they saw a great crowd of canoes filled with savages coming towards them. These were Iroquois. Each side greeted the other with yells of hatred. They did not, however, begin to fight at once, but spent the night dancing, singing, and shouting insults at each other.

When day came Champlain and his few white men lay down in the bottom of the canoes to watch the savages land and begin the fight. Both sides advanced slowly, uttering their horrible war shout or scalp cry, "aw-oh-aw-oh-aw-o-o-o-o-h." But suddenly the ranks of the Algonquins opened, and Champlain with his loaded gun marched down the centre. The Iroquois, who had never before seen a white man, paused in fear and astonishment. Champlain took aim, fired, and two chiefs fell dead. Then the fear which took hold upon the savages was great indeed. What was this awful thunder and lightning which struck men dead in a moment? They knew not. Never before had they seen such magic. Champlain paused to reload, and one of his men fired. Again a savage fell dead. Then fear was turned into wild terror. The Red Men took to their heels and ran madly to the shelter of the forest, pursued by their shrieking, victorious enemies.

So ended the first battle between the French and the Indians. It was fought at a place called Ticonderoga, which means the meeting of the waters, and which afterwards became famous for another great battle.

The Algonquins took many prisoners, whom they treated with abominable cruelty. Champlain at last cried out in horror against it, and himself shot one prisoner dead, rather than see him tortured more.

To the French this battle was but the firing of a few shots. To the Iroquois it meant the beginning of a bitter hatred, a hatred which was never to be allowed to sleep. Ever after this day they were the enemies of the French and the friends of their old foes, the English.

CHAPTER 7

HOW A BOLD ANSWER SAVED QUEBEC

QUEBEC was founded, and for many years the little colony struggled on in the face of difficulties. There were many comings and goings between France and New France. Again and again Champlain crossed the sea to plead his cause with king and councillors, with merchant and with prince. But in spite of all his pains and trouble, New France grew but slowly, and after twenty years Quebec was still hardly more than a village.

Besides founding a colony, Champlain wished to make the wild Red Indians Christian. "To save a soul," he said, "is of more importance than to conquer a kingdom." So he brought priests and ministers from France, and tried to teach the heathen about Christ. But already Christian people had begun to quarrel among themselves about religion. They were divided into two parties. Those who kept to the old religion called Roman Catholics, those who followed the new were called Protestants. In France the Protestants were called Huguenots.

At first both Roman Catholics and Huguenots came to New France. But they hated each other. Even on board ship while they were sailing over the sea to teach the heathen to love each other, they would quarrel, and the quarrel often ended in a fight. Then the sailors would gather round to watch, some crying, "Down with the Huguenots," others, "Down with the Papists." The sailors thought that it was good fun, but it made Champlain sad. "I know not which was the bravest, or which hit hardest," he says, "but I leave you to think if it was very pleasant to behold."

On land things were not much better, and once, when a minister and a priest died at the same time, the sailors buried them in one grave "to see," they said, "whether being dead they would remain in peace, since they could so little agree whilst living."

At last, for several reasons, the King of France forbade any Huguenots to go to New France. This was a pity, for the Huguenots were good merchants, many of them were rich, and they would have been a great help to the new colony. Besides, the Huguenots were ready to go through much toil and to suffer many hardships for the sake of their religion. Had they been allowed to worship God in their own way in the new land, many would have gone there gladly, and the colony would have grown quickly. On the other hand the French Catholics had to be persuaded to go, as they were quite comfortable at home. So the colony grew slowly.

At this time the Stuart kings were ruling in Great Britain. They too, like the French king, tried to force all their people to be of one religion.

But the people would not be forced, so many of them sailed away over the sea to the New World in the hope of finding freedom. They found it too, for although the Stuart kings were despots at home, they allowed much freedom to the colonies, indeed they paid little attention to them. So it came about that the British colonies grew much faster than the French. And soon the British wanted all the land in North America, even Canada which the French claimed.

In the year 1628 France and Britain were at war. For the people in Quebec, the winter had been long and hard. Nearly all the food which the colonists had had was eaten, and Champlain was anxiously looking for more from home, when bad news reached him. He heard that British ships were sailing up the river seizing all the French ships they met. A farm upon which Quebec depended for food had been attacked and burned, and all the cattle carried off. This was bad news indeed. As soon as Champlain heard it he prepared for battle. Each man in the fort was given a post. Guns were loaded and the walls strengthened as well as might be. When evening fell every man was ready for the foe.

That night all was quiet, but next day a little boat flying a white flag was seen sailing up the river. It brought a letter from Captain Kirke, the leader of the British ships. Calling all his chief men together, Champlain read the letter aloud to them.

It was very polite. It told how Captain Kirke had been sent by the King of Great Britain to take possession of all the country of Canada. It told how he had already taken many ships, and how, knowing that there was but little food within the walls of Quebec, he had also destroyed the farm. "And in order that no vessel may reach you, I have made up my mind to stay here till the end of the season so that you may get no more food. Therefore see what you wish to do, if you intend to give up the settlement or not. For, God aiding, sooner or later I must have it. I would desire for your sake that it would be by courtesy rather than by force, to avoid blood which might be spilt on both sides.

"Send me word what you desire to do.
"Waiting your reply, I remain, gentlemen,
"Your affectionate servant,
"DAVID KIRKE."

What was to be done? Yield? There was but fifty pounds of powder in all the fort, and hardly any food. Seven ounces of peas was all that was served out to each man daily. Weak, pale and thin, the French could not hope to hold out against the British for more than a few hours. But their hearts were stout and strong. Not a man was willing to yield without a struggle.

"If Captain Kirke wants to see us near at hand," they said, "he had better come, and not threaten us from so far off."

Then Champlain sat down and wrote as bold and polite a letter as that he had received. "My fort is well furnished with food," he said. "It and we are in good condition to resist you. My soldiers and I would deserve severe punishment from God and man did we yield without a fight. We will await you from hour to hour, and when you come will try to show you that you have no claim to our fort. Upon which I remain, sir, Your affectionate servant,

"CHAMPLAIN."

The letter was sealed and sent, and each man stood to his post, ready to sell his life as dearly as might be. But boldness won the day. When Captain Kirke read the letter he sat gravely thinking. No man, it seemed to him, who was in great straits would have answered as Champlain had answered. He must have been deceived. He was not strong enough to risk a siege and perhaps a defeat. So up sails, and away sped handsome, swaggering Captain Kirke, down stream.

The brave hearts at Quebec waited hour by hour for death which did not come. And at last the good news, that the British had sailed away, was brought to them. They were saved.

CHAPTER 8

HOW THE UNION JACK WAS HOISTED UPON THE FORT OF ST. LOUIS

BY his boldness, Champlain had saved Quebec. But almost at once another misfortune fell upon the brave little garrison. As Kirke sailed down the river he met a fleet of ships bringing food, powder, shot, fresh soldiers and colonists to Quebec. These he attacked and after a desperate fight he captured every one of them. Some of the ships Kirke burned and sank, two he sent back to France with the new colonists who had just come from there, and the rest he carried in triumph to England.

Months went on. In those days news travelled but slowly. The little garrison at Quebec knew nothing of what had happened to their ships, and they waited in vain for the promised food from home. The men haunted the woods for roots and berries. They trapped wild animals and fished the river. But soon they had few hooks or lines left and their powder they dared hardly use for killing game. It was a terrible time. The little children in the fort cried with hunger, and their mothers had nothing to give them. At last the famine became so dreadful that some of the settlers left the fort and went to live among the wild Indians until help should come.

Then one July morning a ship came sailing up the river. A white flag, in sign of peace, floated from the mast. Champlain, as soon as he saw it, hoisted a white flag upon the fort too. The ship came to anchor. A little boat put off and made for the shore. A young British officer sprang to land and asked to be led to Governor Champlain. He was the bearer of a letter from Kirke's two brothers, Louis and Thomas.

"Sir," said this letter, "our brother told you last year that sooner or later he would have Quebec. He has charged us to assure you of his friendship as we do of ours. Knowing very well the extreme need in which you are, he desires that you shall surrender the fort to us. We assure you that you will receive every courtesy from us, and honourable terms."

The state of the garrison was desperate. Yet Champlain would not give in without a struggle. So he sent a priest to talk to Louis and Thomas Kirke. But nothing he could say would move the swaggering, reckless British sailors.

"If Champlain gives up the keys of the fortress," said Louis, "we will treat you well and send you all home to France. If he will not give them up peaceably we will take them by force."

"Give us fifteen days' grace then," begged the priest.

"No."

"Eight days."

"No sir, not a day. I know well your miserable condition. You are all starving. Your people have gone to gather roots in the forest lest you die of hunger."

"Still give us a few days," begged the priest.

"No, no," said Thomas, "yield the fort or I shall ruin it with my cannon."

"I want to sleep within it to-night," said Louis, "and if I do not I shall waste the whole country round."

"Have a care," said the priest proudly. "You deceive yourselves if you think that you can win the fort so easily. There are a hundred men within it well armed and ready to sell their lives as dearly as may be. You may not conquer so easily. You may find defeat and death instead of victory. Once more I warn you. Be careful."

Once again, as a year before, bold words had an effect. Thomas and Louis Kirke hesitated. Could it really be as the priest said? Was the garrison still so strong? They were doubtful what to do, so they asked the priest to go aside a little while they talked to their officers. These all agreed that Champlain must be made to give in at once. "Let him have three hours in which to make up his mind," they said.

So the priest returned to the fort with this sad news. Champlain now saw that it was useless to hold out any longer. Indeed it was worse than useless, for if he yielded without firing a shot the Kirkes had promised that every man should be spared, but if they resisted they need hope for no mercy. Champlain had only fifty men and they were weak and ill. There was not ten pounds of flour left in the fort and hardly any gun powder. To fight would only mean the throwing away of life. So he decided to yield.

But the people were angry. They still believed that they could fight the British. "Even if we lose the fort," they said, "let us show them that we have courage."

"How can you be so foolish?" replied Champlain. "Are you tired of living? We cannot hope to win. We have no food, no powder or shot, and no hope of getting any. Would you throw your lives away?"

Truly, how could the strongest fort hold out when in its walls there were neither soldiers, shot, nor food?

When at last the bitter talk, this way and that, was over, it was evening, so no more could be done that night. The worn-out garrison spent a last sad night within the fort. The British lay in their ship opposite. Next morning Champlain stepped on board the waiting vessel. There he gave up the keys and signed away his right to the town which he had founded, and cherished, and loved. So without the firing of a shot Quebec became a British possession. The *fleur-de-lis* of France was hauled down from the Fort St. Louis, as the house which Champlain had built for himself was called, and in its place floated the Union Jack.

This is called the first siege of Quebec, although it was really no siege, for not a shot was fired.

In their own rough way the conquerors treated Champlain with courtesy. They made a list of all that was found in the fort and gave Champlain a receipt for it. "As for a list of provisions," said Kirke, with grim humour, "we will not need to waste paper and ink upon it. I am not sorry, for it is a great pleasure to us to give you all that you need."

"I thank you," said Champlain bitterly, "but you make us pay dearly for it."

Some of the Frenchmen went back to France, others chose to remain with their new masters. Louis Kirke took possession of Quebec and Thomas sailed triumphantly homeward with the spoils of war. But his triumph was short-lived, for as he landed, he was greeted with the news that in April peace between France and Great Britain had been signed. Quebec had been taken in July. It must therefore be handed back to France, as it had been taken unlawfully when the two countries were at peace.

But Charles I. did not lightly let go what he had seized. He was bland and courteous, promised much and delayed much. Meanwhile the British kept possession of Quebec and of Canadian fur trade. Not until three years had come and gone did Champlain once more land upon the shores of his beloved New France as governor. He was then sixty-six years old. As a soldier, as a sailor, as a traveller and explorer, he had suffered all the hardships of life. He had endured bitter cold, scorching heat, wounds and famine, but, in spite of all, he was as eager as ever to fight and labour for New France.

If Champlain was glad to return, his people were no less glad to receive him. Frenchmen and Indian alike joined to welcome him home. As the grey-haired governor stepped on shore the air was rent with cheers. Then with drums beating and colours flying they led him up the steep and winding pathway to his old fort of St. Louis. There once more he received the keys which three years before he had given up with so much bitterness of heart.

Three years later, after nearly thirty years of labour and hardship, Champlain died. He died as he would have wished, in the service of his country, still Governor of New France.

CHAPTER 9

THE FEAST OF EAT-EVERYTHING

AFTER Champlain came many rulers. Some of them were strong and brave, others were weak and foolish. All of them had to fight against their deadly enemies the Iroquois; and for many years the story of New France was one of suffering and terror. The hate of the Red Man never rested, and time after time he fell upon the French with savage strength. He swept through the land, leaving behind him a memory of blood and torture.

When the whites first came to Canada, the Indians were as wild and ignorant as our forefathers had been when the Romans first landed upon the shores of Britain. In some ways, indeed, the Red Man was more savage, for the Britons in that far-off time had swords of iron and copper. The Red Man knew nothing of metals. His tomahawk was of stone, the head being fastened to a wooden handle by thongs of leather. His arrow heads were of flint. His greatest treasure was "wampum," that is, beads made of shells. These beads were used for making belts, and a belt of wampum was the grandest present which an Indian could give to any one.

The Indian soon found out that for a few skins he could buy shining steel axes and long, keen knives from the Pale faces. For many skins he could buy the magic sticks which spoke death at great distance. And the Red Man was clever. He learned quickly. Soon he was as good a shot as the white man. Then the rattle and bang of firearms was added to the war-cry of the Indians, and the wonder is that the few white men were not swept from the face of Canada. Indeed, it seemed at times as if it was not the courage of soldiers and settlers, but of the priests, which kept them from being utterly blotted out. Champlain was a very religious man, and many priests had come with him, until Canada had seemed more of a mission than a settlement. The early story of Canada is full of the brave deeds of the "black robes," as the Indians called the priests.

In 1642 Montreal was founded at the place which, A hundred years before, Cartier had called Mount Royal. It was founded, not by traders, but by men with the zeal of saints and the spirit of martyrs. It was founded by men eager to carry the news of the story of Christ to the wild heathen, and both ready and eager to die for the Cross. Some of these brave priests went far into the country, among the tribe called the Hurons, teaching them to be Christian. For many years they lived and worked among them. But the Iroquois, who were the deadly enemies of French and Hurons alike, waged war against these missions. They ravaged and slew, burned and tortured, until the Hurons as a nation were utterly destroyed. The few who remained fled, seeking shelter now with one tribe now with another. But wherever they fled the Iroquois followed, and at last by famine and war, the race was blotted out.

Many of the brave priests found the death of martyrs. Those who were left returned sadly to Quebec, taking with them a few remaining Huron converts. They had worked hard and endured much; and at the end of fifteen years they had nothing to show for all their suffering and struggle.

The Iroquois were fierce, and strong, and treacherous. They cared not what means they used, so long as their enemies were tortured and killed. Now one of the Five Nations pretended that they would be pleased if some of the "black robes" would come to live among them, and teach them as they had taught the Hurons. The French could hardly believe that these fierce enemies really wanted to be taught. But they were glad at the thought of peace, and about fifty brave men, ten only of whom were soldiers, resolved to go and live among the Iroquois.

They were received with much joy. The savages danced and feasted, smoked the pipe of peace, sang songs, and made speeches, and pretended to be so glad that one of the priests said, "If after this they murder us, it will be from changeableness and not from treachery." But he little knew the blackness of the Iroquois heart.

Soon the forest rang with the sound of axe and hammer as the Frenchmen, priest and soldier alike, worked side by side to build their new homes. Meanwhile another of the Five Nations heard what the French priests had done, and they were angry and jealous. In their anger they took to their war-canoes, and paddling down the St. Lawrence to the Isle of Orleans they attacked, killed, and took prisoner, the helpless Hurons who were now living there. Before the town of Quebec the whole river was black with canoes filled with naked savages, howling, dancing, and singing. And as they howled and yelled they taunted the governor, making a great show of their prisoners, who were the white men's friends. And the governor, who was weak and fearful, dared do nothing. He dared not fire a shot to protect his red-skinned friends, lest their savage foes should revenge themselves by attacking the brave priests who had gone to live among the Iroquois. At last, tired of insulting the helpless Frenchmen, and full of scorn and contempt for the white man, the Indians paddled away up the river with their prisoners.

Days and weeks went past; the priests who had gone to live among the Iroquois taught, and worked, and prayed. In the great forest this handful of white men lived alone among the prowling savages, "who came like foxes, fought like lions, and disappeared like birds"—but in their faith they had no fear.

At length, however, dark whispers of treachery came to them. Friendly Indians warned them that the chiefs had met in council, and had vowed to kill them all. The black robes found it hard to believe that the men who treated them with such smiling kindness meant to kill them. But they were not left long in doubt, for a dying Indian, repenting of his treachery, told them all the plot. Every man was to be killed before the spring.

The Frenchmen now knew that they must escape, and that quickly. But how? All day long the Indians strolled about, following their every step, watching their every movement, in make-believe friendliness. At night they slept around the gate of the mission, ready to spring awake at the slightest sound. To try to escape through the forest was impossible. There was but one hope, and that was to cross the lake near which the mission was built and sail down the river to Montreal. But to do this they needed boats, and they had only eight canoes, which were not nearly enough to carry them all.

The Frenchmen were desperate but not hopeless. Over the mission-house there was a large loft. There the Indians seldom came, and there the priests began in secret to build two large boats. They were soon ready. The next thing was to find, or make, a chance to use them.

Among the Frenchmen was a young man of whom the Indian chief had become very fond. One morning he went to the chief pretending to be in great trouble. "I have had a dream, my father," he said. "It has been shown to me by the Great Spirit that I shall certainly die. Nothing can save me but a magic feast."

The Indians believed very much in dreams. They thought that those who did not do as they told them would be sorely punished. So the chief at once replied: "Thou art my son. Thou shalt not die. We shall have a feast, and we shall eat every morsel."

These magic feasts were called Feasts-of-eat-everything. At them each guest was bound to eat all that was set before him. No matter how much he had eaten, no matter how ill he felt, he was bound to go on until the person whose feast it was said he might stop.

As soon as the day was fixed the priests set to work with right good will to make a great feast. They killed their pigs, they brought the nicest things out of their stores, they concocted the most tempting dishes. But the chief thing they thought of was to have a great quantity.

The evening came. Great fires were lit around the mission-house. About them the Indians gathered. First there were games, dances, and songs. One game was to see who should make the most noise by screaming and yelling. The Frenchmen gave a prize to whoever could yell loudest, so that the savages exhausted themselves trying to win the prize. At last, wearied with their efforts, they all sat down in a circle. Great steaming pots were brought from the fires, and each man's wooden basin was filled. As soon as they were empty they were filled again and yet again. The Indians were hungry, and they ate greedily. While they gorged the Frenchmen beat drums, blew trumpets, and sang songs, making as much noise as they could. This they did to cover any strange sound that might come from the shade of the forest to the sharp ears of the savages. For in the darkness, beyond the glare of the firelight, a few white men were straining every muscle to carry the heavy boats unseen and unheard to the lake. With beating hearts and held breath, now stopping fearfully, now hurrying onward, they reached the lake. The boats safely launched.

The hours went on, and still the feast did not end. The gorged savages could eat no more. "Is it not enough?" they cried. "Have pity on us and let us rest."

"Nay," replied the young Frenchman, "you must eat everything. Would you see me die?"

And although the Indians meant to kill him, perhaps the very next day, they still ate on, for this was a magic feast. It had been ordered in a dream by the Great Spirit whom they must obey. Making strange faces, rolling their eyes wildly, choking, gulping, they ate till they could not move.

"That will do," said the young man at last. "You have saved my life. Now you may sleep. And do not rise early to-morrow. Rest till we come to waken you for prayers. Now we will play sweet music to send you to sleep."

Stupid with over-eating, dazed with drink, the savages slept. For a little time one of the Frenchmen played softly on a guitar. Soon loud snores told him that there was no more need of his music, and he crept silently to the boats. Meantime the priests had fastened the doors and windows of the mission-house, and locked the gate in the high fence which surrounded it. Then one by one they glided stealthily to the boats, until the last man was safe aboard.

It was March and still very cold, and now snow began to fall so that their footprints were covered over.

The lake was still lightly frozen over, and as the first boat pushed off men leaned from the bow and broke the ice with hatchets. The rowers pulled with all their strength, forcing the boat through the shattered ice. The second boat followed in its track. Last of all came the canoes. Thus they crossed the lake, and reaching the river were soon carried swiftly down stream. On and on they went through the dark night, fleeing from death, and torture worse than death. When the sun rose, shedding pale wintry gleams on dark forest and swift-flowing stream, they were far away.

All through the night the Indians slept their sleep of gluttony. When late in the morning they awoke they still felt dull and stupid. But at last arousing themselves they found that all around was still and silent. No sound came from the mission-house, no smoke rose from its chimney. What could it mean?

Full of curiosity the Indians pressed their faces against the fence, trying to see through the cracks in the wood. There was nothing to see. A dog barked in the house, a cock crew in the yard. All else was still.

At last, impatient to know what was happening within, the Indians climbed the fence, burst open the door, and entered the house. It was empty.

Great was the anger of the savages, greater still their astonishment. How could the Black Robes have escaped? they asked themselves. They had no boats, so they could not escape by water. There was no trace of them on land so they had not escaped by the forest. There was only one explanation. This was the work of the Great Spirit. The Black Robes and their followers had flown away through the air during the night. And with this thought, fear fell upon the heart of the Red Man.

Meanwhile the Black Robes were speeding on their way down the river. On and on they went, hardly pausing for rest, until a month later they reached Quebec. They were saved, but the mission had been an utter failure.

CHAPTER 10

A KNIGHT OF NEW FRANCE

"Where a northern river charges
By a wild and moonlit glade,
From the murky forest marges,
Round a broken palisade,
I can see the red man leaping,
See the sword of Daulac sweeping,
And the ghostly forms of heroes
Fall and fade."
A. LAMPMAN.

THE Red Terror grew and spread. There seemed no hope of taming the savage, no safety for the white man but within stone walls. At last the Iroquois began to gather in force, swearing to sweep through Canada and utterly crush their enemies.

Then it was that a little band of seventeen brave men went out to fight the savages. They were headed by a young French noble of twenty-five, named Adam Daulac.

In olden days, when knights rode forth against fell giants and awful beasts, they spent the night in some quiet church, kneeling in prayer. So now these brave men who knew that they were going to certain death, knelt for the last time in the little wooden church of Montreal, confessed their sins and received the holy sacrament. Then, after a solemn farewell, with the prayers and blessings of the people ringing in their ears, they rowed slowly up the river and passed from sight. They were knights, as true and fearless as ever laid lance in rest.

Up the stream they rowed, beneath the bending branches of dark and ancient trees, through wild and almost unknown regions, until they came to a ruined and deserted Indian fort. Here they resolved to await the foe, and here they were joined by some thirty friendly Indians.

They had not long to wait. Soon a whole fleet of war canoes, filled with two hundred yelling savages, came leaping down the rapids. The Frenchmen had not expected the enemy so soon. They were taken by surprise, and were outside the fort, cooking their dinner by some fires which they had just lit. So suddenly had the savages come upon them that they had no time even to seize their pots and kettles, but were obliged to leave them behind and run for the fort.

The Indians expected an easy victory, but from behind their ruinous fort the Frenchmen met them with such a steady fire, that the savages fell back in confusion.

The Indians then began to build a fort opposite the French camp. While they were busy with this, the Frenchmen strengthened and repaired their own fort. They heightened the wooden palings and strengthened them with earth and stones, leaving loopholes all round through which to fire upon the enemy. But before the work was finished the Indians were upon them again.

Calmly the Frenchmen awaited the attack. At the word of command their guns rang out. Every shot told, many a savage warrior fell dead, and, seized with a nameless terror, the others fled. But again and again they rallied, again and again they returned to the attack, answering the cannonade of the Frenchmen with a hail of bullets. Then seeing that in spite of all their efforts they could not take the fort by storm, they made up their minds to burn it. With yells of savage glee they seized upon the Frenchmen's boats, smashing them to pieces before their eyes. Of the splintered fragments they made torches, and each man carrying a flaring, smoking light, they rushed to the wooden walls of the fort. But the fire of the Frenchmen was so sharp, their aim so true and deadly, that not a savage got near enough the fort to set it on fire.

The fight went on. At length the savage chief was shot. Then fury of revenge and desire of blood maddened the Iroquois. Night and day they howled and yelled around the little fort. Night and day the Frenchmen fought and prayed by turns. Worn by want of sleep, tortured by hunger and thirst, shivering with cold they still fought on. They had nothing to eat but a coarse kind of meal made from Indian corn. They had nothing at all to drink. With blackened tongues and dry, parched throats it became impossible to swallow the meal. Frantic with thirst, a few made a rush for the river. For two hundred yards they ran through the spattering fire of the enemy. They risked death for a few drops of water. For their big kettles and pans had all fallen into the hands of the savages, and they had only cups in which to carry the water, and what they brought back was scarcely enough to wet the lips of the gasping garrison.

For seven days the terrible fight lasted. The Frenchmen's supply of shot was growing smaller and smaller. They knew that they could not hold out much longer. The friendly Indians grew weary of the struggle, and they leapt over the wall and fled to join the enemy. So the seventeen Frenchmen were left with only five Indians to help them against hundreds.

On the seventh day of the siege the air rang with cries more loud and savage than before, and the earth, and river, and sky, seemed to tremble with the echo and re-echo of gun shots. Five hundred more savages had arrived and their war-cries mingled with the shouts of welcome from their friends.

Armed with new courage, the whole force of nearly seven hundred savages rushed to the attack. But every loophole of the fort belched forth fire, and many a Redskin fell. Half dead though they were with want and weariness, the Frenchmen still fought fiercely. Three more days passed; days of prayer and agony within the fort, while without, thrown back again and again by the steady fire, the dark savages surged and yelled.

At last the Indians made a yet more determined assault. Protected by huge wooden shields, which covered them from head to heel, they rushed upon the fort with axe and firebrand. In spite of the Frenchmen's fire, the savages were able now to reach the walls. There they hacked and burned trying to make an entrance.

The case of the defenders was now desperate. Daulac then made a bomb by setting a slow match to a small barrel of gunpowder. This he tried to throw over the wall, hoping that it would explode among the Indians. But the Frenchmen were weak with famine and weariness. They could not throw the barrel high enough. It caught upon the top of the wall, and rolling back, burst within the fort, wounding many and blinding others, so that for a few minutes they could not see to fight.

In the confusion which followed, more Indians crowded to the walls, and they gained possession of the loopholes. One moment showed their savage, triumphant faces in the openings, the next the shining barrels of their guns gleamed there, and a hot rain of bullets showered upon the Frenchmen. Shut within the encircling walls, there was little for them but to die.

A moment later the men, who had been hacking at the walls, succeeded in making a breach. Indians poured through it, others scrambled over. On all sides the Frenchmen were surrounded. Dearly they sold their lives. Muskets were thrown aside, with sword in one hand and knife in the other they fought the yelling fiends, till the dead lay thick about them. At length the ghastly fight was over, and the last white man fell dead upon the heaps of slain. Thus fighting against fearful odds, died valiant Daulac and his brave followers. Nor did these gallant Frenchmen die in vain. It was a splendid defeat, far more glorious than many a victory. It saved their fellow-countrymen in Canada. "If seventeen white men behind a wooden fence can hold seven hundred warriors at bay, what will they not do behind stone walls?" the Indians asked. And so, cowed for the time, they turned homewards to mourn their dead and await a day of revenge.

CHAPTER 11

THE BEGINNING OF THE HUDSON BAY COMPANY

AFTER Henry Hudson, many English explorers sailed for Hudson's Bay seeking the North-West Passage. They suffered much and learned little. Then, as if weary with the cruel struggle with ice and snow, these bold adventurers ceased their voyages for a time, and not for forty years did a British ship steer its way among the icebergs of the great inland sea. Then again adventurers sailed to the Far North. But this time they came not to explore, but to trade.

Prince Rupert, the dashing cousin of King Charles II., helped to fit out the expedition, and himself became the governor of the new land which was now claimed by the British. And this land was called after him Prince Rupert Land.

The adventurers received a charter or writing from King Charles, giving them leave to trade and found colonies wherever they would around the shores of Hudson Bay. The company was called the "Honourable Company of Adventurers of England trading into Hudson's Bay," and later it became famous as the Hudson Bay Company.

Soon a British fort was built upon the barren shore, and the red flag of St. George fluttered out in the lonely waste. But the French were ill pleased that any man should set foot in the land they wished to own. So the next year the French king sent a gentleman named De Lusson to take possession of the great North-West. This gentleman did not trouble to go to the North-West, but upon a hill at the Saulte St. Marie, where the three great lakes meet, he held a solemn ceremony.

Here many tribes of Indians were gathered together hideous with paint of various colours, bedecked with feathers and wampum. They were feasted, they danced and played games and smoked the pipe of peace. And at last one sunny day in June they climbed the hill, and upon the top, with much pomp and little understanding what it meant, set their names to a paper. In this paper the great White King claimed the whole of North America from the Arctic Ocean to the Gulf of Mexico, and from the coast of Labrador as far west as land might be, for then the west was but a pathless wilderness, no man knowing how far it might reach.

It was a wild and strange scene. Gay Frenchmen in bright uniforms, priests in rich robes, half-naked savages gaudy in paint and feathers, all were there. When the paper was signed, a great cross blessed by the priests was raised, and planted near it was a post carved with the lilies of France. Then kneeling around the cross with bowed bare heads, the Frenchmen sang a Latin hymn—

"The banners of Heaven's King advance;
The mystery of the Cross shines forth."

Prayers were said. Then with drawn sword in one hand, and a sod of earth in the other, De Lusson claimed all the countries, rivers, and streams, both those which were discovered and those which at any time might be discovered, for his most Christian Majesty, the King of France. And as he ceased, the silence was broken, the air rang with cries of God save the King, mingled with the roar of gunshot and the savage yells of Indians.

A priest then spoke to the Red Men. He told them that powerful though their chiefs might be, they were as nought to the great White King, whose riches were untold, who walked in the blood of his enemies, and who had slain so many in battle that no man might number them. This he told them to strike awe into their hearts, and greatly marvelling at the power of this fearful unknown white lord, the Red Men scattered to their homes again, uttering wild yells or grunting hoarsely as they went.

So once more France and Britain clashed, and France claimed what Britain had taken. Still for some years the Company built forts, traded with the Indians, and grew rich, undisturbed by the French. Then the French too formed a fur-trading company called the Company of the North, and trouble began. Again and again the British forts were attacked and destroyed. Again and again with dogged courage the British returned to them, and rebuilt them.

Even when they were not fighting, the French did all they could to prevent the Red Men trading with the British. But the Red Men soon found out that the British gave them more in exchange for their furs than the French, and so, of course, were glad to trade with them.

Nowadays, if we wish to buy anything, we must give money for it. But to a savage, money is of no use, for he has no shops to which he may go to buy things. So in exchange for furs the traders gave the Redskins tobacco, guns, beads, hatchets, gay clothes, and blankets. During the winter the savages would hunt and trap the wild animals and gather great stores of skins, then when spring came, and the frozen rivers melted, they would load their bark canoes and paddle away to the Company's forts. They had often to travel hundreds of miles, and the journey was full of difficulties and dangers. In those days, through the wilderness of the Far North, there were no roads at all. The rivers and lakes were the only highways. But upon the rivers there were rapids where the waters rushed in white foam over the river bed. So clever were the Indians in managing their canoes that sometimes they could shoot these rapids, that is row over them. But at other times, when the rapids were more dangerous, they would land, unload their canoes, and carry them and their goods along the river banks, and launch again in the smooth water below the rapids. This was called making a portage. Portage comes from the French word porter, to carry. Sometimes, too, when a river no longer flowed in the direction in which the traveller wished to go, he would unload and carry his canoe over the portage to another river which did flow in the right direction, and there launch anew. Sometimes a portage might only be a few yards, sometimes it was several miles.

Often the difficulties of travelling were so great that the Indians, worn with hunger and fatigue, became too weak to carry their loads. Then, before they reached the trading fort, they would throw away many of the skins which they had gathered with such skill and care during the winter months, thus losing the reward they had hoped to gain for their labour.

But the fort at last reached, all difficulties and dangers of the journey were forgotten. With shouts and firing of guns the Indians landed. Leaving the women to unload the canoes and do the other hard work, the chiefs marched to the fort. There they were received by the white men, and sat in state, while pipes were passed round the circle. Then followed days of drinking and feasting, sometimes of fighting too. For the Redskin, alas! loved the "fire water" of the white man, and when the heat of it warmed his blood, he cared not what he did.

At length came the great day. Dressed in a red coat trimmed with cheap lace, brave in many coloured stockings and feathered hat, the chief and his warriors gathered to smoke the pipe of peace. Its long stem was decorated with bears' and eagles' claws, and bright with feathers, and as it passed around the circle each took a whiff. Then when the tobacco burned low in the bowl, speech began. With much flowery talk, and many flowing words, the furs were exchanged for tobacco and guns. It was a long business, but at length the barter was done. Then the Redskins paddled away again, once more leaving the fort to its wonted stillness, and the traders to pack and store the furs ready to be sent off when the next ship from home should arrive.

Such were the beginnings of the great company which for a time ruled a large territory, and which still exists to this day. It was no easy or safe life, for the French looked upon the whole land as their own. Again and again they attacked the company's posts and swept them away. Again and again the British returned, strengthened their outposts, and pushed their conquests farther and farther into the wilds. At last they gained such a firm footing that neither the rage of the Frenchmen, nor the wiles of the Indian, could dislodge them.

CHAPTER 12

THE ADVENTURES OF LA SALLE

FOR a long time Canada was under the rule of fur-traders and companies, and it did not prosper well. The whole people did not number two thousand. Most of those lived in Quebec, Montreal, and Three Rivers, and in the forts, scattered and few, stretching inland along the banks of the river St. Lawrence to the great lakes. But in 1663 Canada was made a crown colony, and King Louis XIV. took the ruling into his own hands.

Canada was now ruled by a Governor, a Bishop, and a third man called an Intendant. One of the Intendant's chief duties was to look after the money and see that it was properly spent. In a different way he was quite as powerful as the Governor, and the Bishop also had great power.

The Sieur de Courcelle was the first governor under the new arrangement. And now, from having utterly neglected the colony, the king began to take a great interest in it. With Courcelles came the Marquis de Tracy, the Viceroy of all King Louis' western colonies and possessions, in order that be might see for himself what the land of New France was like. He brought with him a famous regiment of soldiers called the Carignan-Callieres, from the names of two of their leaders. They were the first real soldiers that had ever come to Canada. Besides the soldiers, the marquess brought many settlers and a great train of servants and courtiers.

In a day the population of Canada was doubled. Fresh life seemed to have been poured into the colony. The towns were gay with courtiers in ribbons, lace, and feathers, through the trackless woods marched the brightly-clad soldiers of the line. But though they seemed gorgeous as peacocks, they were brave as lions. Soon the pride of the Iroquois was humbled. The white man was no longer bullied by haughty, half-naked savages, and for twenty years Canada had peace from the RedMan.

Louis de Baude, Count Frontenac, was one of the greatest of the governors of New France. Next to that of Champlain, his name is perhaps the best remembered in the history of the colony. He was the first man who tried to give the people of Canada freedom. Until Frontenac came, the people had no say in ruling. Now the governor tried to form a parliament. He asked the townspeople to come to talk about the affairs of the colony together with the priests and nobles. But when the French king heard about it, he was very angry. He did not wish the people to be free. He wished to keep all the power in his own hands, and Count Frontenac was forbidden to call his little parliament together again.

Although Frontenac was not allowed to do all he wished, he was a very powerful ruler. But he was proud and haughty, and often quarrelled with the Intendant and with the Bishop. The Indians, however, dreaded and respected him more than any other "Onontio," as they called the white rulers.

Onontio means "great mountain" in the Indian language. One of the governors of New France had been called Montmagny. The Indians had been told that in the French language that meant Great Mountain, and from his name they called all the governors who came after him, Onontio or Great Mountain.

But never had Onontio been respected as Frontenac was respected. The Indians felt that he was their master. He would not call their great chiefs "Brother," as other rulers had done. He called them his children and he was their Great Father. Yet though they feared him, they loved him too, for he would laugh and jest with them, play with their children, and give their wives strings of beautiful beads. Then, too, at times he would paint his face and dress himself like an Indian chief, and with tomahawk in hand would lead the war-dance; or again he would sit by the council fire making speeches as fine as any savage warrior.

It was while Frontenac was ruler that the great time of Canadian exploration began. In spite of both French and British colonies, little was known of the vast continent of America. The French forts stretched inland along the river St. Lawrence to the great lakes; the British crept along the seashore from Florida in the south to Acadie in the north, and were shut out from the great west by the Alleghany Mountains. But what was behind and beyond none knew.

The British, when they went to live in the New World became fishermen and farmers, settling down quickly to a peaceful home life. Not so the Frenchmen. Priest, soldier, or colonists, each seemed filled with the roving spirit of the forest, the desire for adventure and the thirst for knowledge and conquest. Indeed the desire for a wild and roving life became so strong in some, that they could no longer remain in towns and villages, and they wandered away into the woods to live among the Indians. They dressed like Indians and married Indian women. They were reckless, fearless men, loving the forests and the lonely lakes and rivers, and instead of taming the Redskins they themselves became almost like savages. In vain the King of France made laws forbidding the young men to wander away and live in the woods. The woods called them, and they could not resist the call. These men became known as "wanderers of the woods," or, in the French language, *Coureurs de bois*.

These forest adventurers were great fur-traders. They knew all the haunts and habits of the wild animals. They read the signs of sky and wood as we might read a book. In winter, alone across the trackless snow, they found their way. In summer the pathless forest had no terrors for them. They were warriors and explorers as well as trackers and traders. Lawless and brave, they were looked upon as outlaws, and sometimes in battles they might be seen fighting for Indians, sometimes for the French.

> "Give me freedom, give me space,
> Give me the open air and sky,
> With the dean wind in my face
> Where the quiet mountains lie.
>
> I am sick of roofs and floors,
> Naught will heal me but to roam;
> Open me the forest doors,
> Let the green world take me home.
>
> I am sick of streets and noise,
> Narrow ways and cramping creeds;
> Give me back the simpler joys;
> Nothing else my spirit needs.
>
> For the road goes up and the road goes down,
> And the years go over and by,
> And soon will the longest day be past,
> Soon I must lay me down."

When these wanderers of the woods came to the towns to sell their furs, they brought with them many wonderful stories of the sights they had seen far in the unknown wilds. Among other things, they talked of a "great water" of which the Indians told wonderful tales. They called it the Mississippi or Father of Waters. Then men began to ask what this great water was. Was it perhaps the fabled passage to the Indies, which many a brave sailor had given his life to find? If it could be found, would it lead at last to the Vermilion Sea, to China, to the spice lands, and the glories of the East?

Many people set out to find this great water, and at last a priest named Marquette and an explorer named Joliet discovered the Mississippi. They sailed far down it, past where the yellow, angry waters of the Missouri join it. On and on southward they went, until at length they became sure that the great river did not flow across America and fall into the Pacific Ocean as they had thought, but southward into the Gulf of Mexico. Having made sure of this they turned home again with the news of their great discovery.

Among the many French adventurers was a man named Réné Robert Cavelier, Sieur de la Salle. He is generally called La Salle, and is one of the best known of the Canadian explorers.

Like others, La Salle had heard of the great water and was eager to follow it all the way to its mouth. So with a friend called Tonty he gathered

"ALONE ACROSS A TRACKLESS SNOW."

a company, and went to explore.

Tonty, like La Salle, was brave and fearless, and he was much dreaded by the Indians. He had only one hand, the other having been shot off while he was fighting once in Europe. So he had an iron hand made to replace the one he had lost, and he always wore a glove over it. Once or twice when the Red Men had been unruly he had brought them to order by knocking them down with this hand. Not knowing that it was of iron, they wondered at his power and strength, and called him a "medicine man" and feared him greatly.

La Salle was one of the most unlucky of men, and now he had many and terrible difficulties to fight. He had enemies who did their best to hinder and ruin him. His own men even were not true to him, besides which he had to fight with storms, and cold and heat, hunger and thirst, and not least, with savage Indians. But he was so brave and determined that nothing made him give in.

Before La Salle began his exploration, he built a ship Which he called the *Griffin*. In it he sailed up Lake Erie and Lake Michigan. It was the first time that a sailing-boat had ever been seen on these great inland seas, and the Indians came to wonder and stare at it in astonishment.

La Salle had not much money, so from Lake Michigan he sent the *Griffin* back to Montreal with a load of furs, giving the captain orders to sell them and return with goods needful for the expedition, as soon as possible.

When the *Griffin* had sailed, La Salle journeyed on with the rest of his men to the head of Lake Michigan, and there he awaited the return of his ship.

But the *Griffin* never came again. In vain La Salle waited and watched for a white sail. No white sail ever appeared. What became of the *Griffin* will never be known. Somewhere upon the great lakes it was lost, with all the men on board. Not one returned to tell the fate of the others.

While La Salle waited and watched in vain for the return of the *Griffin*, the good days were passing, winter was coming. At length he gave up hope of seeing his ship again, and made up his mind to go on without the fresh supplies he had sent for. So, through many trials and dangers, suffering from cold and hunger, the little band pushed on. For La Salle, perhaps, the hardest trial of all was that his men did not believe in him. Nearly all were discontented, and many were afraid of the difficulties and dangers of the way. Two, indeed, were so afraid that they ran away.

At length La Salle made up his mind to rest for the winter on the banks of the river Illinois. Here he built a fort which he called Fort Créve-Coeur, or Heart-Break. But in spite of the sad name he gave his fort, La Salle showed that he had not quite lost heart, for he began to build another ship to take the place of the *Griffin*.

But soon La Salle found that he had not many things which were needed for the ship. To get them, some one must return to Montreal, and La Salle resolved to go himself.

Taking with him one Indian and four other Frenchmen, La Salle set out on his terrible walk of a thousand miles. Tonty with the rest—some sixteen men—remained behind to guard the fort and work at the ship until their leader's return.

This journey of La Salle was tiresome beyond belief. With the first days of spring the snow began to thaw, and thawing it turned the prairies into wide and endless marshes, in which the travellers sank to their knees, or sometimes even to their waists. They could not walk upon the rivers, for the melting ice was not strong enough to bear them. Neither could they sail down them, for the broken ice would have smashed their frail canoes to pieces. So they scrambled along the banks, sometimes forcing their way through forests so dense, that their clothes were torn to rags and their faces so scratched and bleeding that they hardly knew each other.

They had to suffer both from cold and heat. The sun at midday blazed upon them, at night the frost was bitter. During the day they were often drenched with rain or half-melted snow, at night their soaking clothes would freeze. At night, wet and weary, they lay down to sleep around their camp fire, in the morning they awoke to find themselves encased in frosted armour.

Worn out with the terrible hardships of the journey, one after another the men fell ill. But at length, after more than two months crowded with pain and toil and danger, they reached Fort Frontenac, and found rest and shelter.

CHAPTER 13

THE ADVENTURES OF LA SALLE CONTINUED

L A Salle's troubles were not ended. At Fort Frontenac he was greeted with the news that a ship from France, laden with goods for him, had been wrecked. This was indeed bad news. But La Salle was not to be daunted. He at once set to work to gather fresh supplies, and made ready to start back to Fort Heart-Break, there to join his friends.

Then the worst news of all came. A letter from Tonty arrived to tell La Salle that soon after he had left, nearly all his men had mutinied. They had destroyed the fort, robbed the storehouse, and what they could not carry away they had thrown into the river. They had gone, leaving Tonty and four or five faithful men helpless and alone in the wilderness.

La Salle had been eager to set out. Now that he heard this evil news he was more eager still. He felt that there was no time to lose, and that he must find and help his friend at once.

But when, after a long and difficult journey, La Salle reached Fort Heart-Break again, there was no sign of any human being. The fort was ruined and deserted, and only the great staring ribs of the unfinished ship were left to show that white men had been there. No sign of Tonty or his faithful few was to be seen.

Never for a moment, however, did La Salle give in. He spent the winter in making friends with the Indians, and in trying in every way to hear news of Tonty, and at last, when spring came again, the two friends met. They had much to tell each other. But it was a tale of sorrow and failure on both sides. Yet La Salle was not beaten, and once more he set out with Tonty on his travels. But now he gave up the idea of building a ship, and the expedition started down the river in canoes.

It was the middle of winter before everything was ready. The river was frozen over, so the men made sledges, put their canoes upon them, and in this way dragged them over the ice. As they went southward it became warmer, spring came, and the ice began to melt. The sledges were of no more use, and for a time neither were the canoes, for the river soon became full of broken floating ice, through which it was impossible to paddle. But at length the ice was nearly all melted; they reached a clear and open stream, and, launching the canoes, they sailed swiftly onward.

Every day as they sailed they left winter further and further behind. The sun shone pleasantly; spring flowers nodded to them from the banks;

the drooping trees put on a beautiful soft green. It seemed as if their troubles were over. On and on they floated easily down stream, through the smiling spring land, which no white man had ever before beheld. At last they reached their journey's end, and stood upon the shores of the Gulf of Mexico.

On that lonely shore these few white men raised a pillar. Upon it they carved the arms of France and the words, "Louis the Great, King of France and Navarre, reigns, 9th April 1682." The white flag of France, with its golden *fleur-de-lis*, floated out upon the breeze, and the silence was broken for the first time by the sound of guns and the shouts of "God save the King."

When the sound of the shouting died away, the men raised their voices once again. This time they sang a hymn of praise to God. Then with drawn sword La Salle stood beside the pillar. "In the name of the most high, mighty, invincible, and victorious Prince, Louis the Great, by the Grace of God, King of France and of Navarre," he cried, "I do now take possession of this country of Louisiana, the seas, harbours, ports, bays, and all the nations, peoples, cities, towns, villages, mines, fisheries, streams, and rivers, within the said Louisiana from the mouth of the great river Ohio along the river Mississippi, and all the rivers which flow into it from its source to its mouth at the sea."

Then a cross was raised beside the pillar. Once more the guns rang out, once more shouts of "God save the King" awoke the silent echoes of the forest, and men's voices raised a Latin hymn of praise. To France a new kingdom had been added.

If you will look on the map you will see what a great region La Salle had claimed. He himself had no idea how great it was. You will see that the British colonies lay like a narrow strip between the Alleghanies and the sea, while the French had claimed all that lay behind; that is, all the country which is now the United States, as well as the whole of Canada.

It was a vast kingdom, and could not be held by France through the mere planting of a pillar. This La Salle well knew, though he himself did not guess how large a tract of land he had claimed. Now he formed a plan by which this kingdom might be held. His plan was to build a town at the mouth of the Mississippi, and forts all along its banks at certain distances. These forts would be resting-places for traders, and would form a barrier against the British, shutting them more than ever out from the unknown west. All the trade of Canada could then be borne down the Mississippi to the town at its mouth, which would thus grow into a great seaport. From there white-winged vessels would glide out to all parts of the world, and so great wealth and glory would be added to the crown of France.

Such was La Salle's dream. But meanwhile he had to battle his way up stream, back through savage wilderness to the dwellings of white men. And it was not until he had passed through many more adventures and dangers that he reached Quebec once more. From there he set sail for France, eager to tell the king of all that he had done, and of all that he hoped still to do.

King Louis received La Salle kindly, and gave him the help he asked. Soon four ships set sail from France filled with soldiers, workmen, and colonists, bringing with them all things needful to found a city.

La Salle sailed for the Gulf of Mexico, and meant to land at the mouth of the Mississippi, which he had reached before by paddling down the river. But coming at it from the sea was very different from coming to it from the land. La Salle could not find the place, and sailed more than a hundred miles beyond it. When at last they landed, the colonists were already disheartened. They had lost two ships: one had run upon rocks, the other had been taken by the Spaniards, who claimed the Gulf of Mexico as their own, threatening with death any who dared to enter it. On the way out, La Salle had quarrelled with his officers. Things from first to last went ill, and so it was with little spirit in the task that the colonists set about building their wooden houses.

Two years of struggle, toil, and misery followed the landing. "This pleasant land seemed to us an abode of weariness and an eternal prison," wrote one of the company. Sickness and death thinned their numbers, till at the end of these two years, of the two hundred men and women who had set sail, scarcely forty remained. And these were but a ragged and forlorn band. Their clothes were in such tatters that they were glad to make coats of sail cloth; their food was near an end. Gladly would they have left their prison, but they knew not how. In vain they strained their eyes seawards, hoping for the sight of a friendly, fearing to see a Spanish, sail. Sadly they thought of their beloved France, which they had left with such light hearts. They longed to return, but no ship came. They were alone, forsaken, and lost in that far land.

At length La Salle made up his mind to try to find his way back to Canada by land, and bring help from there to the forlorn colony. So one morning there was a sad scene within the walls of the little fort, as those who went said farewell to those who stayed. Many tears were shed as last handshakes were given, last good-byes said. Then the little band set out on the long and terrible journey northward.

They were a quaint and ragged party. Some wore the clothes they had brought from France, now much patched and darned; some wore coats of sailcloth; some the skins of wild animals. They were but ill prepared for their long and perilous journey through prairie and forest, by stream and lake. Yet in the brave, unyielding heart of La Salle, there was still hope.

La Salle was brave and strong, and his friends loved him well. But these friends were few. To most people he was cold and haughty, and he made many enemies. Now bitter hate and discontent filled the hearts of some

Of his men. As the difficulties and hardships of the way grew greater, their hatred grew deeper, and at last one morning they shot their leader dead. "There thou liest, there thou liest, great Bashaw," cried one, rejoicing as he saw his enemy lie dead upon the ground. The mutineers then stripped the body of all its clothes and left it naked and unburied, a prey to the wild beasts. So he who would have founded a kingdom and made France great among the nations, lies in a nameless, unknown grave. Of what became of his murderers little is known. By man, at least, they went unpunished.

No help ever came to the little colony La Salle had left behind him. It was attacked by Indians; nearly all the colonists were killed, the rest scattered. La Salle's brilliant dream ended in nothingness, but he had shown his countrymen the way. Other great men followed him who were more successful, and it seemed for a time as if France would indeed hold the great possessions claimed for her in the New World.

CHAPTER 14

COUNT FRONTENAC

WHILE La Salle was struggling down the Mississippi, Frontenac, the great Onontio, was having his troubles too. The Indians who had been at peace for so long were growing restless. It needed all Frontenac's cleverness to keep them quiet. And though he kept peace with the Red Man, he could not do so with his white brother. He quarrelled with the Intendant and he quarrelled with the Bishop. At last the quarrels became so bad, that King Louis in anger called both Frontenac and the Intendant home.

Frontenac was followed by a governor who could not manage the Indians at all. They grew insolent, he grew frightened. Then King Louis, more angry than ever, ordered him to come home.

Again, under the next governor, the troubles with the Indians grew no better but rather worse, till the Iroquois prowled about like wolves, and no white man's life was safe. The French plotted, and the Indians plotted. Treachery was met by treachery, blood was wiped out in blood. The Iroquois' hatred of the French, which for a time they seemed to have forgotten, burst out again with wilder fury than before.

One stormy August night, amid the lashing of hail and the scream of the wind, the Indian war-whoop was heard by the sleeping settlers of Fort La Chine, not far from Montreal. Leaping from their beds they made ready to defend themselves. From all sides yelling, painted warriors poured in upon them. Muskets flashed and roared, tomahawk and hatchet gleamed and fell. Many fled in the darkness, but few escaped the awful vengeance of the Indian. When the sun rose it shone upon the ruined, deserted village in the ashes of which lay the dead bodies of two hundred men, women, and children. More than a hundred others were led away captive, many of them to be done to death with horrible tortures in the Indian encampment.

The people of Montreal were filled with horror, the governor was helpless with fear. For two months the Indians prowled about, ravaging and destroying at will. Then they went off to their own country, carrying their prisoners with them. Before they went they gathered around Montreal, filling the air with hideous yells—giving a yell for every prisoner they had taken, and thus showing their scorn of the governor.

Besides this fearful Indian warfare, quarrels between the British and the French colonies were every day becoming more bitter. For many years, while the French north of the St. Lawrence had been founding scattered colonies and trying to make the heathen people Christian, the British colonies south of the St. Lawrence had been growing stronger and stronger. The British had not claimed so much land as the French, but there were far more people in the small part that they had claimed, and they held it with far firmer hands.

Now there began a struggle between the British and the French for the fur trade, for the possession of the waterways by the rivers and great lakes, and for the friendship of the Indians. The Indians had already found out that the British gave them more for their furs than the French. So even those who were friendly with the French were not unwilling to trade with the British. There is no room in this little book to tell of all the quarrels and of the exciting fights which took place when white men fought against each other, and side by side, with yelling savages whose faces were painted red and green, or spotted with black and white. They were indeed often painted all over, and naked except for tails of wild beasts hanging down their backs. Upon their heads they wore horns, in their noses and ears iron ornaments, and round their necks chains of beads. They were somewhat terrible friends to have, and very fearful enemies.

The Iroquois had nearly wrecked the colonies of New France, when the news came that Frontenac, the great Onontio, was coming back. He was now seventy years old, he was old and grey, but he had not forgotten how to rule. His coming struck terror to the Indian heart. With them he would have made peace, but with the British he waged war. For he believed that they had been to blame for many of the quarrels, and that they had stirred the Iroquois to fight.

So against the British Frontenac sent three armies of French and Indians. It was dead of winter when they set out. Shod with snow-shoes, wrapped in fringed blankets, daubed with paint and decked with feathers, French and Indian alike sped over the snow fields.

The British were not prepared for war. At one fort the gates were open, the doors unbarred. And so secure did they think themselves that, instead of sentinels, there stood by the gateway two snow men. But in the dead of night, over the silent snow, French and Indian stole. With fierce war-whoops they fell upon the sleeping men. The slaughter was awful, and soon the village was a smoking ruin.

All three armies were alike successful, if armies they might be called, for they were rather wild marauders. The Indians began again to respect the French and were no longer so insolent. But the British now gathered in strength to repay the blow. Sir William Phips sailed out from New England, attacked and took Port Royal, and once more claimed Acadie for the British.

Then the New Englanders decided to take Quebec. And one October morning a fleet of thirty-four British ships, big and little, sailed up the St. Lawrence and anchored before Quebec.

A little boat, flying a white flag, put off and made for the shore. In it was an officer carrying a letter to Count Frontenac. As he came to shore the Frenchmen met him, and before he was allowed to land they blindfolded him. Then with a soldier on either side he was led through the streets to the governor.

Up and down steep and stony pathways he was dragged, followed by a jeering crowd of women and children who laughed aloud as he stumbled over rough places, telling him it was but a game of blind man's buff.

At length, bewildered and out of breath, the young officer was led into a room, and the bandage was taken from his eyes. Then he found that he was standing before the governor and his officers. For a moment, dazzled by the sudden light, he gazed in confusion at the crowd of Frenchmen in their gay uniforms, glittering with gold and silver lace. Then recovering himself, he gave the letter which he had brought to Frontenac.

This letter, in very proud words, demanded the surrender of Quebec, in the name of William and Mary, King and Queen of England, Scotland, France and Ireland. It gave Frontenac one hour in which to return an answer.

The letter was read aloud, and when the reading was at an end the British officer pulled out his watch. "It is ten o'clock," he said, showing it to the governor; "I require your answer by eleven."

"By heaven!" thundered Frontenac, "I will not keep you waiting so long! Tell your commander that I do not recognise King William, and that the Prince of Orange, who calls himself so, is a usurper. I know no king of Britain but King James. I will answer your general with the mouths of my cannon. Let him do his best, I will do mine."

With the French commander's proud answer ringing in his ears, blindfolded once more, the British officer was led stumbling down the steep streets to his boat.

So the siege began. But although Phips was brave, he was leading men little used to war. They had courage enough, but little discipline. They were farmers and fishermen rather than soldiers. They threw away their lives, they wasted their shot against the solid wall of stone upon which Quebec is perched, while the Frenchmen riddled their ships with shot and shell.

At last, with splintered masts and torn rigging, the British sailed away. Yet, had they but known it, Quebec had almost been within their grasp. For although there were men enough and powder and shot enough within the walls, food was scarce, and the horror of famine stared the defenders in the face.

CHAPTER 15

THE STORY OF MADELEINE DE VERCHERES

WAR still went on—war between French and British, between French and Iroquois. The houses in the country were deserted, the fields lay untilled, the people crowded to the towns for safety. Here and there the people of a village would gather and work all together. But while they worked, sentinels were on the watch to give warning at the first sign of danger. Everywhere the red terror lurked. No man was safe, no life was sure. The trader paddling downstream with his store of furs, the trapper returning from the woods, each knew that he held his life in his hands. "The enemy is upon us by land and sea," wrote Frontenac; "send us more men if you want the colony to be saved."

Many stories are told of brave deeds done at this time. But one of the most famous is that of Madeleine de Vèrcheres, a girl of fourteen, who held her father's fort against the Indians for a whole week.

It was autumn, and all the settlers at Vèrcheres had gone to work in the fields some miles from the fort. Two soldiers only had been left on guard. Besides them there was an old man of eighty, some women and children, and Madeleine with her two little brothers of ten and twelve.

All seemed peaceful and quiet. But through the thick forest, which already glowed gold and red beneath the autumn sun, Indians were stealing. Thinking that all was safe, Madeleine had gone down to the river which flowed not far from the fort. Suddenly, through the still air, was heard the sound of gun-shots. Hardly had the sound died away when there came a cry from the fort. "Run, miss, run!" shouted the old man; "the Indians are upon us!"

Madeleine turned. There, not a pistol-shot behind her, was a band of forty-five or fifty Indians.

How Madeleine ran! Fear seemed to give her wings. But oh, the way was long! As she ran, she prayed in her heart, "Holy Virgin, Mother of God, save me!" The bullets of forty-five muskets sang and whistled round her as she fled. Would she never reach the fort? Oh, how far off it seemed! "To arms, to arms!" she shouted, hoping that some one would come out and help her. No one came. At last she reached the gate and fled within. With trembling hands she closed and barred it.

For the moment she was saved. But it was only for the moment. Wasting no time, Madeleine ran round the fort to see that all was safe. Here and

'NO MAN WAS SAFE, NO LIFE WAS SURE.'

there logs had fallen out on the palisades, leaving holes through which the enemy might get in. These she ordered to be replaced, herself helping to carry the logs. As soon as that was done she went to the guardroom where the gunpowder and shot were kept. Here she found the two so-called soldiers hiding in abject terror. One had a lighted match in his hand. "What are you going to do with that?" she asked quickly.

"I am going to set the powder on fire and blow us all up," he answered.

"You coward!" cried Madeleine, "go!"

She was only a girl of fourteen, but she spoke so sternly that the soldier was ashamed. He blew out his match and left the room.

Madeleine now threw off the white muslin bonnet which women used to wear in those days. Putting on a steel cap, and taking a gun in her hand, she turned to her two brothers. "Boys," she said, "let us fight to the death. Remember what father has taught you, that gentlemen must be ready to die for their God and their king."

The boys were as brave as their sister, and, taking their guns, they went to the loopholes and began to fire upon the Indians who were now close round the house.

Although Madeleine was so calm and brave, the women of the fort were much frightened. They cried pitifully, and so did the little children. Madeleine comforted them as well as she could, and told them that they must not cry, for if the Indians without heard, they would learn how hopeless the state of the fort was, and would attack more fiercely.

All day long the fight lasted, and with the darkness of night came a terrible storm. The wind howled round the walls, snow and hail beat against the windows. It was a fearful night, and Madeleine anxiously watching the movements of the Indians, became sure that they were making ready to attack the fort under cover of the darkness and the storm.

So Madeleine gathered her little garrison and made a speech to them. "God has saved us to-day from the hands of our enemies," she said. "But we must watch to-night lest we fall into their snares." Then to each she gave his orders, posting her few men as well as she could round the walls. So all night long the Indians heard the steady tread of sentinels on duty. Every hour from fort and block-house came the cry, "All's well." The wily Indians were completely deceived, and thinking that the fort was strongly garrisoned they dared not attack.

Towards morning there was an alarm. The sentry nearest the gate suddenly called out, "Lady, I hear something."

Hurrying towards him, Madeleine peered anxiously through the loophole. Yes, there, against the whiteness of the new-fallen snow, black moving figures could be seen coming close round the house. For a few moments Madeleine watched anxiously. Then soft lowing and snuffling was heard. Madeleine gave a sigh of relief. These were no Indians, but some cattle belonging to the fort which had found their way through the snow to the gate. There were only a few, for the Indians had captured nearly all the herd.

"We must open the gate and let them in," said some one.

"God forbid," replied Madeleine, "you do not know the wiles of these Indians. Very likely they are behind the cattle, wrapped in skins and ready to rush in the moment we are silly enough to open the gate."

But after some talk it was decided to risk it. For if they were long besieged they might be glad of the cattle to keep them from starving.

Calling her two brothers, Madeleine placed them one on each side of the gate, with their fingers on the triggers of their guns ready to fire. Then the gate was carefully opened. One by one the cattle came in, and the gate was again closed in safety.

At last the long night ended. And as the sun rose and the darkness fled, the fears and terrors of the night fled too.

The day passed, and another, and another. The Indians still prowled without, the brave little garrison still kept watch within. Hour by hour Madeleine marched round the posts, always smiling, always speaking cheering words, however heavy her heart might be. For the first two days and nights she hardly slept, never laying down her gun or taking off her clothes.

And so a week went by.

Upon the seventh night Madeleine sat in the guard-room. She was very weary. With her gun lying across her arms, and her head resting upon the table, she fell asleep. Suddenly she started wide awake to hear the tramp of men around the house. Springing up, she seized her gun. "Who goes there?" she called out into the darkness.

"French," came the reply; "it is La Monnerie come to help you."

Ah, that was good news! Running to the gate Madeleine threw it open. But even now she did not forget to be careful. Posting a sentinel, she marched out to meet the Frenchmen.

"Sir, you are welcome," she said, giving La Monnerie the leader, a military salute. "I render you my arms."

"Lady," replied the captain, bowing low before her "they are in good hands."

"Better than you know, perhaps," replied Madeleine proudly.

La Monnerie and his soldiers marched into the fort. Wonderingly he made a tour of the posts and found all in good order, each "man" at his post. It was perhaps the strangest, bravest garrison he had ever seen. Among them were an old man of eighty, and a boy of ten, and their leader was a girl of fourteen.

"Sir," said Madeleine, a little wearily but with a joyful pride, "relieve my men. We have not been off duty for eight days."

"And this is my little garrison, my brothers Louis and Paul;
With soldiers two, and a cripple. May the Virgin pray for us all.
But we've powder and guns in plenty, and we'll fight to the latest breath,
And if need be, for God and country, die a brave soldier's death.

"Load all the carabines quickly, and whenever you sight the foe,
Fire from the upper turret and loopholes down below,
Keep up the fire, brave soldiers, though the fight may be fierce and long,
And they'll think our little garrison is more than a hundred strong."

So spake the maiden Madeleine, and she roused the Norman blood
That seemed for a moment sleeping, and sent it like a flood
Through every heart around her, and they fought the red Iroquois
As fought in the old-time battles the soldiers of Carignan.

And six days followed each other, and feeble her limbs became,
Yet the maid never sought her pillow, and the flash of the carabine's flame
Illumined the powder-smoked faces, ay, even when hope seemed gone,
And she only smiled at her comrades and told them to fight, fight on.

And she blew a blast on her bugle, and lo, from the forest black
Merrily, merrily ringing, an answer came pealing back.
Oh, pleasant and sweet it sounded, borne on the morning air,
For it heralded fifty soldiers, with gallant be la Monniere.

And when he beheld the maiden, the soldier of Carignan,
And looked on the little garrison that fought the red Iroquois
And held their own in the battle, for six long weary days,
He stood for a moment speechless, and marvelled at woman's ways.

Then he beckoned the men behind him, and steadily they advance,
And with carabines uplifted the veterans of France
Saluted the brave young captain so timidly standing there,
And they fired a volley in honour of Madeleine Vèrcheres.
                                                W.H. DRUMMOND.

CHAPTER 16

THE WAR OF THE BOUNDARY LINE

THERE is no room here to tell of all the struggles of Britain and France in America. But you have read enough to see how these two great powers had laid hold of the mighty continent, and how, in spite of all the thousands of miles of prairie and forest, of lake and stream, there was not room for both. One must go. But which? Was it to be the stolid, dogged race, who had painfully felled the trees and ploughed the land, reclaiming it bit by bit from the vast forest, building there, homes and churches and clustering towns? Or was it to be the gay adventurers and earnest black-robed priests, who reared crosses upon the borders of desolation, and claimed with the roar of cannon and singing of hymns, unexplored and unknown countries and peoples, for God and their king?

"Do you not know the difference between the King of France and the King of Britain?" a Frenchman once asked the Indians. "Go, look at the forts which our king has built. You will see that you can still hunt under their very walls. They have been built for your good, in places where you go. The British, on the other hand, are no sooner in possession of a place than they drive the game away. The trees fall before them, the earth is laid bare so that you can scarcely find a few branches with which to make a shelter for the night."

It was true. The British turned the wild forest into meadow-land and corn-fields. The French claimed the forest, and left it forest still, still the Red Man's hunting-ground.

The King of France was a despot at home. He was just as much a despot in his colonies. Everything the French settler did, was done by the French king's orders. In the French colonies there was no more freedom for the people than there was at home. In the British colonies it was very different. British settlers sailed to the New World because they were un-happy at home, because they could not worship God as they wished, or because they could not have the king they wanted. They sought freedom and they found it. At home the people rose against their king. They cut off his head and said they would have no more kings. But after a little they grew tired of having no king, and they asked Charles II. to come to rule over them. Later, the people rebelled again, and a new race of kings came to the throne. But all these changes did not make much difference to the colonies. The colonists remained British subjects whether King or Protector ruled the British Isles, this, too, although they received little help or attention from home.

So by degrees thirteen colonies were founded in America. Little by little they grew strong and prosperous, and at length the king and people at home began to see what a great state had grown up beyond the seas.

Yet although these thirteen colonies were all British, there was very little union amongst them. It was a long time before they learned that if they did not wish to be crushed out by the French, they must join together and help each other.

Years rolled on. There was no peace—there could be no peace between the two peoples. Even when France and Britain were not fighting at home, there was almost always fighting in America. And if the roar of cannon was quiet, and the white man's sword in sheath, the Red Man's tomahawk gleamed and his war-cry made the darkness terrible.

At last the great struggle in America began. It has been called the War of the Boundary Line.

Slowly, as the British colonies grew, they pressed westward. The country where Pittsburg now stands came to be called the Gate of the West. Both French and British wished to possess that gate, and both claimed the land. Here the French built a fort which they called Fort Le Bœuf.

When the Governor of Virginia heard of this, he sent a young man called George Washington to tell the French commander of the fort that he was upon British ground, and that he must leave at once.

After a long and difficult journey Washington reached the French camp one evening just as the officers were sitting down to dinner. They received him most courteously, but they told him that they meant to take and keep possession of the valley of the Ohio. "You Britishers are two to our one," they said, "but you are so slow, you cannot prevent us doing what we want."

The commander himself was grave and polite. "I will send the British governor's letter to Canada," he said, "but in the meantime my men and I will stay where we are. I have been commanded to take possession of the country, and I mean to do it as best I can."

With this answer Washington had to go back to his governor. But in the spring, he returned with about three hundred men. He was not able, however, to dislodge the French, and, after some fighting, he was forced to march away again.

All this time France and Britain were supposed to be at peace. War had not been proclaimed, but now a thousand men were sent out from home to help the colonists. When the French heard this, they too sent men. Yet the King of France and the King of Great Britain kept on being polite to each other, and pretending that nothing was meant.

But at sea the French and British vessels met. Up went a red flag to the masthead of the British flagship. "Is this peace or war?" asked the French captain.

"I don't know," replied the British, "but you had better prepare for war."

And quick to point his words came the roar of cannon. The Frenchmen made good show of fight, but the British were the stronger, and soon the French struck their colours.

So, without being declared, war began.

But at first things went ill with the British in Canada. The home troops were sent out under the command of Major-General Edward Braddock. He was brave, but obstinate and old-fashioned. He had a contempt for the colonial soldiers, and a still greater contempt for their Indian friends. He was so rude to these that the haughty savages, instead of helping the British, stalked away offended, and took no part in the fight. "He looks upon us as dogs," they said.

Before setting out to attack the French, Braddock spent many weeks in making preparations, in gathering men, stores, and wagons. At last all was ready, and the long train of men and horses started for Fort Duquesne.

Braddock was used to fighting in Europe. He knew nothing of fighting in the wilds of America. Never before had he had to face the difficulty of taking an army, with all its train of baggage and ammunition, through pathless forest. Three hundred men with axes led the way, cutting down the trees to clear a path. Slowly behind them, now jolting over stumps and stones, now sinking axle deep in dust or mud, followed the wagons and cannon. So great were the difficulties of the road that the army crawled along at the rate of scarcely three miles a day, and so narrow was the path that the line of march was over four miles in length. But with British doggedness they toiled on; the red coats of the soldiers and the white-covered wagons lighting up the dark forest; the sound of trumpet-calls and the clash of arms awakening the silence.

On this slow and painful march many of the men fell ill. So Braddock resolved to divide his army. Leaving the heaviest baggage, the sick men and some of his soldiers behind, under another officer called Dunbar, he pressed on with about twelve hundred men. But even thus lightened the march was not very fast, and the colonists were disgusted to find that their ideas of what a rough road meant, and those of the British, were quite different. The British, they said, "halted to level every molehill and build bridges over every brook."

News of the march soon reached the French at Fort Duquesne. And when they heard how great the numbers were, they were much afraid, and almost decided to leave the fort and march away before the British arrived. But a brave officer named Beaujeu, said, "No, let us rather gather some of the Indians and go out to meet them." Then council fires were lit, and Beaujeu, dressed like an Indian brave, flung the war-hatchet down and talked to the Red Men until they were athirst for blood and ready to join the fight. So the war-dance was danced. Then daubed with paint and decked with feathers, six hundred red warriors and two hundred and fifty

Frenchmen marched out to meet the British. They were led by Beaujeu, who looked almost like an Indian, wearing a fringed shirt as they did, under his steel breast-plate.

The summer sun was shining, the sky was blue and clear, as the British force wound slowly across the river Monongahela. The men were in good spirits, for their journey was nearly at an end, Fort Duquesne being only nine miles off. Of victory they had no doubt, so to the sound of drum and trumpet they marched gaily along. Then suddenly, from the dark and silent forest, dashed a crowd of Indian warriors, uttering piercing, hideous war-cries. At the same moment a hail of bullets mowed down the British soldiers. Quickly they returned the fire, and shouting, "God save the King," they rushed at the foe.

But the Indians scattered through the forest. Hiding behind trees and bushes they shot in safety at the British, whose red coats made them an easy mark. Gallantly the British fought. But it was like fighting against puffs of smoke. They could not see the foe; they were guided only by the smoke; their bullets tore through the bushes and were buried in the tree trunks, doing little harm, while from every side death rained upon the redcoats.

The British were unused to this savage warfare. Had they scattered like the Indians, and fired from behind shelter as they did, there might have been some hope. The American colonists, who were with the army under George Washington, knowing the ways of the Indians, fought them in their own manner. But to Braddock, that seemed unsoldierly and cowardly. If his men tried to scatter, he drove them together again, so they stood a brilliant target in the sunshine to be mown down by the murderous fire of savages.

Braddock himself fought and shouted like a madman. Horse after horse was shot under him, and at last he fell, sorely wounded.

For two hours or more the slaughter lasted. Then the troops could stand no more. They fled, leaving more than half their number dead or dying upon the field. All night they fled, pursued by the savage foe. Day came, still on they fled until they reached Dunbar's camp. Even here their panic did not cease. Dunbar and his men were seized with terror too. But it was not possible to flee with such baggage as they had. So stores were destroyed, barrels of gunpowder were thrown into the river, wagons were burned, lest they should fall into the hands of the enemy. Then the whole army marched back the way it had come. The rout was complete.

But meanwhile, swept along with the fleeing host, Braddock was dying. His life was ending in the darkness of defeat and disaster. Gloomy and silent he lay in his litter. "Who would have thought it?" was all he said. Then, as if with some returning hope, he murmured: "We shall know better how to do it another time." Then he died. For him, there was to be no "other time."

THE PATH OF GLORY

"Quebec, the grey old city on the hill,
Lies with a golden glory on her head,
Dreaming throughout this hour so fair, so still,
Of other days and all her mighty dead.
The white doves perch upon the cannons grim,
The flowers bloom where once did run a tide
Of crimson, when the moon was pale and dim
Above the battlefield so grim and wide.
Methinks within her wakes a mighty glow
Of pride, of tenderness—her stirring past—
The strife, the valour, of the long ago
Feels at her heart-strings. Strong, and tall, and vast,
She lies, touched with the sunset's golden grace,
A wondrous softness on her grey old face."
                                        B.BISHOP.

THE story of the first years of the great struggle in America is a story of mistakes, defeat, disaster, ill-luck, and bad management. "I dread to hear from America," wrote Pitt the great Commoner. "We are undone both at home and abroad. We are no longer a nation," sighed another gloomily. These were dark and perilous days for Britain and her colonies. There was war, there was disaster abroad; there was discord at home.

Then Pitt came into power. He was very certain of himself. "I am sure that I can save the country," he said, "and that no one else can." Then he set himself to the task.

Pitt cared not one jot whether people had great names or fine friends. He looked only for men—men fit for the work to which they were sent. So he recalled the blunderers, and sent in their places men whom he could trust.

Soon the tide began to turn. Soon, in place of news of disaster and defeat, came news of victory. Louisburg, the strongest fortress possessed by the French, fell. Frontenac was taken, so, too, was Fort Duquesne, and the memory of Braddock's defeat was wiped out. The name of the fort was changed to Pittsburg in honour of the great statesman. It bears that name still.

But while the outposts of Canada were falling, while British officers were drinking to "British colours on every French fort, port, and garrison, in America," Quebec, perched high upon its frowning rock, guarded the St. Lawrence. It was the key of Canada. So with eight thousand men at his back, Major-General Wolfe was sent to take it.

Up the St. Lawrence sailed the British warships making their way safely through the rocks and sand-banks of the treacherous passage, passing where the French would hardly have dared risk small merchant vessels. "Ay, ay, my dear," laughed one brave old salt, "I'll convince you that an Englishman shall go where a Frenchman dare not show his nose."

Wolfe made his camp upon the Island of Orleans, just below Quebec, and the siege began. But the days and weeks went past, and in spite of all that he could do, Quebec seemed no nearer being taken. The country round about was a desert. The houses of Quebec were shattered and ruined by the British guns, but safe within the walls the brave and wary French general, Montcalm, waited and watched. He waited the coming of winter, when the mighty St. Lawrence would be one frozen mass. For before then, he knew that the British ships must sail away, or be crushed like matchwood in the hungry jaws of the ice king.

"You may ruin the town," said one Frenchman, "but you will never get inside."

"I will have Quebec if I stay here till the end of November," replied Wolfe.

Day by day the British army was weakened by disease and death. Wolfe, himself, who had never been strong, became so ill that he could no longer go among his soldiers cheering them with brave words and smiles. He lay in bed, helpless and in pain, downcast, and almost in despair.

But as he lay there he resolved to make one more effort to gain the town. Up the steep cliffs there led a little pathway, so narrow that only one man could go at a time, so dangerous that it was but carelessly watched. Up this pathway Wolfe determined to lead his men. It was a plan daring almost to madness. Had it failed, it would have been called madness. It did not fail.

When Wolfe had once made up his mind, no danger made him afraid. Soon his plans were ready. Yet he had little hope of success. Before he made the attempt he wrote home to Pitt a letter showing how sad he was, "despairing as much as heroes can despair," it was said of him.

The night chosen for the adventure was dark and clear. There was no moon, but thousands of stars glittered and twinkled, as silently Wolfe's men stepped into the boats, and were carried across to the point where they were to land.

No one spoke, the gentle dip of muffled oars was the only sound. Wolfe, pale and thin, feeble of body, but eager of spirit, sat among his officers. As the boats moved slowly along, he repeated softly a poem called "An Elegy in a Country Churchyard," which had been written not long before by the poet Gray. "Gentlemen," said Wolfe, as he finished, "I would rather have written that poem than take Quebec."

Slowly the boats drifted on through the silent darkness. Suddenly a voice rang out through the night. "Who goes there?" cried a French sentry from the shore.

"France," replied a Highland officer, who was in one of the first boats, and who could speak French well.

"What regiment?" asked the sentinel.

"'The Queen's,'" replied the officer. Fortunately he knew that the French were expecting some boats with food to come down the river, and that "The Queen's" regiment would be guarding them.

The sentinel was satisfied. "Pass," he said, and the boats passed on with their loads of anxious, eager men.

But the danger was not over. Again they were challenged. Again the Highland officer replied. He spoke softly, fearing to speak too clearly lest his accent should betray him. But the sentinel was suspicious. "Why don't you speak louder?" he asked.

"Hush!" said the Highlander, "we are boats with food. Don't make a noise, the British will hear us."

Once more the sentinel was deceived, and in safety the boats at length reached the landing-place.

Wolfe was among the first to spring to shore. Quickly the men followed. For a moment their leader stood looking up at the rugged, frowning cliff which rose two hundred feet sheer above him. It was far more steep than even he had thought. "You can try it," he said calmly to an officer near him, "but I don't think you will get up."

Not get up! With such a leader! The climb began. Hot and panting, clinging to roots of trees, branches, bushes, slipping and stumbling, the men went on.

As they neared the top, the rustling of the bushes caught the ear of the sentinel above. "Who goes there?"

"France," replied the same Highland officer who had already saved the boats from discovery.

But this time the sentinel was not deceived. A few shots were fired at random into the darkness. It was too late. The first man had gained the top. In a few minutes Highlanders swarmed over the edge of the cliff. The French guard was overpowered and silenced, and when the sun rose it shone upon four thousand red coats drawn up in battle array upon the Heights of Abraham, as the place was called.

Breathless, panic-stricken messengers hurried with the news to the brave French commander. With white set face, and eyes hard and fixed, Montcalm looked across the plain to where the silent army stood. The long, red line showed clear against the dark wood and heavy sky, and where the sun broke through the clouds it caught the glitter of steel.

"We must crush them," said Montcalm.

Not till ten o'clock did the battle begin. Then Montcalm's men advanced. Indians terrible in war-paint and scalps, gay French soldiers, daring reckless Canadians, on they came. In quivering silence the British awaited them. Then the order to charge was given. The air was rent with British cheers, and the defiant scream of the bagpipes mingled with the Indian war-cry.

The fight was short and deadly. Everywhere amid the havoc strode Wolfe, pale and calm. A shot struck him in the wrist. Hastily tying his handkerchief round it, he went on. Again he was struck. Still he kept on. A third shot sent him staggering to the ground.

Quickly his officers carried him out of the fight. "It is all over with me," he said, as they laid him gently down. Then he lay still.

Suddenly one of the officers who stood beside him cried out, "They run! they run!"

"Who run?" asked Wolfe, raising himself.

"The enemy, sir," replied the officer; "they give way everywhere."

"Now, God be praised!" cried Wolfe, "I die in peace!" Then he turned on his side and spoke no more.

Carried along by the rush of fleeing soldiers, Montcalm, sorely wounded, was borne back to Quebec. Streaming with blood, reeling in pain, he still sat upon his horse, and so was hurried within the gate. There all was terror and confusion. "Alas! Alas!" cried a woman in the crowd, as she saw the general's stricken face and blood-stained coat, "Alas! Alas! the Marquess is killed!"

"It is nothing, it is nothing," he replied. "Do not trouble about me, my good friends." But even as he spoke he fell from his horse.

Montcalm too, like his gallant foe, was dying. "So much the better for me," he sighed; "I shall not live to see Quebec surrender." So he died, and with him died the hope of France in America.

Montcalm was buried in a convent within the walls of Quebec in a coffin hastily made, in a grave more hastily dug. Years later a British governor placed a marble slab over the spot. Upon it were the words, "Honour to Montcalm. Fate robbing him of victory gave him a glorious death."

When the great news of the taking of Quebec reached England there was much rejoicing. But it was a sort of mournful triumph, and although bonfires blazed and bells rang, hearts were sad for the loss of the brave young leader.

In one village there was no rejoicing. No bonfire was lit, no bell was rung, no cheer was heard in the street, for there, in a darkened house, a widowed mother mourned her boy. And the villagers, who had known and loved him too, felt her loss greater than a nation's triumph.

Upon the Heights of Abraham there stands a monument. It was placed

"SLIPPING AND STUMBLING, THE MEN WENT ON."

there in memory of the heroes of the siege of Quebec. Upon the one side is carved "Montcalm," upon the other, "Wolfe."

"The breezy call of incense-breathing morn,
    The swallow twitt'ring from the straw-built shed,
The cock's shrill clarion, or the echoing horn,
    No more shall rouse them from their lowly bed.

For them no more the blazing hearth shall burn,
    Or busy housewife ply her evening care;
No children run to lisp their sire's return,
    Or climb his knees the envied kiss to share.

The boast of heraldry, the pomp of power,
    And all that beauty, all that wealth e'er gave,
Awaits alike th' inevitable hour,
    The paths of glory lead but to the grave.

Can storied urn or animated bust
    Back to its mansions call the fleeting breath?
Can Honour's voice provoke the silent dust,
    Or Flatt'ry soothe the dull cold ear of Death?"

These are a few verses of the poem which Wolfe repeated as he crossed the St. Lawrence. Perhaps no more beautiful words could be found in which to mourn a hero's death.

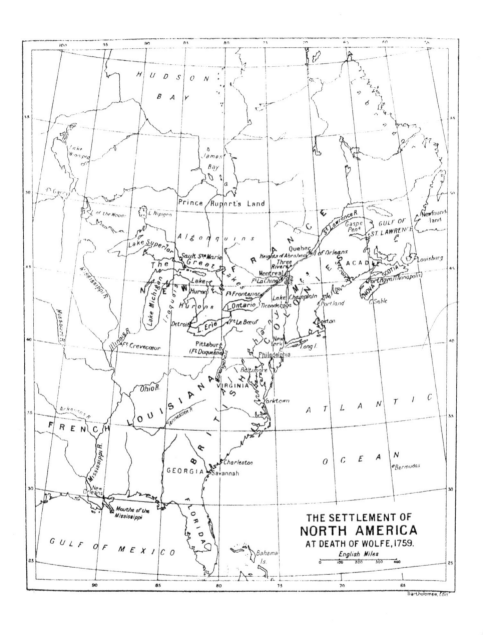

THE SETTLEMENT OF
NORTH AMERICA
AT DEATH OF WOLFE, 1759.

English Miles

CHAPTER 18

FOR THE EMPIRE

"There where the Loyalists came,
And the houses of men were few,
Little was all their wealth,
And great were the hardships they knew.

But greater the hardy faith
They kept unflinching and fine,
And chose to be naught in the world
For the pride of a loyal line."

BLISS CARMAN.

AFTER the taking of Quebec the war dragged on for another year. Then Montreal fell, and on 8th September 1760, the Marquess of Vaudrenil, the French Governor, gave up Canada to the British. In 1763, the Peace of Paris was signed, and by it, all Canada, and all the land east of the Mississippi, became British Possession.

"With a handful of men," said Pitt, "General Wolfe has added a Kingdom to British rule." By the Peace of Paris the story of New France was ended, and the story of British Canada began.

Britain is a Protestant country. It is also a free country, where no man is made to suffer for his religion. But at this time, the Roman Catholics were harshly treated. They were not allowed to hold any public office. They could not be members of parliament, or officers in the army or navy. In no way were they allowed to serve their country. King George wanted to make these same rules for Canada. But nearly all the people in Canada were Roman Catholic, and many saw how unfair this would be. So in 1774 the Quebec Act was passed. Among other things, this Act did away with the differences between Protestant and Catholic, and gave the Canadians many of their old French laws again. Thus their religion was left to the people of Canada, and in many other ways they had far more freedom than ever before.

This pleased the Canadians, but it made many of the old British Protestant colonists angry. They declared that the French rebels were treated better than they were. They grew angry about other things too, and at last they rose in rebellion against the mother country. Then the great war began which ended in the loss of all the British colonies in America except Canada. For Canada, which had been so lately won, not only refused to join the rebellion, but fought against the United States, as these lost colonies are now called. Once again Quebec was besieged. This time it did not fall. The Americans were driven away, and Canada became more surely a British possession.

But although the Americans had rebelled against their king, there were many among them who were still loyal, that, too, in face of scorn and persecution. After peace was made, these loyalists would not remain in the United States. They would not be ruled by a rebel President. To prove their loyalty to king and country, they chose rather to leave land, houses, money, friends, and all that they had. Some went home to England, but most journeyed across the boundary line and found a refuge in Canada.

Many a weary mile they trudged on foot, carrying their children and the few things they had been able to save on horseback. Houseless and tentless they slept at night under the open sky. They suffered from cold, hunger and weariness, often having to beg their bread, glad to accept kindness from the Indians on the way. But no hardship made them turn back.

The British were, and are, proud of these Loyalists. Parliament voted a large sum of money to help them in their troubles, and they were allowed to put the letters U.E. after their names. These letters mean United Empire.

The money sent from Britain was spent on food, clothes, and tools for the United Empire Loyalists. To each was given a hoe, spade, and axe. A plough and a cow were given between each two families, and many other things to help them to begin life over again were divided amongst them. Each one, too, received two hundred acres of land in Canada. But in spite of all that was done, the first few years were very hard for the Loyalists.

A great part of the west of Canada was still unknown. It was wild prairie-land or dark and tangled forest. But there, most of the United Empire Loyalists found a home. But at first it was a life of hardship. Many of them had left rich and beautiful homes where they had been accustomed to every comfort. Now before they could find a shelter for their heads, they had to fell the trees and build their houses. They had to clear the ground and sow and reap, before they could get corn for bread. They had to hunt and trap wild animals for food, often in the end having scarce enough to eat. One year the harvest failed, and things were so bad that r it was called the Famine Year. That year, many of the Loyalists had to live on roots, wild berries, and nuts. But, through all the suffering and the struggle, none wished to go back to America. And we may be proud to remember that it is from such brave and loyal men and women, that many of the Canadians of to-day are descended.

Some of the Loyalists scattered through Canada, some went to what is now Nova Scotia, but most went to the west. That part became known as Upper Canada, and the part along the St. Lawrence already settled by the French, Lower Canada. So it came about that Canada was really divided into two. Upper Canada was peopled by British Protestants, Lower Canada by French Catholics. Each part had its own Legislative Council and Assembly, that is, a kind of parliament. In the one there was British law, in the other, for the most part, French law. One would think that there was no union, or likelihood of union, between the two. But they had one bond of union—loyalty to their king. And out of these widely different peoples came the United Canada of to-day, and the French Canadians, through every storm and trouble, have proved themselves as staunch and true as any Briton born.

CHAPTER 19

THE STORY OF LAURA SECORD

AT home the great Napoleon was fighting Britain. He was fighting her on many a bloody battlefield; he was fighting her in other ways, doing his best to ruin British trade and shipping. He forbade any country to trade with Britain, and his ships watched the seas, ready to attack any ship carrying goods to Britain.

King George replied by forbidding any nation to trade with France, and threatening to seize all ships carrying goods to French ports. Here was a state of things likely to ruin the trade of many lands. The United States did much trade with France, and the Americans were very angry with King George for his Orders in Council, as his decree was called. They quite forgot that Napoleon had begun the quarrel by forbidding people to trade with Britain.

Great Britain, being an island, needs a large navy to watch her shores. At this time it was difficult to find enough sailors to man her ships, and sometimes, too, the sailors would run away. So the British claimed the right to search all ships belonging to neutral lands (that is, all lands taking neither one side or the other, in the quarrel), in order to find runaway sailors. Countries at war have always had this right, but it made the Americans angry, and on 18th June 1812 they declared war against Britain once more.

But the Americans of course did not sail over to Britain to fight there. They had no thought of that. But they longed to possess another and much nearer land. They marched into Canada and fought there. The Canadians had really nothing to do with the quarrel, and it was hard that they had to suffer. The Americans thought, too, that Canada having been so lately conquered, would not want to fight for Britain. They were much mistaken.

If you look on the map, you will see that all across the continent of America the United States and Canada lie side by side. The line where one country touches another is called a frontier. Canada had seventeen thousand miles of frontier to defend, and not six thousand men with which to do it. And Great Britain fighting at home against Napoleon had few soldiers to spare.

But the people of Canada, both French and British, gathered to defend their homes. Many Indians too, well pleased with British rule, joined them, and the Americans found they had no easy task in front of them.

One of the great heroes of this war is Major-General Sir Isaac Brock. He was not a Canadian born, for he had been only about ten years in the country. But he was a true Canadian at heart. He was a gallant soldier and a wise general, and his men loved him, and were ready to follow him anywhere. Again and again he led his soldiers to victory, beating armies twice or three times more numerous than his own. But at last at the battle of Queenston Heights on the Niagara he was killed. "Don't mind me!" he cried, as he fell, "push on, boys!" And with a cry of "Revenge the general!" his men rushed on, scattering the enemy in flight. Swearing, cheering, sobbing, they pursued the fleeing foe till night fell. It was a victory indeed, but one dearly bought the life of their brave commander.

There were many other men who in this struggle won for themselves great and honourable names. But it was difficult to find another commander as brave and as clever as Brock. So back and forth the fortune of war swayed, now one side winning, now another. Many battles were fought, many brave deeds done, but I must tell of how a woman once saved the British from defeat. A British officer named Fitzgibbon had been sent to hold a post called Beaver Dams, about twelve miles from Niagara. He had only sixty men, half of whom were Red Indians. The post was important, and the Americans made up their minds to seize it. With great secrecy they made their preparations in order to take the post by surprise, for a few miles off, at a place called Twelve Mile Creek, lay another force of two hundred men. But the Americans hoped to surprise Fitzgibbon, so that he should have no time to get help.

The secret, however, leaked out. A Canadian named James Secord overheard their talk and learned their plans. But he was lying ill. He had fought with Brock at Queenston where he had been badly wounded, and he was still unable to move.

With five hundred men, fifty horse and two cannons, the Americans were marching upon the handful of men at Beaver Dams. Secord knew it, but could do nothing. To the helpless sick man the knowledge was torture. Only twenty miles away, his fellow-countrymen were awaiting certain death, and there was no means of warning them. There was no man he could send, for all the country was watched by American sentries. Even if any man had been willing to risk his life, Secord knew of none he could trust—none but his wife. And to her he whispered the thought that tormented him. "They must all die," he said, "for lack of a word of warning."

"But that shall not be," said Laura Secord, "I will go."

So as the sun rose on a still June morning, Laura Secord started on her long and dangerous walk. There was no sign of haste, nothing to show that she was setting out upon a journey. Slowly driving a cow before her, as if she were taking it home to be milked, she passed the American sentries. Slowly down the country road she passed. The birds were singing in the dawn, the air was sweet with the scent of wild flowers, and as Laura walked, her dress brushed the dew from the grass. But no eyes had she, or ears, for the beauty of the day. With beating heart, and breath that came and went sharply, she strolled along. At last the edge of the forest was reached. Under the shadow

"Driving a cow before her, Laura Secord passed the American sentries."

of the great trees passed the woman and the cow. Soon they were deep in the forest, shut from all eyes. Then there was no more need of pretence. Leaving her cow to find its way home as best it might, Laura ran. On and on she went, panting, breathless, gasping, now stopping a moment to rest, now hurrying on again, startled by a rustle in the bushes, trembling at the howl of some wild animal.

A walk of twenty miles along a level, well-made road may not seem a great task for a strong woman used to a country life. But to go twenty miles through pathless forest, over bridgeless streams, through mire and swamp, haunted every moment by the fear of discovery, needed all the strength and all the courage of a right brave woman.

Hour by hour Laura walked, and ran, and scrambled onward. The sun rose high, and sank again, and the moon shone out ere she reached her journey's end. Then, just as she thought that her labour was over, Red Men rushed out upon her from behind a tree, and barred her path. For a moment it seemed to Laura that her pain and toil had been of no use, and that a death of torture was to be her fate. Then joyfully she saw that the Indians were friendly. In a few minutes she was led before Fitzgibbon.

Quickly Laura's story was told, and as the soldier listened, he bowed in reverence before the brave lady. Then with glowing words of thanks and praise ringing in her ears, Laura was led away to a farmhouse near to rest.

Quickly Fitzgibbon made his plans. First he sent a messenger hurrying towards Twelve Mile Creek to ask for help. Then he ordered his Indians to scatter through the wood, and watch for the approach of the enemy.

The night passed quietly, but as the day dawned, the gleam of steel was seen, the tramp of men heard. As the Americans came on, the Indians, yelling horribly, fired upon them from all sides. They made so much noise, they fired with such deadly sureness, keeping out of sight all the time, that the Americans believed that there were hundreds against them. For two hours the fight against an unseen foe lasted. Then the Americans began to waver. Their leader was uncertain what to do. Believing himself surrounded, he hesitated whether to go on or to go back. At this moment Fitzgibbon, at the head of his thirty redcoats, appeared bearing a flag of truce. The firing ceased, and after a few minutes' parley the American commander gave in.

Fitzgibbon had hardly expected to succeed so easily. Now he scarcely knew what to do. How could thirty soldiers and a few savages guard five hundred prisoners? But soon two hundred men arrived from Twelve Mile Creek, and his difficulties were at an end.

Canada did not forget Laura Secord and her brave deed. Nor did Britain forget her. Years later, when King Edward, then Prince of Wales, visited Canada, he found time, in the midst of balls and parties, to go to see an old woman, and hear from her own lips how, when she was young, she had carried a message through wood and wilderness to save her country from defeat.

CHAPTER 20

RED RIVER SETTLEMENT

FOR two years the war of 1812, as it was called, went on. From beginning to end it was a wicked, useless war, thrust upon an unwilling people. And when at last peace came, neither side seemed to have gained anything. The boundary lines were hardly changed, and in the treaty of peace, the pretended causes of the war were not even mentioned.

But Canada did really gain something. The population of Canada was now very mixed. There were French Canadians, United Empire Loyalists, English, Scottish and Irish settlers, and they had often been jealous of each other, and had misunderstood each other. Now that a common danger had drawn them together, they had all joined in fighting for their country, and Canada had shown, as she has shown ever since, that she was "for the Empire." Strange to say, too, when the heat of battle was past, the bitterness which had been between America and Canada began to pass away, for each nation had learned to respect his neighbour beyond the frontier.

But while the war was going on, a struggle of another kind was taking place in the Great North-West.

You remember how the Hudson Bay Company had been founded, and how, in spite of fearful difficulties it had grown and prospered. Soon after the Conquest (that is the conquest of Canada from the French), another fur company was formed called the North-West Company, and later still there was a third called the X.Y. Company. Soon all these three companies began to quarrel, and whenever their men or officers met, there was sure to be fighting. They stole each other's furs whenever they could, and often the skins passed through the hands of all three before reaching the market.

Things were in this state when a Scottish nobleman, the Earl of Selkirk, began to take a great interest in the fur trade and in the Hudson Bay Company. From the Company he got a grant of a large piece of land near Lake Winnipeg, and began to form a settlement there.

Lord Selkirk brought his settlers from the Highlands of Scotland. They were men and women used to a rough climate and a hard life. But hard as their life had been, they came to a much harder. On the way out they suffered from fever and hunger on board ship. When they arrived they had to pass a winter on the icy shores of Hudson Bay in clothes warm enough perhaps for Scotland, but not half warm enough for the icy north.

At last, however, the bitter cold winter passed, spring came, and the settlers journeyed to Red River, where they were to build their new homes, and begin life afresh.

But the Nor'-Westers were the sworn enemies of the Hudson Bay Company, they were the enemies too of these new settlers. They wanted to keep the North-West to themselves, and they vowed to root out these "gardeners" and shepherds who came to turn their hunting-grounds into wheat-field and pasture. Besides the Nor'-Westers, Lord Selkirk had another enemy in the Métis or Bois-Brulés. These were a race half French, half Indian, the children of the roving Coureurs de Bois. They loved the wild wastes and solitudes. Their home was the rolling prairie, their roof the sky. They wanted no towns and churches, no herds and wheat-fields, and as more and more land was settled by farmers, as trees were felled, and the earth furrowed by the plough, the Métis retreated to the wilds. Now they gladly joined the Nor'-Westers in ousting the new comers, who wanted to turn yet more of their beloved wilderness into ploughed land.

So scarcely had the Scottish settlers arrived when there swooped down upon them an armed company of Nor'-West men, fierce in Indian war-paint, and very terrible to the eyes of these simple Highlanders.

The Nor'-Westers succeeded in what they had set out to do. The little band of settlers were so terrified that they fled for refuge to the Hudson Bay Company's fort at Pembina, leaving all their scanty wealth in the hands of the enemy.

But Highlanders are not easily beaten. They bided their time, and the next year they returned to Red River, built their houses, ploughed and sowed their land, and settled down in peace.

But the peace was not for long. Once again the Nor'-Westers swooped down upon the new colonists. Again, they were scattered, and, where their homes had been, lay a heap of black and smoking ruins.

But the struggle was not over. More men came from Scotland, many of the scattered colonists returned, and once more Red River rose from its ashes.

Then followed months of hardship and struggle, a fight with cold and hunger, with difficulties and dangers of all kinds. Even to these sturdy Highlanders, bred to hardship and toil, the life proved too dreadful. Many of them gave up the struggle, and fought their way back through wilderness and forest to Canada, or died on the way. Others, false to their friends, took the easier way, and joined their enemies, the Nor'-Westers.

But the Nor'-Westers were not content. They had sworn the utter destruction of the colony, and they meant to keep their word. So one June day, three hundred half-breeds, fearfully bedaubed with paint, gay in savage splendour, rode down upon the settlement. The governor and about thirty men went out to meet them. They were quickly surrounded, and he and about twenty of his men were shot dead.

Those who were left fled back to the fort, where soon all was terror and confusion. Children cried out in fear, women wept for their dead, or, stricken and white, awaited they knew not what fate.

Two days later, robbed of all they possessed, the remaining colonists left their homes to the flames and the destroyer, and wandered forth again houseless and penniless.

But while the Nor'-Westers drank and sang, and rejoiced at the utter downfall of Red River, Lord Selkirk was on his way to avenge his people. With about a hundred men he arrived at Fort William, the chief post of the Nor'-Westers. Forcing the gate he took possession of the town, and the murderers were soon made prisoner and sent to Montreal to be tried.

Again the colonists returned to their ruined, forsaken homes, but the summer was gone, and the harvest poor. Famine stared them in the face, and after fearful sufferings and long endurance, they once more took refuge at Pembina.

In the spring, however, they came back again. This time all seemed to go well. In peace the fields were ploughed and sown. In peace the corn sprang up, grew and ripened. Then one summer afternoon the sky was darkened. The air was filled with the hum and buzz of insects, and a flight of locusts settled on the land.

They covered the trees and the fields, they swarmed in the houses. At night the earth was smiling and green. In the morning it was a grey wilderness.

Once again ruin and famine stared the settlers in the face. The onslaught of wild half-breeds had been easier to bear than this. They at least could be fought. But against this new enemy the stoutest arm, the bravest heart, was helpless. Stricken with despair, many a strong man bowed his head and sobbed as if his heart would break.

Once more, with weary feet, the colonists trudged the well-known way to Pembina, there to spend the winter on the charity of the Hudson Bay Company.

The next year it was found to be useless to plough or sow, for the locusts still swarmed everywhere, killing each green blade as it sprang to life, and poisoning both air and water with their dying millions. But the colonists lit great fires which attracted the locusts; they fell into the fires in thousands, and at last the plague was burned out. The land was sown once more, and after eight years of struggle and disaster Red River Settlement began to prosper. Then tired of fighting, the Hudson Bay Company and the North-West Company joined together and shared the fur trade between them. So there was peace.

But the struggles of the Red River colonists were by no means over. For many a year their life was full of hardship, but bit by bit they won success. And to-day the great corn prairies of Manitoba stretch mile upon mile. The golden grain ripens in the summer sun, falls beneath the sharp knives of the reaping-machine, and is carried far and wide to give food to the world and bring wealth to Canada. And we look back, and remember with pride, the Scotsman who first saw that these lands were good for corn-growing, and the brave colonists who would not be beaten, and who returned again and yet again with unconquered courage, until at last they won the battle against misfortune.

CHAPTER 21

LOUIS RIEL

DURING the war of 1812 Upper and Lower Canada had been drawn together. French and British forgot their differences and jealousies. But when peace had once more come these differences and jealousies were felt again, and the French especially thought that they had not enough voice in the ruling of the land. Many of them were still very ignorant, being able neither to read nor write. These scarcely knowing what they wanted, but easily led by a handful of clever and discontented men, rose in rebellion.

This Rebellion they called the Patriot War. There was never any real reason for it, and it was soon over. But it made wise people see that something must be done to prevent such discontent in the future. So it came about that Canada, which, in 1791, had been divided into British Canada and French Canada, was, in 1841, united again. It was decided that there should be only one Parliament, to which both French and British should come in equal numbers. It was also decided that the colony should have "responsible government." Responsible government means government by those who are responsible, or answerable to, the greater number. They may continue to rule only so long as the greater number of the people wish them to do so. When they can no longer get the greater number to vote for them they must cease to rule. Then there is a "General election," and people choose again those whom they wish to have power.

The Assembly of Upper Canada had met at Toronto, that of Lower Canada at Quebec. The new parliament now met at Kingston, on Lake Ontario, which was between the two, and beautiful romantic Quebec was left lonely on its rock.

For the next few years parliament was moved from place to place, no one being able to fix which was best. At last Queen Victoria was asked to settle the question. She chose a little village on the river Ottawa. And there at Ottawa fine new buildings were built, and there the Parliament of the Dominion of Canada has sat ever since.

But this union of Upper and Lower Canada did not mean the whole of Canada as we see it marked on our maps to-day. It meant only the two states of Ontario and Quebec. Nova Scotia, New Brunswick, and all the great land known as the North-West Territory were still separate provinces. But gradually these lands joined the union, and now the Dominion of Canada stretches all across the north of America from sea to sea. Ontario, Quebec, New Brunswick, Nova Scotia, Manitoba, British Columbia, and Prince Edward Island, are the names of the provinces which make up the great Dominion. Newfoundland alone has a separate government.

As time went on and Canada grew into a united whole it was no longer thought well that any province should be ruled by a company, and all the lands belonging to the Hudson Bay Company were brought under the direct rule of the Canadian Government.

Since the days of Lord Selkirk Red River had prospered. Bit by bit the wild prairie had been reclaimed. It had been ploughed and sown, and now corn-fields waved where lately the bison had roamed. Houses, schools, and churches stood where pine and hemlock tree had towered their dark heads for ages. The wild Métis had forgotten their hate, and side by side thrifty Scottish settlers and adventurous French half-breeds lived in peace, the one careful and saving, the other careless, passionate and spendthrift.

But most of these half-breeds knew, and cared, nothing for Canada. To them the Company was everything, and they were content to live beneath its rule. But when they heard that Canada, not the Company, was to rule in future, they thought that they were being given over to some foreign power.

The Métis were very ignorant, and it was a pity that no one was sent to explain to these simple people what was really happening; it might have saved the shedding of much blood and many tears. No one was sent, and so they rose in rebellion, led by a man called Louis Riel.

Louis Riel, himself a Méti, was a clever, but half-educated man. He thought himself a patriot, and soon had an army of six or seven hundred men behind him. They took possession of Fort Garry, one of the strongest of the Hudson Bay Company's forts. They made many of the settlers prisoners, and proclaimed a new government, of which Riel was president.

Backed by his army the new president did as he liked, taking prisoner and banishing whom he chose. One of the worst things he did was to condemn a young man named Scott to death, because he had spoken scornfully of his government. After a mere mockery of a trial, Scott was led out and shot mercilessly by some half-drunk Métis.

The news of this murder rang like a war-cry through all Canada. It roused to indignation every fair-minded Canadian, and Colonel Garnet Wolseley, a young British officer then in Canada, was sent to Fort Garry to put down the rebellion. But when Riel heard of his coming he ran away to the United States, and the rebellion was at an end.

This disturbed part of the dominion was now made into the province of Manitoba, and many of the things for which Riel had fought were granted by the Manitoba Act.

But fifteen years later Riel came again, and there was another and far more serious rebellion. It is difficult to explain all the causes for this rebellion. The Métis thought that they were being badly treated by the Government. They thought that their land was being taken from them, and that they had not enough power in Parliament. They could get no one to listen to their grievances, so at length they sent to Riel, and asked him to come to help them.

Riel came, but this time he seemed more like a madman than a patriot. He called himself "The Liberator," and said that he was the bearer of a message from God. He lived in a curious fashion, eating chiefly blood boiled in milk, and did many things to try to make people think that he was truly the messenger from God that he said he was.

But in spite of his mad antics, or perhaps because of them, Riel had soon a large army of Métis at his back. And not only Métis, but Red Men followed him. Tribe after tribe smeared their faces with war-paint, danced the war-dance, and set out to join the rebels. The North-West was full of the nameless horror and terror of the Red Man, as Canada had been long years before. Great and terrible as their names, were some of the chiefs who took part in the war—Big Bear, Wandering Spirit, Yellow Mud, Bare Neck, and Man-Who-Wins were some of them—and there were many more with as strange and high-sounding names.

As soon as the rebellion began, the news of it flashed like wild-fire over Canada, and from all sides volunteers came, eager to fight for their country. For weeks and months the rattle of firearms and the terrible Indian war-cry was heard in the North-West, and all the land was filled with blood and tears. But in the end the rebels were beaten. Riel was taken prisoner, tried, and condemned to death for high treason, for he "did maliciously and treacherously levy and make war against our Lady, the Queen."

With Riel were hanged eight Indians, and a few others were imprisoned. So ended what is known as the Saskatchewan rebellion.

With this rebellion, war in Canada came to an end, so that since then the country has found time and strength to grow great. And thus we leave a united and peaceful Canada. From that June day, hundreds of years ago, on which John Cabot landed to plant the red cross of St. George upon "the new isle," it has grown step by step until it is a mighty Dominion, stretching from sea to sea. It is a nation within a nation, strong and prosperous in itself, and yet a part of our great Empire.

LIST OF KINGS AND GOVENORS

KINGS OF GREAT BRITAIN AND IRELAND.	KINGS OF FRANCE.	RULERS OF CANADA.
James VI. . . 1603	Henry IV. . . 1589	
	Louis XIII. . 1610	Samuel de Champlain . 1608
Charles I. . . 1625		
		Chevalier de Montmagny 1636
	Louis XIV. . 1643	
		Chevalier d'Ailleboust . 1648
Commonwealth 1649		
		Jean de Lauzon . . . 1651
		Vicomte d'Argenson . . 1658
Charles II. . 1660		
		Baron D'Avaugour . . 1661
		Sieur de Mésy 1663
		Chevalier de Courcelles . 1665
		Comte de Frontenac . . 1672
		Sieur de la Barre . . . 1682
James II. . . 1685		Marquis de Denonville . 1685
William and		Comte de Frontenac . . 1689
Mary . . 1689		
William III.		
(alone) . . 1694		
		Chevalier de Callières . 1698
Anne . . . 1702		
		Marquis de Vaudreuil . 1703
George I. . . 1714		
	Louis XV. . . 1715	
		Marquis de Beauharnois 1726
George II. . . 1727		
		Comte de la Galissonière 1747
		Marquis de la Jonquiere 1749
		Marquis Duquesne . . 1752
		Marquis de Vaudreuil . 1755
		BRITISH GOVERNORS
George III. . 1760		Lord Amherst 1760
		Sir James Murray . . . 1763
		Sir Guy Carleton . . . 1766
	Louis XVI. . 1774	
		Major-General Haldeman 1777
		Henry Hamilton . . . 1785
		Lord Dorchester . . . 1786
		(Sir Guy Carleton)
	Republic . . 1792	

Kings of Great Britain and Ireland.	Kings of France.	Rulers of Canada.
		Gen. Sir R. Prescott . . 1796
	Napoleon I. . 1804 (Emperor)	
		Sir James Craig . . . 1807
		Sir George Prevost . . 1811
	Louis XVIII. . 1814	
		Sir J. Sherbrooke . . . 1816
		Duke of Richmond . . 1818
George IV. . 1820		Lord Dalhousie . . . 1820
	Charles X. 1824	
		Sir James Kempt . . . 1828
William IV. . 1830	Louis Philippe 1830	Lord Aylmer 1830
		Lord Gosford 1835
Victoria . . 1837		
		Sir John Colborne . . 1838
		Lord Durham 1838
		Hon. C. Poulett . . . 1839
		GOVERNORS-GENERAL OF UNITED CANADA
		Lord Sydenham . . . 1839 (Hon. C. Poulett)
		Sir Charles Bagot . . . 1842
		Lord Metcalfe 1843
		Earl Cathcart 1845
		Earl of Elgin 1847
	Republic . . 1848	
	Napoleon III. 1852 (Emperor)	
		Sir Edmund Bond Head . 1854
		Viscount Monck . . . 1861
		GOVERNORS-GENERAL OF THE DOMINION.
		Sir John Young . . . 1868 (Lord Lisgar)
	Republic . . 1870	
		Earl of Dufferin . . . 1872
		Marquis of Lorne . . . 1878
		Marquis of Lansdowne . 1883
		Earl of Derby 1888
		Earl of Aberdeen . . . 1893
		Earl of Minto 1898
Edward VII. . 1901		
		Earl Grey 1904

AUSTRALIA

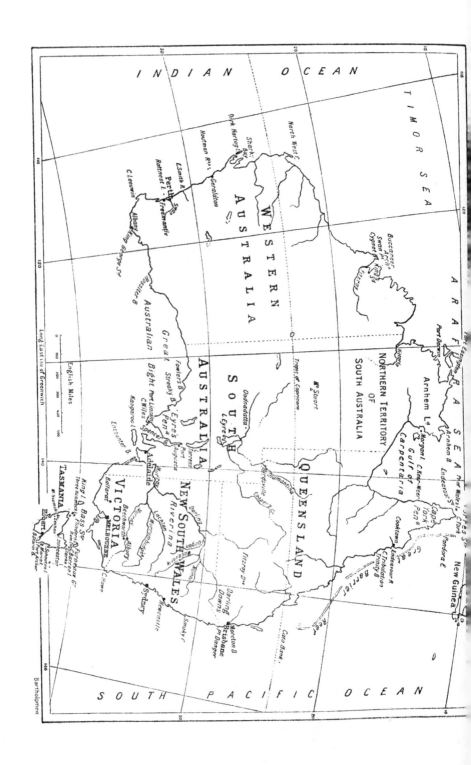

CHAPTER 1

"THERE IS NOTHING NEW UNDER THE SUN"

WISE people tell us that the land of Australia is perhaps the oldest in the world. At a time when the wide ocean swept over the continent of Europe, when our little island still lay far beneath the rippling waves, the land of Australia stood above the lone waters.

Yet to us Australia is a new discovered country. Long ages ago indeed travellers and learned men told tales of a Great South Land which lay somewhere in the Southern Seas. But no eye had seen that fabled country, no ship had touched that unknown shore It was a country dim and mysterious as fairyland. On ancient maps we find it marked with rough uncertain lines, "The Southeme Unknowne Lande," but how it came to be so marked, how the stories about it first came to be told, and believed, we shall very likely never know.

It is hard to tell too, who, among white men, first set foot on this great island. If one of the brave sailors of those far-off times did by chance touch upon its shore, he found little there to make him stay, or encourage him to return. For in those days what men chiefly sought was trade. And in Australia there was no place for trade. It was a great, wide, silent land where there were no towns, or even houses. It was peopled only by a few black savages, who wore no clothes, who had no wants, and who cared for nothing but to eat and drink.

But in the seventeenth century, when Holland was mistress of the seas, and the Dutch planted their flag on every shore, they found their way to the Great South Land.

It was a Dutchman who discovered Tasmania. He called it Van Dieman's Land in honour of the Governor-General of the Dutch East Indies. But the name was afterwards changed to Tasmania, by which name we know it now. The great Gulf of Carpentaria is named after another Dutchman, and all round the northern, western and southern shores, here and there may be found names to remind us of those old Dutch adventurers. But the name New Holland which the Dutch gave to the whole land has long since been forgotten.

The Dutch did little more than discover the coast. They founded no colonies, they built no towns, and so their hold on the land was hardly real. They marked New Holland upon their maps, but they knew little about it. No man knew what a vast land New Holland was, or how far stretching were the rolling plains of which they had had only a glimpse.

Soon Holland as a great sea power gave way to another which was to become still greater. Van Tromp the Dutchman was beaten by Blake the Englishman.And after that the Dutch seem to have lost all interest in the Great South Land.

Then in 1699 a British sailor called Dampier set out on a voyage of discovery to the Southern seas. He was more than half a pirate and had led a life of wild adventure. But he was a daring seaman, and had already been to New Holland more than once. And so King William III. chose him to lead an expedition of discovery.

One February day Dampier sailed out from England, and six months later anchored in a bay on the west coast of New Holland, which he called Shark's Bay, because his men killed and ate many sharks there. It is still called Shark's Bay.

For some time Dampier cruised along the shores taking note of all that he saw, of the land, the birds, and beasts. Among the birds, Dampier saw gaily coloured parrots and cockatoos, and black swans. Among the beasts, the chief was a curious-looking animal with a long tail and long hind legs upon which it leaped and hopped about. The natives called it Kanguro.

He saw a few natives. They were tall, thin, and black, with blinking eyes and frizzled hair. They had no weapons except wooden spears, they wore no clothes, and their houses, which he only saw in the distance, looked to him like haycocks. But some had no houses at all. "They lay in the open air without covering, the earth being their bed and heaven their canopy. They had no possessions of any kind. Not soe much as a catt or a dog." With such people there was no hope of trade, and in those days no one thought of taking possession of a land unless there was some trade to be done.

Having cruised about for some time and finding no fresh water, Dampier feared to stay longer, lest his men should fall ill in that desert land. So he steered away to the East Indies and from thence sailed homeward.

Many years passed. Now and again a ship touched upon the shores of New Holland but no one took much interest in it. It was a barren, useless land most men thought, a stony desert for the greater part, good enough for the few wild black fellows who lived there, but never a home for white men. Besides this, the British, who were now the great sea power, were busy fighting in India and America, and had little time and few ships to spare for peaceful exploration.

But in the long reign of George III. , when after much fighting Britain was at length at peace with all the world, men once more turned their thoughts to peaceful things. Then in 1768 Captain James Cook was sent upon an exploring expedition.

James Cook had had a very exciting life, but there is no room to tell about it here. As a small boy he was sent to serve in a draper's shop, but at the age of fourteen he ran away to sea, and from then till now when he was forty, his life had been full of excitement and adventure.

In this voyage, Captain Cook sailed all along the eastern coast of Australia, a thing which no white man had ever done. He landed in many places, naming capes, bays, and points, as he passed. One great bay he named Botany Bay, because of the many plants and flowers to be found there. And here he set up the Union Jack, cut the name of his ship and the date of his landing on the trees near, and claimed the land for King George.

Cook and his men had many adventures. At one time they were nearly wrecked. The ship struck upon a rock and stuck fast. The water began to come in so quickly, that although the men worked hard at the pumps, it seemed as if the ship would sink. But luckily the sea was smooth, and there was little wind, and after much hard work they were able to steer into a safe harbour. Here they ran the ship ashore, and found a hole in the bottom big enough to have sunk it. But by good fortune a piece of coral rock had stuck in the hole, and this had saved them.

Having mended the ship as best they could they once more set sail, and at last readied what is now known as Torres Strait, having explored the whole eastern coast of Australia.

At Torres Strait Cook landed. Once more he set up the British flag and claimed the whole eastern coast with all its bays, harbours, rivers, and islands, for King George. And to this great tract he gave the name of New South Wales. There in that far-off land, their little ship, a mere speck between blue sky and bluer sea, this handful of Britons claimed new realms for their king. And to attest their claim, volley upon volley of musketry rolled out, awakening the deep silence of that unknown shore. There was none to answer or deny the challenge, and when the noise of cannon died upon the quiet air there was only the sigh of trees, the ripple of waves, and the scream of wild birds to break the stillness.

CHAPTER 2

THE FOUNDING OF SYDNEY

AFTER Cook sailed away the great island-continent was left once again to silent loneliness. Cook made other voyages, but did not discover much more of Australia, and for many years few white men touched upon the shores of the Great South Land.

Then came the war in which Britain lost all her American colonies. It was a great loss, how great at the time perhaps few knew. But in one way the loss soon began to be felt.

The British in those days instead of keeping evil-doers in prison at home, used to send them to work upon the farms or plantations in America. When America was no longer a part of the British Empire, convicts, as such evil-doers were called, could not be sent there. The prisons at home became full to overflowing. Something had to be done, and at last it was decided to make use of New South Wales and found a colony there to which convicts might be sent.

So on 13th May 1787, the "First Fleet," as it afterwards came to be called by Australians, sailed out on its long voyage. In the eight or ten ships there were about a thousand people. Nearly eight hundred of these were convicts, both men and women, the rest were soldiers and marines to guard them.

With the fleet, as Governor-General of the new colony, went Captain Arthur Phillip.

On the way out the ships stopped at Teneriffe and at Cape Town, where the Dutch Governor received them kindly. Here they took aboard so many cocks and hens, sheep and cattle, that the ships looked more like Noah's arks than anything else.

In June 1788 the new colonists arrived at Botany Bay, where it had been decided to found the colony. But Captain Phillip did not think it a good place, and went exploring in a small boat further north until he found the beautiful Jackson Bay.

Here Captain Phillip decided to found the new colony. He landed and set up the Union Jack, and gathering round the flagstaff, he and his officers drank to the king's health, and to the success of the colony.

The convicts were landed, the soldiers were drawn up in line, guns were fired, and Captain Phillip made a speech to the convicts. He told them that now under a new sky, in a new home, they had once again a chance to forget their evil ways, and begin a new life. Once again they had a chance to prove themselves good British subjects. This was the first speech in the

English language that had ever been made in that far-off land, and when Captain Phillip had finished, a British cheer rang out.

Thus the city of Sydney was founded.

Now began a busy time. The stillness of that silent land was broken for ever. All day long the woods rang with the sound of the axe. All day long the ring of hammer and anvil was heard, the tinkle of the mason's trowel, the sighing of the carpenter's saw. There was everything to do. There were houses to build, roads to cut, harbours to make. The land had first to be cleared of trees, and wood and stone had to be quarried and hewn for building. With all this to do, there was little time left for farming.

Besides, among the soldiers, and sailors, and convicts, there were no farmers. None among them knew how to set about the work. The season was dry, the seed which was sown did not sprout, or was eaten by rats, and there was little or no harvest. The sheep and cattle died, or ran away into the forest and were seen no more.

Soon the food which had been brought from home grew scarce, and the promised ships which were to bring more, did not appear. The little colony began to starve. Convicts and freemen alike grew gaunt and pale. The governor himself knew what it meant to go hungry, for he would not fare better than the others, and he gave up his private stores for the use of all. "If any convict complains," he said, "let him come to Government House, and he will see that we are no better off there."

Hollow-cheeked and faint, every man looked eagerly, longingly, out to sea, straining weary eyes to catch a glimpse of a white sail upon the blue waste of water. Day after day passed. No sail appeared. Little work was done, for men who are always hungry cannot work.

The colonists had brought food for two years. Now three had passed, and still no help came from home. With hundreds and hundreds of miles between them and Britain, they seemed to be cast away and forgotten. They knew nothing of what was happening in the world. They had no means of knowing if they were really forgotten, or if some mischance had befallen the ships sent out to them. There was no way by which they could send a message home. They could do nothing but wait.

At last one morning a ship came in sight What joy there was! The women wept, the men cheered.

Eagerly the colonists crowded round the new arrivals asking for news of home. They heard with joy that they had not been utterly forgotten and neglected. Ships with stores had been sent, but had been wrecked on the way.

Soon another ship arrived, then another and another, The long pain of hunger was at an end, and for a time at least the little colony was saved from starvation. But famine came upon them again, and at one time things were so bad that people who were asked to dine at Government House were told to bring their own bread with them.

With the ships bringing food to the colony came a regiment of soldiers. They were called the New South Wales Corps. The Marines and their officers, who had come out in the "First Fleet," then went home; and Captain Phillip was not sorry that they should go, for although they had been sent out to help to keep the convicts in order, they had themselves been very unruly, and had added much to the governor's difficulties. These difficulties were great, for it was no easy matter to rule a colony made up of wild, bad men, sent there in punishment of their misdeeds. But, as will be seen, the New South Wales Corps was not much help to the governor.

In December 1792 Governor Phillip, worn out by five years of hardship, gave up his post and sailed home.

He was succeeded by Captain Hunter, but until he arrived the colony was left in the hands of Major Grose, leader of the New South Wales Corps.

Captain Phillip had been gentle and just. He had shared every hardship with the colonists, and had tried to make the convicts better. Grose cared nothing for the improvement of the convicts, and he was utterly unfit to rule. He allowed the soldiers to do as they liked, and they very soon became wild, riotous, and drunken. They took everything into their own hands, and soon from being merely soldiers, they became the merchants and rulers of the colony. Everything coming into the colony had to pass through their hands. But the thing they traded in most, and made most money out of, was rum.

Some free settlers had now come to Sydney, and they were allowed to have convicts to help them on their farms. The officers and men of the New South Wales Corps also took land, and had convict labourers, whom they paid for their work in rum. The soldiers made friends of these convicts, and they drank and gambled together, so that the convicts, instead of becoming better, became worse, and when Governor Hunter arrived, he found that all the good that Governor Phillip had done was destroyed. The whole colony was filled with riot, disorder, drunkenness, and misery.

Captain Hunter tried to put things right again. He tried to stop the trade in rum, but he was not strong enough to do it. The "Rum Corps," as the soldiers came to be called, had got the upper hand, and they meant to keep it. So during the whole time of Hunter's rule, he had to fight the men and officers of the Rum Corps.

This was the darkest time in the whole history of Australia. But dark though it was, it was now that the foundation of Australia's greatness in trade was laid.

With the New South Wales Corps there had come out a Captain John MacArthur. He, like so many others, received a grant of land, and began farming. He soon saw that the land was very good for rearing sheep, and began to turn his attention to them. But whereas others thought of rearing them for food, he thought of them for their wool After a great deal of trouble he got "wool-bearing sheep," first from the Cape, and then from King George's own famous flock of Spanish merino sheep.

At this time the British got most of the wool they needed for their great factories from Spain. But Napoleon, who was fighting Britain in every way possible, now tried to ruin their trade by forbidding all the people of Europe to trade with them. When they could no longer get wool from Spain, the British wool trade began to suffer. Then it was that MacArthur stepped in. From his sheep-farm he was soon able to send shiploads of wool to the factories at home, thus preventing the ruin of British manufactures, and bringing wealth to Australia. From then till now the industry has grown, and now millions of pounds' worth of wool are exported every year.

CHAPTER 3

THE ADVENTURES OF GEORGE BASS AND MATTHEW FLINDERS

> "See! girt with tempest and wing'd with thunder,
> And clad with lightning and shod with sleet,
> The strong waves treading the swift waves, sunder
> The flying rollers with frothy feet.
> One gleam like a blood-shot sword swims on
> The skyline, staining the green gulf crimson,
> A death stroke fiercely dealt by a dim sun,
> That strikes through his stormy winding-sheet.
>
> Oh! brave white horses! you gather and gallop,
> The storm sprite loosens the gusty reins;
> Now the stoutest ship were the frailest shallop
> In your hollow backs, on your high arched manes."
>
> A. LINDSAY GORDON.

IT was not until the town of Sydney had been founded for some years that anything was known of the great island upon which it was built. But at last people became curious to know more about their new home.

When Captain John Hunter came out from home as Governor of New South Wales, there came with him two daring young men. The one was George Bass, the ship's doctor, and the other Matthew Flinders, a midshipman. Flinders was only twenty-one, and Bass a few years older.

These two soon became fast friends. They both were eager to know more of the land to which they had come, and about a month after they arrived in Sydney, they set out on a voyage of discovery in a little boat of eight feet long. They called it the *Tom Thumb*, and the whole crew was themselves and a boy.

In this tiny boat they sailed out into the great Pacific, and made for Botany Bay. Here they cruised in and out of all the creeks and bays, making maps of everything, and after an adventurous time they got safely back to Sydney. But they were not long content to remain there. Soon they started out again, and again had many adventures.

Once they got into such a storm that their little boat was nearly swamped. They themselves were soaked to the skin, their drinking water

"Natives gathered round them."

was all spoiled, and, worst of all, their gunpowder was wet and useless.

So they rowed to shore, meaning to land and dry their things, and look for fresh water. As they landed, several natives gathered round them. Bass and Flinders hardly knew what to do. The natives about were said to be very fierce, if not cannibals. There were about fifty of them, armed with spears and boomerangs, against two white men and a boy, who had no weapons, for their guns were rusty and full of sand, and their gunpowder wet.

A boomerang is a native Australian weapon made of hard wood. It is made in peculiar shape, and the black fellows throw it in such a wonderful way that it hits the object it is aimed at, and returns to the hand of the thrower.

Although very uncertain what would happen to them, Bass and Flinders put a bold face on matters. They spread out their gunpowder to dry on the rocks while the natives looked on. They next began to clean their guns, but at this the black fellows became so angry and afraid that they were obliged to stop.

As neither could understand the other's language, talking was rather difficult. But the white men made the savages understand that they wanted water, and they were shown a stream not far off where they filled their cask. They would now have been glad to get away, but their gunpowder was not dry.

Then Flinders thought of something to keep the savages interested. A few days before he had cut the hair and trimmed the beard of a savage, much to his delight. So now he produced a large pair of scissors and persuaded some of those round to let him play barber.

Flinders did not make a very good barber, but that did not matter as the savages were easily pleased. They were very proud of themselves when the cutting and snipping was done, but some of them were very much afraid as the large scissors were nourished so near their noses. Their eyes stared in wild fear, yet all the time they tried to smile as if they liked it, and they looked so funny that Flinders was almost tempted to give a little snip to their ears just to see what would happen. But the situation was too dangerous for such tricks.

At last the powder was dry. Everything was gathered and put into the boat, and the three got safely away, well pleased to have escaped while the savages were still in good humour.

A few nights after this they were nearly wrecked. They had anchored for the night when a terrible storm arose. The waves dashed high over their tiny boat, there were cliffs on one hand, reefs on the other. They hauled up their anchor as quickly as they could and ran before the gale. Bass managed the sail, Flinders steered with an oar, and the boy bailed. "A single wrong movement, a moment's inattention, would have sent us to the bottom," says Flinders.

It was an anxious time, and the darkness of the night added to their danger. But suddenly, when things were so bad that they thought they had not ten minutes more to live, the boat got through the breakers, and in three minutes the adventurers found themselves in the calm waters of a little cove. In thankfulness for their escape they called it Providential Cove. A few days later, having explored thirty or forty miles of coast, they reached Sydney in safety.

It was not long before Bass set out exploring again. This time Flinders could not go, as he had to attend to his duties on board ship. Alone Bass discovered more of the coast, but the greatest thing that he did was to make sure that Tasmania was not joined to Australia, but was a separate island. And the strait between Tasmania and Australia is called Bass Strait after him.

It would take too long to tell of all that Bass and Flinders did, and of all the adventures they had. After a little. Bass sailed away to South America on a trading expedition, and was never heard of more. It is thought that he was captured by the Spaniards, and made to work as a slave in the silver mines. If that is so, it was a terrible end for this brave sailor who loved the free life upon the ocean waves. It is pitiful to think that he, who had felt the sting of the salt spray upon his cheek, and the taste of it upon his lips, had henceforth to toil in a dark, close mine, a broken-hearted captive.

Even after his friend had gone, Flinders did a great deal of exploring. He sailed all round the coasts of Australia in a rotten, little boat called the *Investigator*. "A more deplorable, crazy vessel than the *Investigator* is perhaps not to be seen," said the captain who later, with great difficulty, brought her home to England. When Flinders reached Sydney he found that some of the planking was so soft that a stick could be poked through it. It was in such ships that those brave sailors dared the stormy seas! But Flinders was anxious to reach home, for he had made many maps of the coast, and had filled many note-books, and he wanted to have them published. So he left the *Investigator*, and sailed home as a passenger in another ship.

They had not gone far, however, when one dark and stormy night they were wrecked upon a coral reef. All night the storm raged, the winds blew, and the waves dashed over the wretched, weary men. But when morning came they saw a sandbank near, and upon this they managed to land, only three men being lost in the storm.

Luckily they were able to save most of the food and water out of the wrecked vessel, and were soon settled on their sandbank. They made tents of sails and spars, planted a flagstaff, and ran up a blue ensign with the Union Jack upside down as a signal of distress. And so they prepared to wait until some passing ship should find them and take them off. But it was by no means a likely place for ships to pass, and after a few days Flinders decided to take one of the ship's boats which had been saved from the wreck, and sail back to Sydney to bring help.

They named the little boat the *Hope*, and one fine morning Flinders, with thirteen other men, set sail. As they launched out they were followed by the cheers and good wishes of their shipwrecked comrades, and one of them, having asked leave of the captain, ran to the flagstaff, tore down the flag, and ran it up again with the Union Jack uppermost. This he did to show how sure they were that the voyage would be a success, and that Flinders would bring help.

So it was with cheerful hearts that Flinders and his brave followers began their long journey of two hundred and fifty leagues in an open boat. And like heroes they bore every hardship which came upon them. The weather became rainy and cold, and they were often drenched to the skin and had no means of drying or warming themselves. Tossed about on the huge, hollow waves like a cockle shell, in danger from sharks and whales, they yet escaped every peril, and after ten days of hardship and toil they arrived safely at Sydney.

Flinders at once went to Government House. Captain King was by this time governor, and he was a good friend to Flinders, who now found him sitting at dinner. The governor stared in astonishment at the wild, unshorn, ragged man with lean, brown face and bright eyes, who walked into the room. It was some minutes before he knew him to be his friend Matthew Flinders, who he thought was many hundreds of miles on his way to England. But when he realised who it was, and listened to the tale of disaster, his eyes filled with tears.

At once the governor agreed to send help to the ship-wrecked men, but it was some days before ships could be got ready, and every day seemed to Flinders a week. He was so afraid that if he did not get back quickly the men on the sandbank would grow tired of waiting, give up hope, and try to save themselves in an open boat, and so perhaps all be drowned before help came.

But at length everything was ready. Three ships set sail and safely reached the narrow, sea-swept sandbank, and all the shipwrecked men were rescued.

Flinders then went on his way to England with his precious maps and plans, a few only of which had been lost in the wreck. But the ship in which he went was so small and so leaky that it could not carry enough food and water for so long a voyage. Flinders was therefore obliged to stop at every port he came to for fresh supplies. The French and British were again at war, and at Mauritius, which then belonged to France, he was taken prisoner, in spite of the fact that he had a passport from Napoleon.

Flinders was treated as a spy, and all his journals and maps were taken from him. And now his fate was little better than that of his friend Bass. For seven long years he was kept a prisoner, eating his heart out with desire for freedom. At last he was set free, and after some more adventures he reached home.

But his troubles were not at an end. He now discovered that a French sailor had stolen his maps and journal, and that he had published them in France as his own, having changed all the names which Flinders had given the places into French names. The name Australis, which Flinders had been among the first to use, he had changed to Terre de Napoleon—that is, land of Napoleon. And for many a long day Australia was marked in French atlases as Terre de Napoleon.

It was a bitter blow. But broken in health and worn with long hardships and imprisonments though he was, Flinders was not yet beaten. He gave up the rest of his life to writing an account of his travels, which he called *A Voyage to Terra Australis*. But, sad to say, upon the very day that it was published, he died. To the end he was a sailor and adventurer. Almost his last words were, "I know that in future days of exploration my spirit will rise from the dead and follow the exploring ships."

It was by such men of daring, by such deeds of valour and of long endurance, that the outlines of Australia were traced upon our maps.

CHAPTER 4

A LITTLE REVOLUTION

IT was in 1800 that Captain John Hunter was recalled and Captain King took his place. The new governor set himself at once to stop the trade in rum, which was bringing ruin on the Colony. Men sold everything to get it They bartered away their sheep and cattle and even their growing corn, until they who had been prosperous farmers became ruined beggars. But in putting down the trade in rum King brought upon himself the hatred of the soldiers who made a great deal of money out of it, and who were very angry to see their gains thus disappear. He had to crush rebellions among the convicts too. The work was not easy, but King was firm, and soon he brought some kind of order out of wild confusion. And although, as he said, he " could not make pickpockets into good farmers," he forced them to be less drunken and made them try to work, and so by good behaviour earn freedom.

It was during the time of Governor King's rule that the island of Tasmania was first colonised. For sixteen years, in all the wide island-continent, it was only in the few miles round Sydney that the white man had planted his foot and built his home. But French ships were now seen cruising about, and the British began to fear that the French meant to found a colony in Tasmania, which, since the discoveries of Bass, they knew was not joined to Australia, but was a separate island.

So to be beforehand with the French, King sent a lieutenant with a few soldiers, convicts, and freemen, to found a colony there. They landed and began to build a little town, which they called Hobart Town, in honour of Lord Hobart, who was then Secretary of State for the Colonies.

The new colony had its troubles and trials just as Sydney had had, but it conquered them all and began to prosper.

About this time, too, an attempt was made to found a town near where Melbourne now stands. But these first colonists did not think it a good place for a town. So they left their half-built houses there and went across to Tasmania, and settled down about fifteen miles from Hobart. Thus a beginning was made, and by degrees other towns were founded, and the lonely spaces of Australia began to be peopled by white men.

In 1806 Captain Bligh succeeded Captain King as governor. He was a stern, hard man with a fearful temper. He was known as "Bounty Bligh," because when he had been captain of the *Bounty* his men had mutinied and cast him adrift, with eighteen others, in an open boat in the Pacific Ocean. But however stern and cruel Bligh might be, he was a clever seaman.

Now, in this terrible plight, he showed it. With wonderful skill he steered his boat and ruled his men, and after a voyage of almost four thousand miles they readied land safely. This journey of his is one of the wonderful things of the story of the sea.

But although Bligh was a good seaman he was not a good governor. He soon made himself hated by nearly every one in the colony. He quarrelled, too, with Mr. MacArthur who, you remember, had brought wool-bearing sheep to the colony and who was now, after the governor, perhaps the chief man in all Australia.

Soon after Bligh arrived MacArthur went to him to talk about his farm and his hopes that sheep and wool would bring wealth to the colony. But Bligh flew into a temper at once. "What have I to do with your sheep and cattle?" he cried. "You have such flocks and herds as no man ever had before. You have ten thousand acres of the best land in the country. But, by heaven, you shall not keep it!"

Instead of help and sympathy, MacArthur only got angry words. So a quarrel was begun which as the months went on grew worse and worse. The fault was not all on one side, and these two strong and powerful men did not try to understand each other. At last Bligh put MacArthur into prison for refusing to pay a fine which he considered unjust. He threatened to put six officers of the " Rum Corps" in prison too, as they encouraged MacArthur.

At this, the barracks was in an uproar. Both men and officers declared that the governor was trampling on their liberty and rights, and that instead of keeping law and order he was upsetting both. They resolved not to suffer it and they rebelled.

So about half-past six one midsummer evening, which in Australia, you must remember, is in January, they gathered at the barracks. Then with fixed bayonets, drums beating, and colours flying, they marched to Government House, followed by a crowd of people all eager to see the downfall of the governor.

At the gate the governor's daughter tried to stop the soldiers. But she was told to stand aside, and the men marched unhindered into the house, for the very sentries had joined the rebels.

"I am called upon to do a most painful duty," said Major Johnston. "You are charged by the respectable inhabitants of crimes that make you unfit to rule another moment in the colony. I hereby place you under arrest by the advice of all my officers, and by the advice of every respectable inhabitant of Sydney."

Thus Bligh was taken prisoner and his rule was at an end. No one was sorry, for he had no friends. For some weeks he was kept prisoner, then promising that he would go direct to England, he was allowed to go on board a waiting vessel. But he broke his word and went to Tasmania instead.

There he tried to make the colonists receive him back as governor. But although at first they treated him with all due honour, they soon grew tired of him. Bligh was then forced to leave Tasmania as he had left Australia, and for some time he cruised about in his ship.

Meanwhile Major Johnston ruled New South Wales. But after a time the news of the revolt reached England. A new governor, Colonel Macquarie, was at once sent out with a Highland regiment to restore order. Macquarie was told to make Captain Bligh governor again for twenty-four hours, just to show the mutineers that they could not do as they liked. Then he was to become governor himself and send home the whole of the New South Wales Corps, and every one who had had a part in the revolt, to answer for their misdeeds.

This was done; and the Rum Corps, which for years had been the greatest power and at times the greatest terror in the colony, went home for good and all. But no very heavy punishment was given to the mutineers. Major Johnston was expelled from the army, but he returned to Australia and became one of its most important settlers. MacArthur was forbidden to return for eight years, as he had been the chief cause of all the disturbance. But at the end of that time he did return, and his name is remembered as one of those who did most for Australia in the early days.

As for Bligh, he was made an admiral; and that, he no doubt felt, made up for all that he had gone through.

CHAPTER 5

THE FIRST TRAVELLER IN QUEENSLAND

ONE day in February 1846 a ship sailed out from Sydney on its way to China. It was a cargo boat, but, as was common in those days, it carried a few passengers too, and with the captain went his wife. A fair wind blew, and all hoped for a quick and pleasant passage.

But as the ship sailed on its way the wind became ever stronger and fiercer, until, when a week from home, a terrible storm was brewing, and the ship with bare masts was scudding before the blast.

At last the storm calmed and the danger seemed over. But the ship had been driven far out of its course, and a careful watch was kept lest it should run upon some unknown rock or reef.

For a few days all went well, then suddenly one night the watchman saw something loom ahead of the ship, whether land or dark cloud he could not tell. Before anything could be done there was a fearful shock, the ship shivered from stem to stem, and then lay still.

Every one except the watchmen was in bed. The shock made them spring from their beds and rush in terror to the deck. All was black darkness. There was nothing to be seen around but the night and the cruel white-crested waves. In the darkness nothing could be done, and so in shivering misery, the waves lashing over the ship, men waited for the dawn.

The night seemed long, but at last a cold, grey light crept into the sky. Then it was seen that all around the ship sharp points of rock showed above the water. Upon one of these the ship had struck. But nowhere was there the faintest sign of land.

As soon as it was light enough, the captain ordered the boats to be lowered. But almost as soon as they reached the water, they were dashed to pieces and swept away by the savage waves.

All hope was gone, and the shipwrecked people gave themselves up to despair. But the captain was a man who did not easily give way. He ordered all hands into the cabin, and when they were gathered he bade them pray. And so there knelt together, three pale-faced women and their frightened children, with a handful of brave, rough men who well knew that they had sailed their last voyage upon this earth.

But the captain's calm voice and earnest prayer put new courage into the men. They rose from their knees and set to work to make a raft strong enough to live in that wild sea. Long they toiled, cutting and sawing, hammering and lashing spars and planks together. All the time they worked at the risk of their lives, for every wave swept the decks.

At last the raft was ready, and with great difficulty launched. What food there was, was placed upon it. But, alas, it was very little, for most of the provisions had been washed overboard or spoiled by the salt water. One cask of water, a little brandy, and nine tins of preserved meat, these were all that could be found. And with this little store the poor wrecked men set sail upon the cruel waste of waters.

Including women and children, there were twenty-one people upon the raft. They knew their food would not last long. They had all heard terrible tales of shipwrecked people, who, when they were starving, had become cannibal and had eaten each other. So now, face to face with death, they each promised solemnly to keep from anything so horrible, whatever tortures they might suffer.

At first things were just endurable. Three tablespoonfuls of meat a day were served out to each person, and four little drinks of water carefully measured. To help to eke out their stores they caught the sea-birds which now and again alighted upon the raft. These they had to eat raw, but they were looked upon as great dainties.

Three weeks passed. Both food and water were nearly done, when a sail came in sight. Eagerly the weak, worn crew waved and signed. The ship was too far away and the sailors did not see them. Hour after hour they watched and beckoned, but the sail grew smaller and smaller, and at last it vanished altogether in the dim distance, and the little raft was left once more alone on the empty sea.

The portion of meat, the measure of water, grew less and less day by day, until at last one morning there was no more meat, and no more water left. Still there was no sign of land, still there was nothing all around but the cruel, vacant sea.

"I shall die now," said one man wearily. And die he did.

Remembering their promise the others quickly threw the body overboard. They feared that the terrible pangs of hunger which had come upon them might make them forget.

But now, when there seemed nothing but an awful death before them, the poor castaways caught a fish for the first time. Each day after this they caught some fish. Then rain came and eased their terrible, burning thirst. But day by day, unable to endure longer, some of the company died. The children, two of the women, and many of the men each followed one after another.

At length, after six weeks of fearful suffering, land came in sight. Although they did not know it, the castaways had reached the shores of Queensland. They only guessed that they were somewhere on the coast of Australia.

Now when at last the raft reached the land, there were only seven left of all who had set out from the ship. These were the captain, his wife, and five men. They were little more than skeletons, and when they were once more on dry land, they lay down upon the beach and slept from sheer weakness and weariness.

Next morning the captain managed to make a fire, at which they cooked some shark which they had caught. It was the first cooked meat they had eaten for more than six weeks. Then they crawled about and found some oysters. But they were all so sick and faint with hunger and exposure, that they could with difficulty drag themselves about even in search of food.

Now again a sail was seen. With all the strength they had left, they tried to signal to it. But their efforts were in vain. Sitting on the rocks, with despair in their hearts, they watched the ship slowly sail out of sight.

Three more of the party died, and there were only four left when, to add to the terrors of the fight with death, a party of black fellows came upon them. They proved, however, in their own way, friendly. They took, it is true, everything the shipwrecked men had left, even to their clothes, leaving them almost naked. But they brought them roots to eat, and signed to them to join in their wild dance called a corrobboree.

This, of course, the white men could not do, and as the black fellows did not seem very pleased at their refusal, one of the sailors offered to sing.

This greatly delighted the savages who sat round grimacing, while the four wretched white people stood together and sang,

> God moves in a mysterious way
> His wonders to perform;
> He plants His footsteps in the sea,
> And rides upon the storm.

Thus were the white people received into the tribe. For two years they lived with the savages in great misery. They had now enough to eat, it is true, but they had to live as savages. At the end of three years all had died except one man called Murrell. He seemed better able to bear the hardships, and for seventeen years he lived among the black fellows, talking their language and living their life, until he forgot his own tongue and even his own name.

But at last, after many weary years, ships began to come, and white men, it was told Murrell, had built a hut not far off.

When he heard this news, Murrell decided to try to escape from his fearful life. So one day he set off to find the white man's hut. Having lived so many years under the burning sun of Queensland, wearing no clothes, he was very brown and very dirty too. But now when thoughts of his old life had awakened in him, he went to a pool and washed himself as white as he could.

Round the white man's hut there was a fence, and when Murrell reached it dogs ran out barking and snapping at him. So, to keep them from biting him, he climbed upon the fence and called out as loud as he could.

Three men lived in the hut, and at the sound of Murrell's call, one of them came out. He stared at this strange being in wonder. Then, "Bill," he cried, "here's a naked, yellow man standing on the fence. He isn't a black man. Bring the gun."

"Don't shoot!" cried Murrell, in terror. "I'm a shipwrecked sailor, a British object."

He really meant to say "subject," but it was so long since he had spoken English, and he was so frightened and excited, that he hardly knew what he was saying.

When the men heard him speak English they put down their gun, and brought him into the hut, listening in astonishment to his story. They gave him some breakfast, but Murrell found that he no longer liked tea; and bread, which he had not eaten for seventeen years, now seemed to choke him.

Murrell was, however, very glad to get back to civilisation once more, but he returned to his black friends to say good-bye to them. And when they understood that he was going to leave them for always they were filled with grief and cried bitterly. Murrell, too, when he thought of all the rough kindness they had shown to him these many years, was sorry to say goodbye. But the sight of white men, and the sound of his own language, had awakened all his old longing for home, and he left his black friends.

He was taken to Brisbane and made much of. He became a storekeeper, married, and settled down to a quiet life, but the terrible hardships he had passed through had left him weak and feeble, and he did not live long to enjoy his new found comforts.

Such were the adventures of the first travellers in Queensland. But things have changed. Were a traveller to land now where Murrell was shipwrecked, he would find pleasant homes and smiling pastures. And perhaps on the very spot where, seventy years ago, only the black man hunted, where Murrell wandered naked and miserable, he might find a train waiting to take him back to Brisbane.

CHAPTER 6

THROUGH THE GREAT UNKNOWN

UP to the time when Macquarie came to govern New South Wales nothing at all was known of Australia inland. The Blue Mountains, beautiful and rugged, defied every attempt to cross them. Among others, gallant George Bass had tried. But he was less successful by land than by sea and he discovered nothing.

But now the colony was growing larger, and the settlers began to feel themselves cramped between the mountains and the sea. They had need of larger pastures to feed their sheep and grow their corn, so three young men determined to find out what lay behind the mountains. And, taking with them food enough to last six weeks, they set out.

They had a hard task before them. They had to cut their way through woods where no white man at least had ever passed before. Across dark valleys, up and down steep cliffs, now crawling along narrow ledges, now clambering up rocky heights, they reached at last the western side of the hills. There they saw the land open out in rolling, fertile plains, and knew that they had found what meant new life and wealth to the colony.

> "The dauntless three! for twenty days and nights
> These heroes battled with the haughty heights;
> For twenty spaces of the star and sun
> These Romans kept their harness buckled on;
> By gaping gorges, and by cliffs austere,
> These fathers struggled in the great old year;
> Their feet they set on strange hills scarred by fire;
> Their strong arms forced a path through brake and briar;
> They fought with nature till they reached the throne
> Where morning glittered on the great UNKNOWN.
> There, in the time of praise and prayer supreme,
> Paused Blaxland, Lawson, Wentworth, in a dream;
> There, where the silver arrows of the day
> Smote upon slope and spire, they halted on their way.
> Behind them were the conquered hills—they faced
> The vast green West, with glad, strange beauty graced;
> And every tone of every cave and tree
> Was as a voice of splendid prophecy."

Returning home, the three told the governor of their discovery, and he, after making sure that what they said was true, set convicts to work to make a broad road across the hills. It took two years to make. Many a valley had to be bridged over, the solid rock had to be blown up. But at last the great work was finished. Then the colonists led their flocks and herds along the road to the grassy plains beyond, which were soon dotted with homesteads, and the town of Bathurst was founded.

After this many travellers set out, eager to fill the great blank of the map of Australia, and it would take many books to tell of all their adventures. With patient courage and wonderful endurance they found, and marked, and named tract after tract of the vast island, each man stealing his little corner from the Unknown and adding it to the Known. To the great work these pioneers gave their health and money and all that they had. Some of them even gave their lives, and lie lost for ever in the great, silent land, no man knowing to this day where their bones rest. Australia has no battlefields. Its peaceful soil has never been soaked in the blood of thousands, its blue skies have never been darkened with the smoke of war. No heroes have fallen to the sound of trumpet and of drum fighting for King and Country. But the men who fought with nature, who suffered hunger and thirst, and all the woes of the desert, who day by day, and hour by hour, showed the courage of endurance, are as well worth remembering as those who, in one quick moment of fervour, thought life well lost for the sake of some great cause. And the names of Hamilton, Hume, Sturt, Eyre, Leichardt, Mitchell, Kennedy and many others stand out in the story of Australia as men who were not afraid to suffer and to die.

We cannot follow all these explorers, you must read their stories elsewhere. But I will tell the story of two, not because they were the greatest or did most, but because they are among the best known, and because they were the first to cross the island-continent from south to north all the way from sea to sea. For when the island had once been crossed from shore to shore there was an end to the wonderful stories that had grown up about the marvels to be found in the middle of it. Some said that there was to be found a great and fertile land, where white people lived in the wealth and luxury of a sort of fairyland; some again said there were great inland seas, boiling rivers, and mountains of fire to be found there. But when the land had been crossed, these stories were at an end, although there was then, and is still, much to be learned.

By the year 1860 the fringes of Australia had been peopled, and although little was known of the interior, the land was divided into five colonies, broken off from the mother colony of New South Wales. Each of these colonies had a capital and a governor of its own. Victoria had its capital, Melbourne; South Australia its capital, Adelaide; Western Australia its capital, Perth; Queensland its capital, Brisbane.

Now the Colony of Victoria decided to send out an expedition to cross the continent As its leader, an Irishman named O'Hara Burke was chosen. No expense was spared to make the expedition a success. Camels were brought on purpose from India, for they, as is well known, can go for a longer time without water than perhaps any other beast of burden. And one of the worst dangers and difficulties in Australian exploration was the want of water. It is to-day the greatest drawback to Australia.

The expedition set off from Melbourne in high spirits. Crowds of people turned out to see it start The mayor made a speech, Burke made another, and amid a storm of good wishes and cheering the long procession of men, laden camels, and horses wound out of sight.

But the expedition which had begun so brightly was soon overshadowed. The leader of the camels quarrelled with Burke, and went back to Melbourne saying that no good would ever come of the expedition under such a leader. And indeed, brave though he was, Burke was not a good commander.

A man named Wills was now made second in command, and the expedition continued its way.

When Menindie on the Darling river was reached, it was found that some of the men and camels were already knocked up and unable to travel fast. But instead of waiting here to rest for a short time, or going on slowly, Burke, who was hot-headed and eager, divided his party into two. Leaving one half under a man named Wright to come on slowly, he pushed on quickly with Wills and six other men to Cooper's Creek. It is not easy to see what Burke hoped to gain by this, for at Cooper's Creek he arranged to wait for the others.

Here there was plenty of grass and water, and while waiting for Wright and his party to arrive, Burke and Wills made many short expeditions, exploring the country round. They found stony deserts and waterless tracts, and nothing very encouraging.

In this way a month went past. Then Burke, impatient at the slowness of Wright, decided to again divide his party. Leaving four men under a leader named Brahe to await Wright, he, with Wills and two others, again set out northward. The men left behind were told to wait three months, and if Burke and Wills did not return they might then give them up as lost and go home.

Having made all their arrangements, the little party set out. On and on, day after day, they trudged. Sometimes they met with bands of natives who, however, were friendly enough. Sometimes the way lay through stony desert, sometimes through fertile plains, or swamps and thick forest. At last they reached the seashore. But a forest of trees and a thick undergrowth of bushes lay between them and the sea, and although Burke and Wills made gallant efforts to struggle through it, they were obliged to turn back without having really seen the water or having stood upon the northern shore.

It was now two months since they had left Cooper's Creek. They were weary and worn. Their food was nearly at an end. And so they made haste to return, lest the men left at Cooper's Creek should, as they had been told, go home believing their leader to be lost in the wilds.

The way northward had seemed hard and long, the way back seemed yet harder. Soon there was nothing left to eat. One camel after another had to be killed for food. The men fell ill, and worn out with hardships, one died.

The three remaining gaunt, lean skeletons struggled on. At last they, with two skinny camels, arrived at Cooper's Creek.

There was no one there.

Upon a tree was a note telling the wretched, weary travellers that the others had left that very morning, and that Wright, who had been left behind at the Darling, had never arrived at all.

It was heart-breaking. Sick and hopeless were the men who that night lay down to sleep in the deserted camp. Burke had mismanaged the expedition badly. Perhaps he knew it, and that made the hardships no easier to bear.

Fortunately Brahe and his party had left some food behind them. They had marked a tree with the word "Dig," and here the travellers found the buried stores.

Now that they had food enough, Wills and the other man, who was called King, proposed that they should rest for a few days until they had regained some strength. But Burke with his impatient spirit would not listen. He proposed to start off again and try to reach home by going through South Australia instead of back as they had come. He wanted to go by way of Mount Hopeless, which had been reached by another explorer some years before.

There was now a sheep farm there, and Burke thought it could not be more than one hundred and fifty miles off.

It seems to us, reading of it long after, a mad and foolish idea. And so it seemed to Wills and King. But they gave way to their leader and the journey began. It was a dismal failure. They lost their way and, at last worn out and once more starving, were obliged to go back. On this return journey Burke and King became so weak that they could go no farther, and alone, Wills returned to Cooper's Creek to bring food to his dying comrades.

Meanwhile, had they only known it, help had been very near. For Brahe, having at last met with Wright, had returned to Cooper's Creek. But finding no one there, and believing that no one had been there in their absence, they all started homeward with the news that the others had perished.

The news was true enough. But it need not have been true if only things had been better managed.

Now, of the three left alone in the wilderness. Wills was the first to die. A few days later Burke followed him, and King alone was left. He kept himself from utterly starving by eating the seeds of a plant called Nardoo. Then he fell in with some friendly blacks who had already helped the forlorn party. With them he stayed until he was found and rescued, for he was not left to die unaided. When Wright and Brahe reached home with their sad news, search parties were at once sent out to find the bodies at least of the brave, misguided men. So King was found. But he was pale and thin, more like a skeleton than a living man, and so weak that he could scarcely speak. But after a few days of care and nursing he grew much better, and was able to tell the sorry story of all his pains and hardships.

The dead bodies of Burke and Wills were found where they had died, and were buried in the wilds. But afterwards they were brought to Melbourne, where they were buried with great ceremony and a monument in their memory was raised.

King received a pension, and the relatives of Burke and Wills were cared for. It is pleasant, too, to know that the kindly blacks were rewarded, although it was only with beads and ribbons, looking-glasses and sugar. To them such things seemed very precious, and they were well pleased.

"Set your face toward the darkness—tell of deserts weird and wide,
Where unshaken woods are huddled, and low languid waters glide;
Turn and tell of deserts lonely, lying pathless deep and vast;
Where in utter silence ever Time seems slowly breathing past—
Silence only broken when the sun is necked with cloudy bars,
Or when tropic squalls come hurtling underneath the sultry stars!
Deserts, thorny, hot and thirsty, where the feet of man are strange,
And eternal Nature sleeps in solitudes which know no change.
Weakened with their lengthened labours, past long plains of stone and sand,

Down those trackless wilds they wandered, travellers from a far-off land,
Seeking now to join their brothers, struggling on with faltering feet,
For a glorious work was finished, and a noble task complete;
And they dreamt of welcome faces—dreamt that soon unto their ears
Friendly greeting would be thronging, with a nation's well-earned cheers;
Since their courage never failed them, but with high, unflinching soul
Each was pressing forward, hoping, trusting all should reach the goal.

Ye must rise and sing their praises, O ye bards with souls of fire,
For the people's voice shall echo through the wailings of your lyre;
And we'll welcome back their comrade, though our eyes with tears be blind
At the thoughts of promise perished, and the shadow left behind;
Now the leaves are bleaching round them—now the gales above them glide,
But the end was all accomplished, and their fame was far and wide.
Though this fadeless glory cannot hide a nation's grief,
And their laurels have been blended with a gloomy cypress wreath.

Let them rest where they have laboured! but, my country, mourn and moan;
We must build with human sorrow grander monuments than stone,
Let them rest, for oh! remember, that in long hereafter time
Sons of Science oft shall wander o'er that solitary clime!
Cities bright shall rise about it. Age and Beauty there shall stray,
And the fathers of the people, pointing to the graves, shall say:
Here they fell, the glorious martyrs! when these plains were woodland deep;
Here a friend, a brother, laid them; here the wild man came to weep."

H. C. KENDALL

CHAPTER 7

"THE TRACTS OF THIRST AND FURNACE"

AS years went on and Australia grew, great farms stretched out from the towns into the wilds. Many a farmer owned a sheep- or cattle-run as big as an English county, and the yellowing cornfields reached for miles waving and beautiful in the sunshine.

The soil of Australia is in many places so fertile and the climate so good that farming is easy. But the farmers have one great trouble. That is the want of a good water supply. In Australia there are no high mountains to catch the rain clouds. There are no big inland lakes or rivers, and a curious thing about the Australian rivers is that many of them instead of flowing to the sea flow inland. When a drought comes, some of these rivers disappear altogether, and sometimes a drought will last for months or even years.

The years 1839-1840 were years of terrible drought. The grass became browner and browner, and at last it was burnt up altogether and only the dry, sandy earth remained. The leaves withered on the trees and shrivelled up. There was no coolness anywhere. The wind was hot like the blast of a furnace, and, as it swept through the forests, the leaves hissed and crackled against each other instead of whispering gently with a cool, soft sound. No green thing was to be seen, the still air quivered with heat, and the silent birds fell dead from the branches.

The cattle, daily growing thinner and thinner, wandered farther and farther over the plains in search of food and water. As the water pools dried up, the weaker animals sank into the mud and sand left on the edge, and having no strength to struggle out again died there. And there they lay, their dead bodies poisoning the air until the plain was strewn with bleaching bones.

Corn, too, ceased to grow, and flour was sold at £100 a ton. Starvation and ruin stared many a farmer in the face. At first they tried to drive their cattle to Sydney to sell them to the butchers there. But as every one wanted to sell, there were not enough people to buy, and the cattle before they reached Sydney were often little more than skin and bone.

It was then that a Mr. O'Brien thought of a plan by which something might be saved. He had heard that in Russia, when farmers had too many cattle, they killed them for their fat, for though the butchers in a town could only buy a certain amount of meat, a market for tallow could always be found, for it could be sent to distant lands. So now factories and places for boiling down sheep and cattle were built both in Sydney and in the country, and to the farmers' great delight they found that they could make a little out of their starving cattle. Valuable cattle were killed merely for their skin and tallow, but it was better to make even a few pounds than nothing at all, and the poor beasts were put out of misery. The meat of course was wasted, but some of it was used as manure for the land. And sometimes a butcher would buy a hundred or two legs of mutton at 1*d.* each, and make a good profit out of them by selling them to his customers for so much a pound. Thus many of the colonists were saved from utter ruin, and able to live until the rain came again.

When at last the rain did come in a few weeks, the earth was, as if by magic, covered with green once more. Then the cattle, which had wandered in helpless pain, dull-eyed, pitiful skeletons, again became sleek and lively. But in places the rain came with such sudden fury that the river-beds could not contain it, and great floods were the consequence. Then perhaps what a farmer had saved from the drought would be torn from him by the flood.

About ten years later another drought withered the land. Rivers and water-pools disappeared, the earth became a sun-baked desert of clay, where great cracks yawned, and where the cattle wandered "with the terror of thirst in their eyes." As the summer went on, the air grew hotter and hotter, the sky a brazen bowl. Then in February came a day which in Victoria is remembered as Black Thursday. From the north a hot wind blew with the breath of a furnace. The sky grew dark, and out in the Bass Straits weather-wise sailors furled their sails, and made ready to meet a fearful storm.

Hour by hour the wind gathered strength and speed, till by midday it tore shrieking through the bare, scorched trees, howling over the plains, where the bones of hundreds of cattle lay bleaching. Then to the howl and shriek of the wind was added the roar and crackle of fire. As if by magic the whole land was sheeted in flame. On it came like some hungry demon, fierce tongues of fire licking the earth, pillars of smoke climbing the sky. The raging wind tore the lifeless leaves from the trees, the arid grass from the plain, and in a whirl of sparks swept them on to kindle into fresh flame wherever they fell.

The fiery monster spared nothing. The great forest trees appeared for a few minutes pillared and arched in flame, then sank together in one huge bonfire. Farmhouses and gardens were swept away, and as the flames rolled on, man and beast fled before them vainly seeking shelter. Wherever water was to be found, there men fled. Standing in the water they waited, blinded and gasping in the smoke-laden air, till the column of fire had rolled past Above the roar of the flames rose the scream and bellow of terrified animals, the thud and patter of a thousand hoofs, as horse and bullock, sheep and kangaroo, all the beasts of field or forest, birds and serpents, and every living thing, fled before the fiery sword of destruction. Driven by a nameless terror, panting to escape from an awful death, they fled.

All day long and far into the night the storm of fire lasted, and when morning dawned, the land in its track lay a black ruin of desolation.

Many men, women, and children, had died in the flames. Many more lost all that they possessed, and, penniless and disheartened, had to begin life over again, had again to build their homesteads and fence their runs, and find money to buy new tools and a fresh stock of cattle. It was never known how much was lost in this great fire, but those who lived in the country at the time never forgot the havoc it made, or the terrible devastation it left behind. But at length rain came again. Then in a far shorter time than we should believe possible, the land that had been a charred and smoking desert was once more green pasture and corn land, dotted with pleasant homesteads, and Black Thursday was no more than a memory.

CHAPTER 8

THE FINDING OF GOLD

NEAR the town of Bathurst there lived a farmer called Hargraves. He had suffered much from the droughts, and at last, tired of the struggle, he gave up his farm and sailed away to California. He went to try his luck at the goldfields which had lately been discovered there. But in California Hargraves was no more lucky than he had been in New South Wales. Although others around him made fortunes, he made none. However, as he dug, and shovelled, and toiled in vain, a strange thought struck him. The hills and valleys of California were very like the hills and valleys of New South Wales, he said to himself. If there was gold to be found in the one, why not in the other?

When this idea had once taken hold of Hargraves he could not get rid of it. So at length he made up his mind to leave his useless toil and go back to Australia to find out if there was anything in his idea.

He had now very little money left, but he managed to get back to Sydney. He arrived there penniless, and had to borrow money in order to hire a horse to take him to the Blue Mountains, for in those days there were no trains.

At a lonely inn on the slopes of the mountains he put up his horse. There he found a boy who knew all the creeks and streams about, and, with him as guide, Hargraves started out early one morning carrying a trowel and a little tin dish.

Soon he came to what he thought was a likely place in which to find gold. Digging up a little of the greyish, sandy soil he went with it to the nearest stream. Here he dipped and dipped his tin in the water until all the sand was washed away. Then, there at the bottom, too heavy to be floated away by the water, lay a few small grains of dull, glowing gold.

As time after time Hargraves filled his little tin pan, and saw the tiny grains of precious metal glow at the bottom, his breath came fast, his eyes sparkled, his cheeks glowed with triumph. He knew that he had found what he sought, and that fortunes for thousands lay hidden in the hills around him.

Tired, but rejoicing, he went back to his inn and wrote down all that he had done, very sure that he had found out something great, not only for himself, but for all Australia.

For two months Hargraves remained among the lonely hills making quite certain of his discovery. Then he went back to Sydney and wrote a letter to the governor, saying that for £500 he would show him places in

New South Wales where gold could be found.

Many people had pretended to find gold before this. So now the governor was not very ready to believe Hargraves. However, he said that if Hargraves would first point out the place, he would be rewarded afterwards.

This Hargraves agreed to, and in a week there were a thousand people digging and washing for gold in that lonely creek, which, a month or two before, had echoed to the shouts of one man and a boy.

The rush to the diggings was tremendous. Farmers left their farms, doctors their patients. Labourers, servants, clerks, workmen of all kinds, thieves and cutthroats, all swelled the stream which poured along the road over the Blue Mountains. It was hardly to be wondered at that people would no longer toil all day long for a few shillings, when, in the same time they might, by scratching the earth a little, win hundreds of pounds. So business came to a standstill, grass grew in the streets, corn stood in the fields uncut, even the ships remained idle in the harbour, for the sailors deserted whenever they could, and made for the diggings.

But although many who went to the mines made fortunes, others, like Hargraves himself in California, returned in a few weeks disappointed and angry. Others, too, went thinking that they had nothing to do but pick up lumps of gold and carry it home in cart-loads. When these found that they had to work hard, to dig, and shovel, and wash, perhaps for weeks, to live in a tent and "do" for themselves, they were disgusted, and they, too, trooped homewards. All these disappointed people thought that Hargraves had fooled them, and could they have found him they would have gladly killed him. But he kept out of the way.

So over the road between Sydney and the diggings there was a constant double stream of people, some going, eager to begin work, others returning, grumbling and discontented.

But although some returned disappointed, the rush to the goldfields continued so great that it seemed as if all the other colonies would be emptied of men, and that their whole life would come to a standstill. So to stop the rush of settlers out of Victoria, the government there offered a reward to any one who would find gold in Victoria. Gold was found, and found in far richer quantities than in New South Wales. The rush was then turned in another direction, but it still went on. Indeed Melbourne was left at one time with only one policeman on duty. But that did not matter much, as all the rascals and thieves had gone to the diggings like other people. Some marched along with a pack on their back holding all that they possessed in the world, picnicking on the way, sleeping in the open air. Others, a little better off, had hand-barrows in which to carry their goods, while those still better off rode along on horseback or in light gigs or buggies. But all hurried in one direction, all had one object—gold.

At first it was only the colonists who swarmed to the goldfields, for it

"All day long the sound of the pick and the rumble of the cradle were heard."

was some months before the news reached home. In those days there was no telegraph to Australia, and boats took three months to cross the seas. But when at last the news did reach home, whole shiploads of men from almost every nation in Europe came thronging to the diggings. There were among them old and young, rich and poor, strong and feeble, and even the lame and the blind.

To find the gold there was little skill needed and few tools. A pick, a shovel, a pan, and a cradle were enough. The cradle was a pan on rockers into which the earth containing the gold was put along with water, and rocked about until all the sand and earth was washed away and only the gold remained.

All over the country new towns sprang up—towns of tents and wooden shanties. There all day long, from dawn to dusk, the sound of the pick and the rumble of the cradle was heard. Then at the sound of a gun all work ceased. The diggers scattered to their tents, fires were lit, and supper was cooked. For a little there was no noise except the clatter of billies or pans in which tea was boiled, and the hum of talk. Supper over, the men sat around the glowing fires smoking and telling tales, and singing songs, while overhead the stars came out and quiet darkness settled all about them. Then after a time the sounds of song and laughter would cease, and silence would reign over the little town till morning.

In those early days many people made great fortunes in a few weeks, or sometimes by some lucky find, in one day. Others returned home as poor as they had set out, and broken in health. And some who made great fortunes spent it as quickly as they had made it. They did all kinds of wild things simply to get rid of their money, such as buying pianos which they could not use, and having champagne in bucketfuls.

Many lumps of gold called nuggets were found, some of them so large that one was enough to make a man's fortune. One called the Kerr nugget was found by a black shepherd near Bathurst. He had heard how white men were going almost mad seeking for gold, so while he guarded his sheep, he amused himself by poking about with a stick to see if he also could not find some of the mysterious treasure. And in this way, one day he came upon a lump so large that even he, who knew nothing of the value of it, grew excited.

Running back to the farmhouse he burst in upon his master and mistress as they were sitting down to dinner. "O massa!" he cried, hardly able to speak for excitement and breathlessness, "white man find little fellow, me find big fellow!"

When the shepherd had explained what he meant, his master put to his horse and drove off to see this wonderful nugget. There, sure enough, was a huge lump of gold sticking out of the ground where every one might see it, and only needing to be picked up. It was truly a "big fellow," and so heavy that it had to be broken in two before it could be carried away. It afterwards sold for £4000.

But although the Kerr was one of the first large nuggets, it was by no means the largest. Others worth more than double were found later, to which people gave names such as Blanche Barkly, Welcome Nugget, and Welcome Stranger.

Soon the tented mushroom towns grew larger and more numerous. Theatres, hotels, and even churches were built. But when a mine became exhausted, or when news of a richer mine reached the diggers, the township would be deserted, and the country sink back to its former peace, only hundreds of little sand heaps being left to show where men had lately toiled like a swarm of busy ants.

Things were not always quiet and orderly on the goldfields. The greed of gain and the thirst for gold brought out man's evil passions, and often dark and dreadful deeds were done.

Every digger, too, had to pay thirty shillings a month to the government for leave to dig. To the lucky ones who were making fortunes that seemed nothing. To the unlucky ones who toiled for days finding little it seemed a great deal, and they tried to avoid paying it. Upon every goldfield there was a force of police. These police could demand to see a man's licence, and if he had none they carried him off to prison. So many of the diggers came to look upon the police as their enemies, and there were often fights between them.

But those days have long since passed. Gold digging still goes on in Australia. But it is very different now. The men no longer work with pick and shovel, they no longer make fortunes in a single day. The mines are owned by companies, the men are paid wages like any other miners, and the work is done by machinery with all the latest improvements and inventions. And the news of the opening of a new mine or the finding of a large nugget no longer drives people from their offices and their desks to seek their fortunes at the diggings.

CHAPTER 9

THE BUSHRANGERS

> "Hunted, and haunted, and hounded,
> Outlawed from human kin,
> Bound with the self-forged fetters
> Of a long career of sin,
> Hands that are red with slaughter,
> Feet that are sunk in crime—
> A harvest of tares and thistles
> For the pending scythe of Time."
>
> JENNINGS CARMICHAEL

IN the early days of Australia one of the great terrors and dangers of a country life was the bushrangers.

"Bush" meant all land unknown and unreclaimed beyond the few towns and settlements. It might be "open bush," "thick bush," or "scrubby bush"—it was all bush, whether dark forest with high trees and tangled vines, or great plains of tall, waving grass. And the bushrangers were the brigands of the wilds—the Robin Hoods of the Australian forests, except that the bushrangers were, as a rule, brutal and bad, and we have come to think that Robin Hood was a good fellow.

Bushrangers were at first convicts who had escaped into the wilds. For as convicts were hired out to farmers and others as servants, it was much easier for them to escape than it is for a gang of prisoners working under the eye of a warder. Sometimes as many as thirty or forty would escape in a year. They fled to the woods, often living with the savages and doing dreadful deeds. They thought little of committing a murder for a meal, but many of their wicked deeds were done out of a kind of wild revenge for having been imprisoned. Now and again, however, the life in the bush would prove too hard even for these criminals, and after suffering fearful hardships they would return, begging to be forgiven and taken back.

But enough remained to become a terror to the peaceful inhabitants. And at one time, both in Tasmania and in New South Wales, the bushrangers became so bad that the settlers worked in the fields with pistols in their belts, and the women in the houses kept loaded guns always to hand.

One of the most famous Tasmanian bushrangers was Michael Howe. He was a convict who had been a sailor, and who had been condemned to seven years' hard labour for robbery. But not long after he arrived in Tasmania, Howe escaped and joined a band of bushrangers. He soon became their chief, and he ruled like a tyrant. He was very haughty, calling himself "The Governor of the Ranges." The governor of the colony he called the "Governor of the Town."

Howe and his gang soon became the terror of the neighbourhood, but although £100 was offered for his head, none dared try to earn it, for most feared him too much, while others admired him.

At last an old sailor named Worral, also a convict, determined to win the reward. Helped by two other men, he hunted his prey for many days, and at last tracked him to his hiding-place. He was a strange figure, this wild terror of the hills. Clothed in kangaroo skin, with a haversack and powder-flask across his shoulders, and a long, dark beard flowing over his breast, he faced his enemies. Howe fought well for his life, but the struggle was short, and he fell to the ground. Then hacking off his head. Worral carried it, a ghastly prize, to the governor, much as in days long, long ago men carried the heads of wolves to the king for a reward. Worral received his promised reward, and was sent home a free man, loaded now, not with fetters, but with the thanks both of colonists and governor.

Years went on, and convicts were no longer sent to Australia. For as more and more free settlers came, they began to object to the convicts being sent there. Into South Australia they had never been allowed to enter. And in 1868, just eighty years after Sydney had been first founded, the last convict-ship sailed for Australia. After that, evildoers were shut up in prisons at home.

But although convicts no longer came, bushrangers did not die out Others took to the wild life. Sometimes they were the descendants of these convicts or of ticket-of-leave men, as freed convicts were called, or others who had a grudge against mankind, and hated law and order, and above all hated work. They were wild, fearless men, splendid horsemen, deadly shots.

In the great pastures of Australia horses and cattle are not shut into small, fenced fields as at home, but each animal has the initial of its owner branded on its hide. There were men who made a trade of stealing cattle. With a hot iron they changed the letters of the brand, and drove the beasts off to some town far enough away where buyers could be found who would not ask too many questions about where they had come from. These men were called "cattle-duffers" or "bushwhackers." They often carried on their trade for years, but when they became known, and the police were in search of them, they would take to the bush and become regular bushrangers.

Then when gold was found bushrangers became yet more rife. For the gold had to be carried to towns or to the coast to be shipped home. It went always guarded by troops or policemen, but gangs of bushrangers banded together and very often managed to carry off the treasure. Or sometimes the coach, which carried miners and others from the mines to the towns,

"THE COACH WOULD BE 'HELD-UP' AND ALL THE PASSENGERS ROBBED."

would be "held up" and all the passengers robbed.

One of the most dreaded of bushrangers was a man called Daniel Morgan. He was a wild, bad man, and, unlike other bushrangers, he was always alone. He was utterly brutal, and his one desire seemed to be to kill. One day he walked into a farmhouse, alone as usual, with a pistol in either hand and demanded brandy. It was given to him. and then, either from drunkenness or mere cruelty, he began firing among the men with his pistols. Three of them were so badly wounded that one man asked leave to go for a doctor. Morgan said he might go, but when the farmer was on his horse he repented, and, firing at him from behind, shot him dead.

With such doings as these Morgan kept the countryside a-tremble. But at last he came to his end.

The dreaded bushranger appeared one evening at a farmhouse called Peachelba, owned by a Mr. MacPherson. He ordered tea, and after tea commanded Mrs. MacPherson to play upon the piano. With trembling fingers the poor lady did her best. But, as you may imagine, at such a time she could not give her mind to piano-playing, and all the thanks she got was to be yelled at and told that she played very badly.

All the household had been gathered into the room by Morgan's orders, so that he might have them under his eye and pistol Only one little child who was ill was allowed to stay in bed. But now the child began to cry, and Mrs. MacPherson begged to be allowed to send her servant to look after it.

Morgan gruffly gave permission, and the servant left the room. Presently the crying ceased, and Mrs. MacPherson, looking out of the window, saw some one running from the house.

It was the servant. As fast as her feet could carry her she ran to another farm near. Panting and breathless, she rushed into the house and told her news. "But I must go back," she added, "or he will miss me."

"All right," said the farmer, and the brave servant fled back again and returned to the sick child before any one, except Mrs. MacPherson, knew that she had been out of the house.

Quickly the farmer sent messages to the country round about, and by morning twenty-eight men had gathered to surround Peachelba, eager to catch Morgan.

It was a long, weary night to the folk at the farm, but at last day dawned. Breakfast over, Morgan picked up his pistols. "Now, MacPherson," he said, "we will go and get a horse."

MacPherson agreed, for he could do nothing else. But as they walked to the yard a man suddenly slipped from behind a tree. He levelled a gun, there was a loud report, and the dreaded Morgan fell to the ground. Then as if by magic men hurried from their hiding-places and surrounded him. A few hours later Morgan died, having hardly spoken except to grumble that he had not been challenged to a fight—had not had a "fair chance."

A very famous band of bushrangers was a gang called the Kellys. The whole family, both men and women, were a wild, horse-stealing, house-breaking lot. So much feared were they that the country they lived in came to be known as the Kelly district. But they, too, came to their end. Ned Kelly was hanged, others of the gang met their deaths in different ways, and the country settled down into peace once more. But so famous had they been that a theatre manager bought their horses, and made a good deal of money by bringing them into a Christmas pantomime in Melbourne.

Now, happily, the bushranger has gone from the land of Australia as pirates have vanished from the seas. And we may be glad. Their doings may make thrilling stories to read, but most of us would rather not meet them in real life. And it is strange to think that they lived so lately. Robin Hood seems a long way off in the story of our little island, but it is less than thirty years since the last Australian bushranger met his death, and there are men still living who can remember the days when Morgan and the Kellys and others like them held the countryside in thrall.

But Australia is a country which makes rapid strides. One hundred and eighty years ago there was no such place, so far as the white man was concerned. Now in the Island-Continent there are more than five million white people. And what is more wonderful is that a whole continent is under one flag, a thing which in the history of the world has never been before, not even in the days of Alexander, of Cæsar, or of Napoleon. And that flag is the red, white, and blue—the Union Jack. For although since 1901, when all the five colonies united in one, Australia has been a commonwealth, it is still a part of the British Empire.

LIST OF KINGS AND GOVENORS

Kings of Great Britain and Ireland.	Governors of New South Wales.
George III., ... 1760	Captain Arthur Phillip, 1787 to 1792 Major Grose, . . . 1792 ,, 1795 Captain John Hunter, . 1795 ,, 1800 Captain King, . . 1800 ,, 1806 Captain Bligh, . . 1806 ,, 1808 Major-General Macquarie, 1808 ,, 1821
George IV., ... 1820	Sir Thomas Brisbane, . 1822 ,, 1825 Sir Ralph Darling, . 1825 ,, 1831
William IV., . . . 1830	Sir Richard Bourke, . 1831 ,, 1838
Victoria, ... 1837	Sir George Gipps, . . 1838 ,, 1846 Sir Charles Fitzroy, . 1846 ,, 1855 Sir William Denison, . 1855 ,, 1861 Sir John Young, . . 1861 ,, 1867 (Lord Lisgar) Lord Belmore, . . 1868 ,, 1872 Sir Hercules Robinson, . 1872 ,, 1879 Lord Loftus, . . . 1879 ,, 1885 Lord Carrington, . . 1885 ,, 1890 Earl Jersey, . . . 1890 ,, 1893 Sir J. Duff, . . . 1893 ,, 1894 Viscount Hampden, . 1894 ,, 1899 GOVERNORS-GENERAL OF THE COMMON-WEALTH OF AUSTRALIA. Lord Hopetoun, . . 1900 ,, 1902
Edward VII., . . . 1901	Lord Tennyson, . . 1902 ,, 1904 Lord Northcote, . . 1904 ,, 1908 Earl Dudley, . . . 1908

NEW ZEALAND

NOTE.—The verses in this part of the book are by New Zealand writers or are translations of Maori songs.

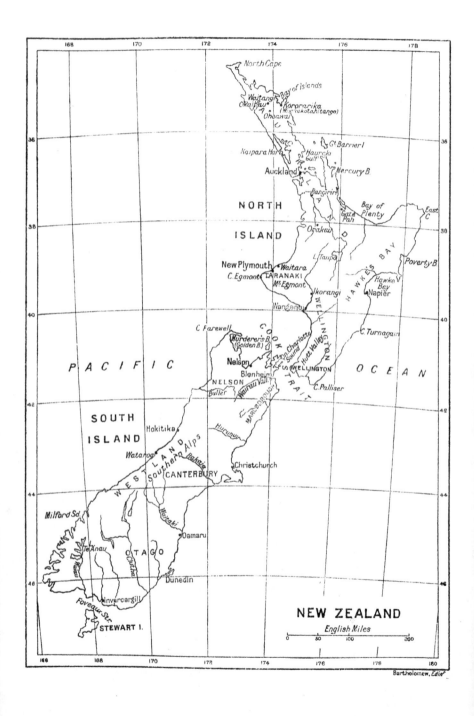

NEW ZEALAND

English Miles

0   50   100   200

Bartholomew, Edin

CHAPTER 1

HOW A GREAT WHITE BIRD CAME TO THE SHORES

IT is doubtful that white man first saw the shores of New Zealand. But the honour is generally given to the Dutch discoverer Tasman. In 1642, returning to Batavia, after having discovered Tasmania, he came upon South Island. Hoping to get fresh water and green food to supply his ship, he anchored. Soon canoes pushed out from the shore, and wild, half-naked savages surrounded Tasman's two ships. They called to the white strangers in loud, rough voices, and blew upon a harsh sounding trumpet. But they would not come within a stone's throw of the ships, although Tasman tried to entice them with presents of linen and knives.

Seeing the natives so many and so warlike, Tasman thought that it would be well to warn the sailors in the other ship to be on their guard, and not let them come aboard. So he ordered a boat to be lowered. But as soon as the natives saw the boat in the water, they surrounded it and drove their canoes crashing against its sides, so that it heeled over. The savages then attacked the Dutchmen with their paddles and short, thick clubs. Three were killed, and one wounded so badly that he died; the others jumped into the water and swam to their ship, while the savages made off, taking one of the dead Dutchmen with them.

Now all hope of friendly barter with the natives being at an end, Tasman sailed away. In memory of this cruel greeting from the savages, he called the place Murderer's Bay, but the name has since been changed to Golden Bay. The whole land Tasman called Staten Land, but that name, too, was soon changed to New Zealand, which name it has kept ever since. And, although we have come to think of it as an English name, it is really Dutch, for the new found land was called after that part of Holland called Zeeland.

But although Tasman had discovered and named New Zealand, no white man had yet set foot upon its shores. The Dutch made no use of their discovery, and for many years the wild Maoris, as the natives of New Zealand are called, were left undisturbed. Now and again a ship touched upon the shores, but little was known of the island until, a hundred years and more after Tasman had sailed away, when another great sailor reached them. This was Captain James Cook.

In 1769 Cook set out upon a voyage of discovery, and before he reached the Great South Land, he came upon the shores of New Zealand. He touched the shores, not on the west side as Tasman had done, but on

"Cook told the Maoris that he had come to set a mark upon their islands."

the east coast at Poverty Bay. Here he landed, being the first white man who is known certainly to have set foot upon these islands.

To the natives the coming of Cook was a thing of fear and wonder. As the *Endeavour*, with outspread sails, came nearer and nearer, they watched the great, white bird, as they took it to be, in amazement, marvelling at the size and beauty of it's wings. Presently the white bird folded it's wings, and from it's side down dropped a tiny wingless bird. This, as it came near, they saw was a curious canoe, filled with white-faced gods. At the sight they turned and fled away in terror. But soon taking courage, they returned brandishing long, wooden spears, and seeming so ready to fight that Cook's men fired upon them. And thus upon the very first day on which the white man came, blood stained the ground.

From Poverty Bay, Cook sailed northward, meeting often with savages. Sometimes they were friendly, and would barter honestly with the ship's crew. At other times they were warlike or thievish, stealing what they could, and singing loud war-songs in defiance.

Cook had with him a South Sea Islander called Tupia, who helped him very much to become friendly with the savages. For although their languages were not quite the same, they could understand each other. So Tupia was able to tell the savages that Cook came in a friendly way, and did not want to fight.

At Mercury Bay, Cook again landed, set up the Union Jack, carved the ship's name and the date upon a tree, and claimed the land for His Majesty, King George. Then sailing onward, he passed all round North Island, and through Cook's Strait (named after himself), proving thus to himself and his crew that these lands were indeed islands, and not part of a continent as had been thought.

At Queen Charlotte's Sound, upon South Island, Cook set up two posts, one on the mainland and one on a little island. Upon these posts were carved the ship's name, the month, and the year, and from the top of them the Union Jack fluttered out.

A few natives came to watch these strange doings, and Cook told them that he had come to set a mark upon their islands, in order to show any ship that might put in there that he had been before them. So the savages allowed him to put up the posts, and promised never to pull them down. They did not understand, however, that Cook, in the manner of those days, was claiming their land in the name of a king who lived in another island, far far away.

After setting up the Union Jack on Queen Charlotte Sound, Cook sailed all round South Island and Stewart Island, and upon 1st April 1770, he left the coast, and steered for the Great South Land.

Cook discovered many interesting things about New Zealand. Among other things, he found out that except a few rats and a few ugly dogs, there were no four-footed animals in the islands at all. Both rats and dogs were used for food, but the natives chiefly lived on eels, fish, and fern-root. New Zealand is the land of ferns, and every valley and hillside is green with them. With the Maoris, fern-root took the place of corn with us, for in New Zealand, although the land was fertile and good, no grain of any kind grew. Fern-root was first roasted, then beaten into a greyish kind of meal, from which bread was made.

The Maoris were tall, strong men of a brownish colour. Their hair was black, and they wore it tied into a bunch on the top of the head, into which they stuck a black, red, or white feather. The faces of the chiefs were tattooed all over in wonderful patterns, the less important people painted themselves with red ochre.

They were a savage and ignorant people, but brave and warlike. Many of them did not care in the least for beads and ribbons and things which usually pleased savages. They thought much more of iron nails, knives, and hatchets. But although they were such fine men, there was one very bad and horrible thing about them. They were cannibals.

The islands were filled with many tribes, who were constantly quarrelling and fighting with each other. Very little was enough to make a quarrel, for the Maoris were terribly proud. A blow was a deadly insult which could only be wiped out in blood, and after a battle the victors would make a horrid feast upon the bodies of their fallen foes. That a chief should be eaten was counted a great disgrace to his tribe, for it was a proof of defeat. And to say to a Maori that his father had been eaten was an insult beyond all words. To have killed and eaten many enemies was a warrior's brightest glory, and great men were often called 'eaters of chiefs.'

In seven years Cook paid five visits to New Zealand. Each time he discovered more of the coast, and learned more of the people and their customs. He brought with him pigs, fowls, potatoes, maize, and other plants and animals likely to be of use to the savages. Some of the plants and animals died, but both pigs and potatoes soon grew plentiful in the land.

CHAPTER 2

THE APOSTLE OF NEW ZEALAND

AFTER Cook, the next visitors to New Zealand were Frenchmen. In those days, as soon as a new land was discovered, wonderful stories were told about it. And the Frenchmen, having heard that the British had discovered an island full of gold and precious stones, came to see, and, if possible, get some of it for themselves. They fell into quarrels and misunderstandings with the natives, and horrible massacres took place. Soon tales of the cruel, man-eating savages who lived in New Zealand spread far and wide. It was not long before the islands got such an evil name that sailors avoided the shores with horror. Men thirsting for fresh water, dying for want of fresh food, chose rather to die than to run the risk of falling into the hands of cannibal savages.

But in spite of its evil name, there were still some roving, daring Britons who ventured to the shores to barter with the savages. For New Zealand flax was so soft and silky that manufacturers were eager to buy it. New Zealand timber, too, was sought after, and above all it was found to be a splendid sealing and whaling ground. So for the sake of wealth men were found to brave the terrors of these shores.

But these old sealers and whalers were among the wildest and most reckless of men. They treated the Maoris and their customs with contempt. They carried them off, both men and women, as slaves, and again and again the proud savages repaid such treatment with a terrible vengeance.

Vainly good men, seeing these things, appealed to King George to put a stop to them. The answer was "The islands are not within His Majesty's dominions." The Governor of New South Wales tried to protect the savages, and threatened those who ill-treated them with punishments. That, too, was vain. For in those days many white men regarded a savage as little better than a beast, to be hunted and hounded as such.

Besides being brave and warlike, the Maoris were a roving, sea-loving people like the Britons themselves. Long ages before white men had touched their shores, they, too, had come from far distant islands, and made a new home in New Zealand. The story of their wanderings had been handed down from father to son, and the names of the canoes in which they had come were still remembered among them.

Now that white men came again and again from far over the seas, the roving spirit awoke once more in many of the Maoris. They longed to see the land from which these white-faced strangers came; these strangers who carried thunder and lightning in their hands, and spoke death to their enemies from afar. They wanted, too, to see the great chief of this power-ful nation, for they thought he must be indeed a mighty warrior. So some of the Maoris ventured on board the whaling vessels and sailed away to England. Some of them, too, saw King George, but when they saw that he was a feeble, old man and no warrior at all, they were greatly disappointed.

Some Maoris, too, sailed to Sydney. There they met a man whose name stands out in the early story of New Zealand almost more than any other. This man was Samuel Marsden, who has been called the "Apostle of New Zealand."

Marsden was prison chaplain at Sydney. He had done much good work among the rough, bad convicts, and when he came to know the wild, ignorant, misunderstood savages, he longed to help them too. "They are as noble a race of men as are to be met with in any part of the world," he wrote to a friend. "I trust I shall be able in some measure to put a stop to those dreadful murders which have been committed upon the islands for some years past, both by Europeans and by the natives. They are a much injured people notwithstanding all that has been said against them."

Among the Maoris whom Marsden met was a chief called Ruatara. He was one of those who had travelled to Europe. There he had had many adventures, and had been cruelly treated by the white men in whom he had trusted. He was returning home, poor and miserable, when Marsden met and befriended him. And when after more adventures he at length reached New Zealand again, he carried with him the story of Marsden's kindness, making his countrymen believe that all white men were not treacherous and base.

Ruatara also carried home with him a present of wheat which Marsden had told him how to sow.

The wheat was sown, and grew, and ripened. But the Maoris scoffed. They did not believe Ruatara's tale that flour could be made from these thin, yellow stalks. But strong in his faith in his new friend, Ruatara reaped and threshed the wheat. Then he came to a standstill. The Maori savages had no idea of the roughest or simplest kind of mill. Ruatara did not know how to grind his wheat, and laughter against him grew louder than ever. But Marsden had not forgotten his friend, and soon a ship arrived bringing the present of a hand-mill.

In great excitement Ruatara called his friends together. They gathered round him, still scoffing. But when a stream of flour flowed from the mill they were lost in wonder. As soon as enough flour was ground it was car-ried off, hastily made into a cake, and cooked in a frying pan. Then the Maoris danced and sang for joy. Ruatara had spoken the truth. Henceforth he was to be believed, and they were ready to receive his friend Marsden with kindness.

Soon after this Marsden got leave from his work in New South Wales and visited New Zealand. He landed in the Bay of Islands, on the north-east coast of North Island. In this very bay, not long before, the crew of a British ship had been cruelly slaughtered, and many of them devoured by the savage victors. Yet without one thought of fear Marsden landed among these man-eaters.

Marsden brought with him, as a present from the Governor of New South Wales, three horses, two cows, and a bull. None of the Maoris, except the two or three like Ruatara who had travelled, had ever seen a horse or a cow. They had never seen any animal bigger than a pig, so they wondered greatly at these large, strange beasts. And when Marsden mounted one of the horses and rode along the sands, they wondered still more.

At this time a fierce war was raging in the Bay of Islands between Ruatara and his uncle Hongi on the one side, and a tribe called the Whangaroans on the other side. Marsden was already known as the friend of Ruatara. Now he determined to make friends with the Whangaroans and bring peace between the foes.

These were the very savages who not long before had killed and eaten the British sailors. Yet Marsden made up his mind to spend a night among them. Taking only one friend with him, Marsden went first to the camp of Hongi. Hongi was a very great and fierce warrior, but Samuel Marsden had won his heart, and with him he was gentle and kind. In Hongi's camp the missionaries had supper and then walked to the enemy's camp, which was about a mile away.

The Whangaroan chiefs received the white strangers kindly. They all sat down together, the chiefs surrounding the two white men. The summer sun was setting, night was coming on, they were alone among cannibals, yet they felt no fear.

Marsden began to talk, telling the Maoris why he had come. He was the friend of Hongi and Ruatara, he said, he wished to be their friend, too, and bring peace among them. Marsden could not speak the Maori language so one chief, who like Ruatara had travelled, and could speak English, translated all that Marsden said.

Long they talked. The sun set, the sky grew dark, the stars shone out. One by one the savages lay down to rest upon the ground. At length Marsden, too, and his friend wrapped themselves in their greatcoats and lay down.

But for Marsden there was little sleep. He lay awake, watching and thinking. It was a strange scene. Above twinkled the bright stars, in front lay the sea, calm and smooth, the waves splashing softly against the shore. Far off in the bay shone the lights of the waiting ship, but close around the white men rose a forest of spears, stuck upright in the ground. All over the plain lay huddled groups of man-eating savages, sleeping peacefully. And who could be sure that they would not suddenly spring up and slay the two white men to make a morning feast?

But the night passed, and with daylight came a boat from the ship to take Marsden and his friend on board again. Marsden asked all the chiefs to come too, although he doubted if they would trust themselves in his power, knowing how often they had been deceived by wicked white men. They showed, however, no sign either of fear or anger, and went on board the ship quite willingly. First Marsden gave them breakfast, then he gathered them all into the cabin. Here, too, came Hongi and Ruatara, and having given them each a present of an axe or something useful, he asked them to make friends and promise to fight no more. Then to Marsden's great joy the rival chiefs fell upon each other's necks, rubbed noses (which is the Maori way of shaking hands), and so made peace. The Whangaroan chiefs then went away much pleased with their presents, and vowing always to love the missionaries, and never more to hurt British traders.

The Sunday after this meeting was Christmas Day and Ruatara was very anxious that there should be "church." So without telling anyone, he began to make great preparations.

First he fenced in about an acre of land. Then he made a pulpit and a reading-desk out of an old canoe, and covered them with black cloth. He also made seats for the white people out of bits of old canoes, and upon the highest point near he set up a flagstaff. Then having finished all his preparations he went to tell Mr. Marsden that everything was ready for a Christmas service.

So on Christmas morning 1815 the first Christmas service was held in New Zealand. Everyone from the ship, except one man and a boy, went ashore. For Marsden was so sure that the Maoris meant to be friendly that he felt there was no need for any one to stay to guard the ship.

The Union Jack was run up, and when Mr. Marsden landed he found the Maori chiefs drawn up in line ready to receive him. They were all dressed in regimentals which the Governor of New South Wales had given them, and behind them were gathered their whole tribes, men, women, and children. And thus, following the white men, they all marched to "church."

The white men took their seats, and behind them crowded the dark-faced savages. The ground was carpeted with green fern, the sky was blue above, and a very solemn silence fell upon the waiting crowd as Mr. Marsden and his friends stood up and sang the Old Hundredth Psalm.

> All people that on earth do dwell,
> Sing to the Lord with cheerful voice.
> Him serve with mirth, His praise forth tell,
> Come ye before Him and rejoice.
> Know that the Lord is God indeed;
> Without our aid He did us make:
> We are His flock, He doth us feed,
> And for His sheep He doth us take.

When the singing was over Marsden read the English Church Service. The people stood up and knelt down at a sign from one of their chiefs, for they understood not a word of what was said.

"We don't know what it all means," they said to Ruatara.

"Never mind," said he, "you will understand later."

"Behold I bring you glad tidings of great joy," was Marsden's text, and when the sermon was over Ruatara tried to explain in Maori language what it was all about. And if the Maoris did not quite understand all, this they did understand, that Mr. Marsden wanted to be kind to them, and bring peace between his countrymen and theirs.

CHAPTER 3

HONGI THE WARRIOR

MR. Marsden could not stay long in New Zealand, for his work was in Australia. But there came with him two missionaries, and they stayed when he left. One of these missionaries taught the Maoris how to build houses and boats; the other taught how to make fishing-lines and other useful things. For Marsden did believe in teaching the savages only to be Christian. He thought it best to teach them first how to live decent and comfortable lives, and how to trade. "You cannot form a nation without trade and the civil arts," he said.

Before he left New Zealand Marsden bought about two hundred acres of land, paying twelve axes for it to the chief to whom it belonged. Upon this the missionaries built their houses and schools, and this was the first piece of land really possessed by the British in New Zealand, and their title to it was duly set down in writing. "Know all men to whom these shall come, that I, Anodee O Gunna, King of Ranghechoo, in the Island of New Zealand, have, for twelve axes to me in hand now paid and delivered by the Reverend Samuel Marsden, given, granted, bargained, and sold, all that parcel of land in the district of Hoshee, in the Island of New Zealand, for ever."

This writing was signed by two Englishmen, and as Gunna could not write, Hongi drew a copy of the tattooing on his face upon the parchment, and Gunna set his mark to it. Thus the white man first set his hand upon the land.

This bargain being settled, Marsden returned to Australia. He was gladly received by his friends there, for they had hardly hoped to see him return alive from the dreaded cannibal islands.

Although Samuel Marsden was a clergyman and wanted to make the Maoris Christian, he thought the best way of doing that was to teach them how to live better lives, how to plant wheat, build houses, and live in peace with their neighbours. "Hoes, spades and axes," he said, "are silent but sure missionaries."

So he encouraged them to trade. But one thing he would not sell to the Maoris. That thing was firearms. He sent a blacksmith to live among the heathen and teach them his trade. But he was forbidden to make or mend any weapon. No missionary was allowed to sell guns, and when Marsden discovered that one had disobeyed his orders he was sent away in disgrace.

But Hongi, although he had made peace at Marsden's bidding, was a fierce, proud warrior. He lived for revenge, and loved power. "There is but

138

one king in Britain," he said, "and there shall be but one in New Zealand."
He resolved that he should be that king. But before he began his conquests
he paid a visit to England.

In England Hongi was feted and made much of. For it was almost as
good as going to a wild beast show to dine with a cannibal chief. He became
a "lion" and went from one fine house to another, being everywhere loaded
with presents. Hongi saw many wonderful things, but he liked best to
watch the soldiers and to wander among the arms and armour in the Tower.

Hongi went one day to see the king, and he, knowing his love for
soldiers, gave him a suit of old armour. Of all the presents he received,
Hongi prized his suit of armour most.

At last, his mind filled with all the splendours he had seen, Hongi
sailed homeward. On his way he stopped ay Sydney, and there he sold all
his fine presents, except only his armour. With the money he bought guns
and ammunition, and once more set out for New Zealand.

Then Hongi began his career of conquest. None now could stand against
him. Battle after battle was fought. Wooden spears went down before his
thunder of guns, and after the battles the victors rejoiced in horrid revelry
upon the bodies of their foes.

Thousands were slain, hundreds more men, women, and children were
led captives as slaves. From end to end, North Island was filled with wrath
and tears. Hongi stalked in conquering pride, glorying in the numbers he
had killed and eaten.

The missionaries were in despair. All the good they had done, all Marsden's peacemaking, seemed to have been in vain. For six years the country
was filled with slaughter and woe, and the beautiful fernland was turned
into a desert, where men wandered seeking revenge and blood.

But at last Hongi's career of war and triumph came to an end. Other
tribes saw that their only safety lay in getting guns to fight guns. And guns
they got. And so the slaughter was made worse, until at length Hongi
was wounded and died. He died a warrior, "Kia toa, kia toa," he said, "be
brave, be brave."

Hongi lived and died in the shedding of blood, yet he never harmed
the missionaries. They were doers of good, he said. He was Marsden's
friend, and he sent his children to the missionary schools, but he himself
never became a Christian.

After Hongi's death the missionaries once more became peacemakers,
and they persuaded the lawless tribes to lay down their weapons. But it
was uphill work, for bad, white men were constantly undoing the good
which the missionaries did. So battles, and murders, and horrid cannibal
feasts went on.

Sometimes, too, without meaning it, white men made the Maoris
angry. It was, for instance, a great crime to touch anything which, for some

reason or another, had been declared to be "tapu," that is sacred. White people did not understand the rules of tapu, and often in sheer ignorance they broke them. According to Maori law this was a sin which could only be wiped out by blood, so, often for seemingly harmless deeds, white men were horribly murdered.

Yet in spite of all dangers, in spite of the dark tales of horror, some settlers were at length lured to the shores. For the land was wonderfully fertile, and people hoped to make great fortunes. So a shipload of colonists arrived, determined to make their homes in New Zealand.

But just at this time the islanders were at war with each other, and soon after they landed the colonists saw a war dance. It was night time. Fires and flaring torches lit up the dusky forms of five or six hundred warriors, who stood in four long rows, swaying and stamping in time to the chant of their leader. With waving arms and rolling eyes they joined in chorus. Thrusting out their tongues, grinning horribly, in the flickering light they seemed like dancing demons. Now uttering loud yells, now hissing like a thousand serpents, now crashing their weapons together, they danced on. Bending, swaying, hissing, yelling, they went through all the actions of war, in fancy killing and eating their enemies. The sight was too much for the new-come colonists. Filled with horror and dread, they fled from the land as quickly as possible.

Yet in spite of all their wild savagery Marsden loved the Maoris. He returned again and again to visit them. Him they always greeted with joy; him they were always ready to obey. When for the last time he came among them he was an old white-haired man, unable to ride or walk far. But, glad to serve him, the Maoris carried him about in a litter, and when he spoke of trying to ride they were quite hurt. Soon after his last visit to New Zealand Marsden died, regretted and mourned by all who knew him, but by none so much as by the Maoris, who had lost in him a good friend.

CHAPTER 4

HOW THE MAORIS BECAME THE CHILDREN OF THE GREAT WHITE QUEEN

ALTHOUGH it was now more than sixty years since Cook had planted the Union Jack and claimed the islands of New Zealand for the British Crown, they were not yet considered part of the British Empire. Many evil deeds were done in the islands by white men, and the British seemed to have no power, or no will to stop them. "The islands are not within His Majesty's dominions" was the convenient answer to all appeals for help.

But at last, in 1832, a British Resident was sent to live in New Zealand. He was told to try and make things better, but he had no power. He did nothing. He could do nothing. "A ship of war without any guns," he was scornfully called.

About this time Baron de Thierry, a Frenchman who had spent much of his life in England, tried to make himself King of New Zealand. He bought, or thought he bought, a great part of North Island for thirty axes. Then he issued proclamations calling himself, "Charles Baron de Thierry, Sovereign Chief of New Zealand, and King of Nuhuheva," and promising his protection and favour to all who would take office under him.

When the British Resident, Mr. Busby, saw this proclamation, he began to be afraid that the French were coming to take the land. So he banded thirty-five of the Maori chiefs together into what he called the United States of New Zealand. These chiefs declared themselves independent, but at the same time they begged the King of Great Britain to protect them against their enemies.

This declaration Busby sent to Thierry. But Thierry replied that New Zealand was not a British possession, that Tasman was there before Cook, and that he as king came to protect New Zealand liberties.

All this time Thierry had lived and written at a distance. Now he arrived in his kingdom. He brought with him only about ninety followers, gathered chiefly from the riff-raff of Sydney. He planted his flag, however, ordered his followers to stand bareheaded in his presence, and to be careful never to turn their backs when they left it. He scattered empty titles and honours around, and began to make a carriage drive from his "palace" to the Bay of Islands.

But the new king soon found that his thirty axes had only brought for him two or three hundred acres of land, instead of the kingdom he had thought. His money came to an end, his followers laughed at him, and his kingship ended in air.

A few years after this some people in England formed a company, which they called the New Zealand Land Company. Hundreds of acres of land were sold in London before it had been bought from the natives or even seen by any white man. Hundreds of people, eager to make money, bought this land without knowing anything about it, except that it was somewhere in New Zealand. Then the Company sent a shipload of settlers out to found a colony.

This was against the law, for, before a British colony can be formed, leave must be given from the crown. No such leave had been asked or given. Indeed the ship was sent off in secret.

Now at last the British Government woke up. It was seen that something must be done. On the one hand British settlers had to be protected from the cruelties of the Maoris. On the other hand the Maoris had to be protected from greedy, land-grabbing white people.

So Captain Hobson was sent out to be the first governor. He was told to make treaties with the native chiefs, and then to declare New Zealand to be a British colony.

On the 29th of February 1840 Hobson landed, and upon the 5th February he held a great meeting of the chiefs at a place called Waitangi.

On a plain near the town a platform was raised, and here at noon the governor took his seat, with the principal white people. Close round the platform sat the grave, dark-faced Maori chieftains, and behind them gathered the rest of the white people. The sun shone from a sky blue and cloudless, the gay tents of the British, decorated with flags, showed bravely against the background of waving trees. It was a scene of beauty and of peace. But there were those who shook their heads and sighed. No good would come of the meeting, they said, for did not Waitangi mean "weeping water"?

When all were gathered, Hobson spoke to the people. But as he could not speak the Maori language a missionary translated what he said to them. He told them how the great white Queen far over the sea loved all her people. He told them that if they would promise to be her children she would love them too. The great white Queen was very powerful, he said, and would protect them from all their enemies, if they would acknowledge her as their overlord.

When Hobson had finished, the Maori chiefs were asked to speak their thoughts. Many of them did not wish to make a treaty. "Send the man away," said one. "Do not sign the paper. If you do you will become his slaves. Your land will be taken from you. You will no longer be chiefs, but will have to break stones upon the roads."

Then an old chief named Waka Nene rose. He was great in battle, wise in council, and his people listened to him willingly. Now he prayed them to hearken to the white lord. "You will be our father," he said, turning to Hobson. "You will not allow us to become slaves. You will keep our old customs, and never allow our land to be taken from us."

Then there was much talk this way and that. Many of the chiefs grew fierce and excited, others sat in sullen anger. At last it was agreed that they should think about it for one day and return then to tell the governor what they had decided.

Next day the treaty was signed. Waka Nene, the wise old warrior who had spoken so well, signed his name as the missionaries had taught him to do. The other chiefs made marks on the paper like the tattooing on their faces. A little later the treaty was signed by many of the chiefs on South Island, and by the end of June Victoria was proclaimed overlord of North and South Islands by treaty, and of Stewart Island by right of discovery. Thus New Zealand became part of the British Empire.

Soon after this the town of Auckland was founded and made the head-quarters of the government. And now that New Zealand had become a British possession, people began to believe that the land would grow peaceful and safe to live in, and in a very short time hundreds of settlers arrived.

In the meantime, a town in the south of North Island had been founded by the New Zealand Company, who, you remember, had secretly sent off a shipload of colonists. They called their town Wellington, in honour of the great Duke.

Wakefield, the leader of the Company, had, by this time too, bought great tracts of land from the Maoris for such things as guns, razors, looking-glasses, sealing wax, nightcaps, jews' harps. Many of the Maoris did not understand the bargains. Many of them had no power to sell the land, and no wish to do so. They only pretended to do so because they wanted the guns and other things. Wakefield, on the other hand, had really no power to buy. For since Queen Victoria had become overlord, land could only be bought through the government. So trouble began. Indeed all the war and trouble there has been in New Zealand has arisen out of quarrels over land. Wakefield did not understand the Maoris, and knew nothing of their land laws, which were very difficult to follow. Sometimes both Maoris and white people would claim the same piece of ground, the one saying that he had bought it, the other saying that he had never sold it. And when the Maoris saw that the white people were taking all the best of the land they grew angry and frightened, and quarrels followed. So the new governor's task was not an easy one. But Hobson was a good and true man, and did his best to be fair both to Maoris and to white men.

Hobson worked hard in spite of illness, for soon after the signing of the Waitangi treaty he became ill. He never got well again, but in spite of that he stuck to his post bravely, until after two and a half years he died.

During these two and a half years New Zealand leaped forward as if by magic. When Hobson first came there were not two thousand white people in all the islands. When he died there were twelve thousand. Besides Auckland and Wellington, the towns of New Plymouth and Nelson, as well as many other villages, had sprung up. There were schools and churches, newspapers, soldiers, and police, where a few months before there had been only one or two missionaries, and wild traders, scattered amongst fierce man-eating savages.

The Maoris, as well as the white people, were sorry when Governor Hobson died. "Mother Victoria," wrote one of the chiefs to the Queen, "my subject is a Governor for us Maoris and for the Pakeha (settlers) in this island. Let him be a good man. Look out for a good man, a man of judgment. Let not a troubler come here. Let not a boy come here, or one puffed up. Let him be a good man as the Governor who has just died."

CHAPTER 5

THE "HEAVENLY DAWN" AND THE "WILD CABBAGE LEAF" MAKE WAR

"Rauparaha's war chant,
Rauparaha's fame song,
Rauparaha's story
Told on the harp-strings,
Pakeha harp-cords
Tuned by the stranger.

No wild hero of romance,
Born in dreamy poet's trance,
    Cradled in some mythic fane,
    Built up in a minstrel's brain
On imagination's plan!—
No such hero was this man.
    He was flesh and blood and bone,
    Standing forth erect, alone,
High above his fellows known!—
Hist'ry paints what he hath done,
Maori valour's bravest son—
Te Rauparaha, Te Rauparaha!

Quick of eye and lithe of limb,
Warriors bent the knee to him!—
    Bold of heart, strong of hand,
    Formed to rule and to command
Suckled on a breast that gave
Milk of heroes to the brave!—
    Richest fruit of Toa's seed,
    Scion of heroic breed,
    Born to conquer and to lead!
Strongest branch of noblest tree
From Hawaiki o'er the sea,
Te Rauparaha, Te Rauparaha!"

THOMAS BRACKEN.

AFTER the signing of the treaty of Waitangi the Maoris lived in peace with the white people. The only quarrels were about land, but these were bitter indeed.

In the north of South Island there lay a beautiful valley called Wairau. This valley Colonel Wakefield claimed; but the chiefs, Rauparaha (the Wild Cabbage Leaf) and Rangihaeata (the Heavenly Dawn), to whom it belonged, declared that he had no right to it. "We have never sold it," they said. "And we never will sell it. We want it for our sons and their sons for ever. If you want our land you will have to kill us first, or make us slaves."

But Colonel Wakefield paid no attention to what the chiefs said. He called Rauparaha an old savage, and vowed soon to put an end to his rule. This, too, in spite of the treaty of Waitangi, by which the white men had promised to protect the Maoris.

Bent on having his own way, Wakefield sent men to mark out the valley of Wairau for farms. But Rauparaha and his followers turned the men off. They were quite polite and gentle about it, but quite firm. They did no harm to any of the white men, or to their belongings. They simply carried all their instruments and tools to their boats and left them there. Next the Maoris pulled up all the flags and stakes with which the land had been marked out, and burned them. They burned the huts which the white men had built, too. "I have the right to do this," said Rauparaha, "for they were built of wood grown upon my own land. So they are mine."

Very angry were Wakefield's men when they returned to Nelson. There they went to the magistrate and told him of the treatment they had received. From him they got a letter or warrant to take Rauparaha and Rangihaeata prisoner, for having burned their houses.

Armed with this warrant they went back to Wairau, accompanied by the magistrate and some workmen. Workmen and gentlemen together, they numbered about fifty; only about thirty-five of them, however, had guns. But even so they thought they would be a match for any number of savages.

When they came to the mouth of the Wairau river, however, they were met by a Christian chief. He warned them to be careful what they did. But they would not listen, and marched on up the river, until they came to where Rauparaha was encamped on the other side.

A few of the party boldly crossed the stream and asked for Rauparaha. "Here I am," he said, rising, "what do you want?"

"You must come with me, to Nelson," said the magistrate, "because you have burned a house, which you had no right to do."

"I will not go," replied the Wild Cabbage Leaf.

"But you must," said the magistrate. "I have brought the Queen's book," he added, showing him the warrant, "that says you must go."

Then Rangihaeata sprang up. He was tall and handsome, his dark face was fierce with pride and anger. Behind him stood his wife Te Ronga, the daughter of Rauparaha. "Are we not in our own land?" he cried angrily. "We do not go to England to interfere with you. Leave us alone."

And so the quarrel waxed, and angry words were bandied back and forth. A pair of handcuffs were brought out. Rauparaha put his hands under his cloak and cried again that he would not go to be a slave.

Then from among the white people a shot was fired. It struck Te Ronga where she stood beside her husband, and she fell dying to the ground.

In a moment all was wild confusion. Volley after volley was fired. "Farewell the light! Farewell the day! Welcome the darkness of death!" cried Rauparaha.

Before the wild charge of the Maoris the British fled. A few stood their ground, but at last, seeing resistance useless, they waved a handkerchief to show that they surrendered.

Rauparaha then ordered his followers to cease fighting. But Rangihaeata was mad with sorrow and hatred. "Do not forget that they slew your daughter, Te Ronga!" he cried, and the unresisting Britons were slain where they stood. In all, twenty-two were killed: the rest, some of them sorely wounded, escaped.

As soon as the heat of fight was over Rauparaha began to fear the white man's vengeance. He had few followers in South Island, so, taking to his canoes, he and they rowed over Cook's strait to North Island, where his tribe lived.

The weather was stormy, and the waves dashed over the canoes as they sped along. But the Maoris were the vikings of the south. Little they cared for the dangers of the deep, for their hearts were hot within them, and as they bent to the oars they sang, their wild voices rising above the roar of the storm.

Wet and weary, Rauparaha landed, and with the salt spray still on his lips, with the song of the storm wind still in his ear, he spoke to his countrymen. Such wild, stirring words he spoke that they were ready to rise and sweep the white man into the sea.

"Now is the time to strike!" he cried. "Now we know what the smooth talk of the Pakeha is worth. You know now what they mean in their hearts. You know now that you can wait for nothing but tyranny at their hands. Come, sweep them from the land that they would water with our blood." And as Rauparaha spoke, he jangled the insulting handcuffs in the ears of his people.

Fortunately there were white men in New Zealand who both knew and loved the Maoris. They soothed the hurt and angry souls of the savages, and the white men, who had begun the quarrel, were told that what they had done was "unlawful, unjust and unwise."

When the new governor, Captain Robert Fitzroy, arrived in New Zealand, he went to see Rauparaha and Rangihaeata, and heard from themselves the story of their wrongs. He listened to all that they had to say, then he told the Maoris that they had committed a great crime in killing men who had surrendered, but because the white men were wrong in the beginning he would not punish them for their deaths. In this way peace was made. But many of the white men were angry that the blood of their brothers had not been avenged. Some of them were so angry that they wrote home and asked that this new governor, who so favoured the Maoris, should be called home again.

CHAPTER 6

THE FLAGSTAFF WAR

BESIDES the land troubles others now beset the governor. After New Zealand became a British colony many changes followed. Gradually the unseen power of Civilisation laid hold upon the islands. The chiefs began to feel uneasy. Something, they knew not what, was rising up around them. Somehow their power was vanishing. Old customs were slipping away. New and strange ones were coming into use. The people were made to pay taxes, a thing they found hard to understand. Ships coming to New Zealand ports had to pay custom duties before landing their goods. So tobacco and blankets grew dear, whale ships almost ceased to come to the Bay of Islands, where once they had crowded, and the trade of the town Kororarika was almost ruined.

A vague fear and discontent spread among the people. Then there were not wanting base white people who pointed to the British flag, and told the dark chieftains that there lay the cause of all their sorrows. And so the idea took root that if only that flag were removed the good old days would return again.

Near Kororarika, on the Bay of Islands, there lived a young chief called Honi Heke. He had married the daughter of the great chief Hongi, and, like him, longed to be powerful among his people. He was restless and clever, and he hated the white people. He was no ignorant savage, for the missionaries had taught him much. But although at one time he became a Christian, later he turned back to his heathen ways.

Proud, wild, and discontented Heke was ready to fight any one. And when one day a woman of his tribe, who had married a white man, called him a pig, he gathered around him a hundred hot-headed young savages like himself, and marching into Kororarika, he plundered the white man's house, and carried off his wife. Then having danced a war-dance, he and his followers cut down the flagstaff, from which floated the Union Jack, and departed rejoicing.

This was serious, and the governor resolved to put an end to Heke's wild tricks. But in all New Zealand there were not ninety soldiers. So he sent to Australia begging for help. Sir George Gipps, the Governor of New South Wales, at once sent a shipload of men and guns. But before they came, Waka Nene and some other friendly chiefs begged Fitzroy not to fight.

"We will guard the flagstaff," they said. "We are old folks and faithful. We will make the young folks be faithful too."

Then at a great meeting twenty-five chiefs apologised for Heke's behaviour, but he himself did not come. Instead he wrote a letter which was only half an apology, for he said the flagstaff was his own. It had been brought, he said, from the forest by his own people, and had been meant, not for the British flag, but for the flag of New Zealand.

However, Fitzroy accepted the apology such as it was. The chiefs, in token of their submission, laid their guns at his feet. He gave them back again making a long speech, in which he warned the Maoris not to believe or be led astray by the tales of wicked white men.

After this, Governor Fitzroy took away the custom duties and made Kororarika a free port once more. He hoped in this way to bring wealth and trade to the town again, and make the people more contented. And when they heard the news, the white settlers were so glad that they used up all the candles in the town to make an illumination to show their joy. So peace was once more made. The soldiers were sent away, a new flagstaff was set up, and again the Union Jack floated out on the breeze.

But before many months had gone Heke once more gathered his men, and the flagstaff was cut down a second time. Heke hated it as the sign that the Maoris had no more power in the land. "God made this land for us and for our children!" he cried. "Are we the only people that God has made without a land to live upon?"

Again Governor Fitzroy sent to Sydney for help. He also offered a reward of £100 to any one who would bring Heke prisoner to him.

This made Heke's followers very angry. "Is Heke a pig," they asked, "that he should be bought and sold?" And he in his turn offered £100 for the governor's head.

Again two hundred soldiers came from New South Wales. Again the flagstaff was set up. And this time it was hooped and barred with iron, and a blockhouse was built near in which a guard was stationed.

All this made the Maoris more sure than ever that the flagstaff was really the cause of their troubles. "See," they said, "the flagstaff does mean power, or why should the Pakehas set it up again and guard it so carefully!"

All the wild and discontented young men now gathered to Heke, who had sworn the downfall of the flagstaff, and of the power of which it was the sign.

It was in vain that the missionaries, who had always been peacemakers, tried to make peace now. Printed copies of the Waitangi treaty were sent to the Maori rebels. But Heke would neither listen nor give in. "It is all soap," he said, "very smooth and oily, but treachery is hidden at the bottom of it." One Sunday morning a missionary went to his camp to preach. His text was, "Whence come wars and fightings." Heke listened to it quietly, then he said, "Go, speak that sermon to the British, they need it more than we."

Days went on, and still the Union Jack floated from the hill above the town. Still Heke and his men lay encamped near, breathing defiance.

The people of Kororarika, well knowing that Heke never broke his word, began to drill, and prepared to give him a hot welcome when he came. But in the end he took them unawares. One morning in March, before the sun was up, two hundred men came creeping, creeping up the hill. The guard was taken by surprise. Before the officer in charge knew what was happening, the enemy were in possession of the blockhouse, and the soldiers were being driven downhill.

Then the axes went to work, and for the third time the flagstaff fell.

The townspeople armed themselves, and with the soldiers and marines from the warship which lay in the bay, defended themselves right bravely. But the Maoris had the best position on the flagstaff hill, and after hours of fighting, men, women, and children fled to the ship, leaving their town to the mercy of the foe.

Great was the joy of the savages when they saw the white folk go. They danced, and sang, and made grand speeches. Then dashing upon the town they began to plunder it.

As the fighting was now stopped, many of the people ventured back again in the hope of saving some of their goods. The Maoris were now perfectly good natured, and did not try to hurt them. Then might be seen the strange sight of Maori and white man carrying off goods from the same house, the one trying to save his own, the other taking whatever he had a mind to take. But before long fire broke out. It raged among the wooden buildings, and Kororarika was soon little more than a blackened ruin.

Homeless and penniless, many of them having nothing left to them but the clothes they wore, the settlers fled to Auckland. Here something like a panic seized hold of the people. Many of them sold their farms for almost nothing and fled from the land in terror.

But the Maoris followed their victory by no cannibal feast. Instead they allowed the missionaries to bury the dead. They even helped some women and children who had been left behind to join their friends. Indeed through all the war the British could not but admire the courteous, generous behaviour of their savage foes.

CHAPTER 7

THE WARPATH

> "When will your valour begin to rage?
> When will your valour be strong?
> Ah! when the tide murmurs,
> Ah! when the tide roars.
> Bid farewell to your children,
> For what more can you do?
> You see how the braves are coming amain,
> Like the lofty exulting peaks of the hills,
> They yield, they yield! O Fame!"
>
> MAORI WAR-SONG.

HEKE'S fame spread far and wide. He boasted of the defeat of the white men, and threatened that when the moon was full he would attack Auckland and sweep it from the earth, as he had swept Kororarika. All the colony was shaken with fear. Everywhere towns were fortified. Everywhere settlers drilled, and practised, and made ready for war.

The governor saw that he must now fight in good earnest. For only after Heke was subdued could there be peace. So again he sent to Australia for soldiers. Meanwhile Waka Nene and the friendly Maoris helped the British, and took up arms against their lawless countrymen.

After the sack of Kororarika, Heke and his warriors marched away to a strong, native fortress or "pah" called Okaihau. There Waka Nene followed him, and there he was joined later by a British force under Colonel Hume.

When the British soldiers arrived they were very much astonished at sight of their allies. Was it possible, they asked, that they were expected to fight side by side with a rabble of half-naked savages? Their astonishment became still greater when the Maoris, in their honour, danced a war-dance, which Waka Nene's wife led, and in which Waka Nene himself joined, dressed in the uniform of a British officer.

It was May when the troops landed. But May in New Zealand is like November at home. The weather was cold and wet. For four days the men marched through almost pathless forest, under torrents of rain. The way was so bad that no baggage-wagons could pass along it. So the men had neither tents nor proper food. Each man carried his own biscuits and slept upon the damp ground. Thus wearied and hungry, they arrived before Heke's pah.

Between a large lake and a wooded hill lay the fortress. It was built of two rows of tree-trunks twelve feet high, and so closely set together that only the barrel of a gun could pass between. The outer fence was covered with flax, and between the two was a deep ditch. Without cannon it was impossible to take such a fort, and the British had only a rocket-tube.

The British began their attack by firing their rockets. The first struck away a strong post, burst inside the pah, and frightened the defenders so much that some of them were ready to flee. But no one being hurt they took courage again. Then as rocket after rocket fell wide of the mark, they watched them with surprise and scorn. "What prize can be won by such a gun?" they sneered, and they were no longer afraid.

Presently they gained so much courage that they came out of their pah to fight. But the British soldiers charged them with fixed bayonets and drove them back again.

So for many hours the fight lasted, the Maoris firing in safety from behind their strong palisade, against which the British vainly wasted their shot. Lead whistled through the air in all directions, the whole country seemed on fire, "and brave men worked their work."

At length the fighting ceased and both sides retired to rest. As the British soldiers sat round their camp-fires they heard a strange sound coming from the Maori pah. the sound of singing. Plaintive and wailing it rose and fell in the still air. It was the Maoris singing their evening hymn. "Fight and pray," had said their priests. "Touch not the spoils of the slain, eat not of human flesh lest the God of the missionaries should be angry. And be careful not to offend the Maori gods. It is good to have more than one God to trust to. Be brave, be strong, be patient." So ignorant and simple, trusting in they knew not what, the Maoris now sang a hymn to the God of the missionaries.

Next day, seeing how hopeless it was to try to take the fort without cannon, Hume marched his soldiers away.

The people in Auckland had been eagerly awaiting the news that Heke was captured. And when instead of that news the worn-out, haggard troops reached the town, they were struck with dismay. Was it possible that two hundred and fifty savages had been more than a match for four hundred well-trained British soldiers? It was the second time that the Maoris had beaten "the wearers of red garments," and now the British began to tremble for their hold on the land.

Meanwhile Heke swaggered about in the glory of victory. He wrote letters to the governor which were about peace indeed, but which breathed war in every line.

More soldiers, however, now arrived from Australia under Colonel Despard. They brought with them four cannon, and the colonists began to feel more cheerful.

The last fight had taught Heke that in the open his soldiers could not stand against British soldiers. He had learned that his safety was in the strength of his fortresses. So now he retired to a pah called Oheawai, which was far stronger than Okaihau.

Here the British resolved to attack him. But it was with great difficulty that the cannon were brought along the rugged path through the forest to Heke's camp, for they were ship's guns, and the wheels were only fifteen inches high. Many a time they stuck fast in the marshy forest, but the friendly Maoris harnessed themselves to the carriages, and at length all difficulties were passed, and in the dusk of a winter's evening the whole army encamped before Heke's fort.

That night there was little sleep in either camp. Through the night as they lay awake on the ground, the British soldiers heard the Maoris in their pah praying, singing, and talking.

In the morning the fight began. The great cannon-balls crashed and crashed against the huge, wooden walls without doing much damage. And when all the heavy ammunition was done only a small breach had been made. But small though it was, Colonel Despard, against the advice of his officers and of the friendly Maoris, ordered a party to storm it.

Bravely the soldiers obeyed his orders. Shouting their war-cry, they charged the breach. Bravely they fought and fell. The breach was narrow. It was defended by hundreds of well-armed Maoris. Fighting valiantly, the British passed the outer fence; but the inner fence was still unbroken. From it a hail of bullets blazed upon the gallant stormers, and man after man went down.

After ten minutes of awful slaughter and confusion the British fell back, leaving half their number dead upon the ground.

Then followed a night of horror. The dead and dying lay untended round the pah. Through the still night air the groans of the wounded were heard, mingled with the songs of triumph sung by the exulting savages.

> "O Youth of sinewy force,
> O man of martial strength,
> Behold the sign of power!
> In my hand I hold the scalp
> Of the Kawau Tatakaha."

Often too, through the night the watch-cry of the pah was heard. "Come on! Come on! soldiers for revenge. Come on! Stiff lie your dead by the fence of my pah. Come on, come on!"

Round their camp-fires the British sat wakeful, watchful, downcast,

"Shouting their war-cry, the British charged the breach."

eating their hearts out in anger and despair.

For two days there was little fighting. The Maoris hung out a flag of truce and told the British they might bury their dead. Then more ammunition having arrived for the great guns, the bombardment again began. Soon the breach already made became much larger, and a second assault was planned.

When morning dawned the pah was to be taken. But during the night the Maoris, seeing they could hold their fortress no longer, slipped quietly away to the forest, leaving their empty pah to the British. So quietly did they go that the British knew nothing about it until they were told by a friend that the Maoris were already ten miles away.

It was hard to fight such a slippery foe. It was useless to try to follow them into the forest wilds, so Colonel Despard marched his men away to Kororarika to rest. And the governor, hoping that now Heke might be persuaded to make peace, told him not to fight any more for the present.

CHAPTER 8

THE STORMING OF THE BAT'S NEST

HEKE was yet far from making peace. He and his friends in their new fastness at Ikorangi were dancing the war-dance, and singing songs of exultation—

> "An attack! an attack! E ha!
> A battle! a battle! E ha!
> A fight on the banks of the river.
> It is completely swept and emptied.
> O you would fight, you would fight.
> You had better stayed at home in Europe
> Than have suffered a repulse from Whareahau.
> He has driven you back to your God.
> You may cast your book behind,
> And leave your religion on the ground.
> An attack! an attack! E ha!
> A battle! a battle! E ha!"

Heke's fame grew greater and greater, for had he not twice defeated "the wearers of red garments." Peace was far from his thoughts, and Governor Fitzroy was about to attack him again, when he was recalled. The British Government were not pleased at the way in which the colony was drifting into war, and Captain George Grey was sent to take Fitzroy's place.

Captain Grey made up his mind to have no more fighting if that were possible. He sent messengers to the rebel chiefs, saying that if they would yield before a certain date, they would be pardoned, and that if they had been in any way wronged, they should have justice.

But Heke would not yield, and once more the war began. This time the Maori forces were divided. Heke was at Ikorangi, and his friend Kawiti at Ruapekapeka, the Bat's Nest. It was upon the Bat's Nest that the attack was made. It was a pah like Oheawai and Okaihau, but far stronger than either. For between the huge wooden fences there was a great mud wall against which cannon balls were of little use.

The British force was now much stronger than before. They had more and heavier guns, but still for days the bombardment went on with little result. Then one day Heke arrived to join his friends, bringing many more warriors with him. The next day being Sunday, the Maoris thought there would be no fighting, for the missionaries had taught them to keep it as a day of rest. So they all gathered in the outworks for prayer, leaving the fort almost unguarded.

The British, however, had no thought of keeping Sunday. A friendly Maori, seeing how quiet it was within the pah, crept close up to the walls. Finding them unguarded, he made signs to the British. Quickly they charged, and before the Maoris realised what was happening, the red-coats had possession of the fort.

Now the very strength of the pah was turned against the Maoris. Secure behind the massive ramparts, the British fired upon the foe. A fierce fight followed. But to dislodge the British from their strong position was impossible, and at last the Maoris fled to the woods.

Tired of the fight, the followers of Heke and Kawiti now scattered and fled. They had little food left; starvation and death stared them in the face. "Can shadows carry muskets?" they said. And so the army melted away. In a few days Heke and Kawiti found themselves almost alone. The end had come. At last the proud chieftains sued for peace.

"Friend Governor, let peace be made between you and me," wrote Kawiti. "I have had enough of your cannon-balls, therefore I say let us make peace. Will you not? Yes. This is the end of my war against you. Friend Governor, I, Kawiti and Heke, do consent to this good message. It is finished."

Now that the rebel chiefs were in his power. Sir George was merciful. He pardoned all who had taken part in the rebellion, and allowed them to remain in possession of their lands. But Heke's proud, restless spirit could not bear the bonds of peace. He pined away, and died at the age of forty-two. As for his old friend Kawiti, he lived to the age of eighty, and then died of measles, a new disease brought into the country by the white men.

There were many who thought that Governor Grey had been too gentle with Heke and Kawiti and the other rebels. Many thought that they ought to have been punished. But time showed that Sir George was right, for the peace was lasting, and left no bitterness behind. Not while Heke or Kawiti lived, however, was the flagstaff at Kororarika put up again. But in 1857 Kawiti's son led four hundred of his people to the spot, and in token of friendship they raised a new flagstaff. They called it Whakakotahitanga, which means "being in union," and to this day the Union Jack floats from it.

CHAPTER 9

THE TAMING OF THE WILD CABBAGE LEAF

WHILE the north was at length settling down to peace, the tribes in the south were growing restless. Their leaders were, as before, Rauparaha the proud "Wild Cabbage Leaf," and Rangihaeata "The Heavenly Dawn." But while the Heavenly Dawn openly showed that he was an enemy, the Wild Cabbage Leaf pretended to be a friend to the British.

Land again was the beginning of the quarrel. About nine miles from Wellington was the fertile Hutt Valley. This Colonel Wakefield thought he had bought. The chiefs said it was still theirs, and they tried to prevent settlers taking possession of it, and soon the land was once more filled with fighting and murder.

So, having made peace in the north, Governor Grey sailed to Wellington, taking with him all the soldiers he could gather.

Soon he discovered that although Rauparaha made great show of friendship, he was really egging Rangihaeata on. In fact, while Rangihaeata was the fighter, Rauparaha was the thinker. So it was resolved to seize him and stop his mischief.

One night a company of a hundred and fifty men silently surrounded the chiefs house. All was quiet. Swiftly and stealthily the men stole into Rauparaha's room, and, while he was still sleeping, seized him. Not a blow was struck, not a shot was fired. The wily old chief was taken prisoner without a drop of blood being shed. But it was not done without a struggle, for Rauparaha bit and kicked fiercely, and his captors carried the marks of his teeth and nails for many a day.

Great was the grief of the Heavenly Dawn when he heard of the capture of his father-in-law. In his grief he made a lament, mourning for Rauparaha as for a dead man.

> "Raha! my chief, my friend,
> Thy lonely journey wend;
> Stand with thy wrongs before the God of Battles' face:
> Bid him thy woes requite.
> Ah me! Te Raukawa's foul desertion and disgrace,
> Ah me! the English ruler's might.
>
> Raha! my chief of chiefs,
> Ascend with all thy griefs
> Up to the Lord of Peace; there stand before his face:
> Let him thy fate requite.

Ah me! Te Tea's sad defection and disgrace,
Ah me! the English ruler's might."

But Rangihaeata did more than idly lament. Gathering his men, he prepared to avenge the capture of his chief. He wrote, too, to the northern tribes, stirring them to battle. "Friends and children, come and avenge the wrongs of Te Rauparaha, because Te Rauparaha is the eye of the faith of all men. Make ye haste hither in the days of December."

But the northern chiefs were slow to move. They told the Heavenly Dawn that it was folly to try to kill the British or drive them from the land. "How could you dry up the sea?" they asked.

But although few joined him, Rangihaeata fought. Although soldiers, sailors, settlers, all were against him, he would not give in. Defeated and hunted he took refuge, as he himself said, "in the fastnesses and hollows of the country, as a crab lies concealed in the depths and hollows of the rocks."

At length, left almost without a follower, Rangihaeata made peace. But his proud spirit never quite gave in. "I am not tired of war," he told Sir George Grey, "but the spirit of the times is for peace. Now, men, like women, use their tongues as weapons. Do not suppose, O Governor, that you have conquered me! No. It was my own relations and friends. It was by them I was overcome."

When Rauparaha had been seized he had been sent to Auckland. There, although he was a prisoner, he was allowed to go about freely. Now, when peace was come again, he was permitted to go home. But the fierce old chief did not live long to enjoy his liberty. Eighteen months later he died.

From first to last, in north and south, the war had lasted for five years. It had cost a million of money.

Sir George now had time to think of ruling the land. He tried to govern well and be just to the Maoris. He protected them as much as he could from land-grabbers, and kept the treaty of Waitangi. He rewarded those who had helped him, and in every way treated them fairly.

One good thing which Sir George did was to make good roads throughout the islands. Even while the war was going on, parties of soldiers and Maoris might be seen peacefully working side by side with pick and spade. The Maoris were good workmen, and the British soon grew friendly with them. They taught the Maoris English, and the Maoris taught them their language. And when the road was finished they parted like old friends.

Then Governor Grey built schools and had the Maori children taught to speak English, and did many other things for their happiness. So when in 1853 another governor was appointed, the Maoris were very sorrowful. They grieved for Sir George as for a lost father, and sang mournful songs of farewell.

"Oh then!
Pause for one moment there.
Cast back one glance on me,
Thus to receive one fond,
One last, fond look.
Thy love came first, not mine;
Thou didst first behold
With favour and regard
The meanest of our race!

Thence is it
The heart o'erflows;
the eye Bedewed with tears doth anxiously desire
To catch one fond, one parting glance,
Ere thou art lost to sight for ever,
Alas! for ever!"

When Sir George Grey came home, too, he was welcomed and thanked. And when at Oxford he received a degree in honour of his work in New Zealand, the students gave three cheers for the "King of the Cannibal Islands."

THE KING OF THE MAORIS

T HE colony of New Zealand grew rapidly greater and stronger. In 1847 Dunedin was founded by a party of Scottish settlers sent out by the Free Church of Scotland. In 1850 Canterbury was founded by the Church of England. These towns would have grown faster than they did, had not gold been discovered in Australia. For many then who had come from home, meaning to settle in New Zealand, rushed away to Australia and the gold diggings.

But things soon righted themselves, for it was not long before the fame of the grassy plains of New Zealand spread to Australia. Farmers there, hearing of these plains where not even a tree had to be cut down to clear the land, sailed over from Australia, bringing flocks with them. Soon the Canterbury pastures became as famous the world over as those of Australia. And since ways of keeping meat by freezing it have been found out, much of the mutton used in Great Britain is brought from New Zealand.

In 1852 New Zealand became a self-governing colony, and in 1854 the first New Zealand Parliament was held.

All seemed prosperous and well with the colony when once more land troubles began.

Some of the Maori chiefs had always been against selling land to the British. "The money the white man gives is soon spent," they said. "The land is gone from us for ever, and we have nothing left." Yet, year by year they saw the white people fence in more and more land for farms. So now many of these tribes banded themselves together into a Land League. The members of this league vowed to sell no more land to the white people.

About this same time too, some of the tribes made up their minds to choose a king. In choosing this king they had no thought of rebelling against the Queen. But they saw that although the governor ruled the white men and the Maoris too, when they quarrelled with the white men, they let them fight amongst themselves as much as they liked. So they desired a king who should rule the Maoris as the Queen far away ruled her people. Within the large tract of land which they had vowed never to sell, the Maori king should rule alone. Within this land no road should be made—for all roads led to slavery.

There was much talk and argument before a king was chosen. For all did not agree that a king would be good to have. But at last a brave old warrior called Te Whero-Whero Potatau was elected. A standard, too, was chosen and raised. It was a white flag with a red border, bearing two red

162

crosses, and the words "Potatau, King of New Zealand."

But many were against the flag, as they had been against the king. "I am content with the flag of Britain," said one old warrior. "It is seen all over the world. It belongs to me. I get some of its honour. What honour can I get from your flag? It is as a fountain without water."

"Let the flag stand," said another, "but wash out the writing upon it. As for me I am a subject of the Queen."

But in spite of all objections the flag was unfurled, the king was chosen.

Potatau was now treated with royal honours. Salutes were fired, his subjects stood bareheaded before him, and backed out of his presence, while he, wrapped in an old blanket, sat upon a mat and smoked his pipe.

And sometimes while his counsellors talked and made laws, he slept peacefully, knowing not what was done.

Governor Browne paid little attention to the "King movement" as it was called. If he had, he might have turned it to good. As it was, it turned to evil.

Soon a quarrel arose which led to fighting. A Maori offered to sell to the governor some land at Waitara, not far from New Plymouth. The governor bought it, but Te Rangitake, the chief in whose country the land was, being among those who had joined the Land League, forbade the sale. "I will not give it up!" he cried; "I will not, I will not, I will not! I have spoken."

The Maori land laws were very difficult for a white man to follow. The chiefs often had a kind of feudal right over the land, and so, although it did not really belong to Te Rangitake, he had a right to forbid the sale. "These lands will not be given by us into your hands," he wrote to Governor Browne, "lest we become like the birds of the sea which are resting upon a rock. When the tide flows the rock is covered by the sea. The birds fly away because there is no resting-place for them. I will not give you the land."

But the governor decided that Te Rangitake had no right to hinder the selling of the land. So he sent men to mark it out for farms. But the men were met by all the oldest and ugliest women in the land, who hugged and kissed them till they were obliged to run away.

Then the governor sent soldiers, and seeing that peaceful means were no longer of use, the whole tribe rose in arms. Rangitake built a pah upon the land, pulled up the governor's stakes and flags and burned them, and war began.

Once more the governor sent to Australia for soldiers. Once more the land was filled with blood and war.

From pah to pah the Maoris flitted as their custom was. Settlers in terror fled from their farms, leaving their homes, their flocks and herds, to the mercy of the Maoris. Some fled from the country altogether.

At first this quarrel had nothing to do with the King movement. Indeed Te Rangitake had refused to join that. But now the king tribes came to help their fellow countrymen. The king himself was old and feeble, so the men were led by a young and warlike chief called Te Waharoa. It was he, indeed, who had been one of the principal upholders of the king, and he was called the king-maker.

In the midst of all the trouble the king died, and his son Tawhiao was chosen in his stead. But he had not the fame of his father, and had little power among the natives.

For many months the war went on, but at length, in May 1861, peace was made, the governor promising to look into Te Rangitake's claims once more.

CHAPTER 11

TO THE SOUND OF THE WAR-SONG

THE peace was a mere truce. Things seemed drifting again to war when the government at home recalled Browne, and sent back Sir George Grey, who had already proved so good a ruler.

Sir George Grey, when he came, decided that the land at Waitara had been unjustly taken, and must be given back. But it was now too late. Misunderstandings and blunders grew worse and worse, and the second Maori war broke out. From India and from Australia, troops came to help the settlers, while the Maori tribes gathered to the sound of an old war-song.

Soon the fight began. The Maoris fought well and fiercely. It was the story of Oheawai and of the Bat's Nest over again. In a night the Maoris would build a fort strong enough to keep the British for a month at bay.

For days they would defend it, and when it seemed about to be taken would forsake it and flee to another as strong or stronger. They were always far outnumbered by the white men. Yet never once did the white men gain a great victory.

It seemed of little use to capture or destroy a pah, for the Maoris fled to another a few miles off, where the attack had to be begun afresh. The whole country seemed dotted with strong fortresses.

But at length at Rangiriri, a strong fort surrounded by a river and by swamps, many of the Maoris were captured. From dawn to dark on a wintry July day the thunder of war lasted. Shot and shell were poured upon the fort from every side. Again and again the British soldiers dashed at the walls, only to be thrown back again like waves broken upon a rock. But when night fell, the fort was completely surrounded. And when day dawned the Maoris hung out a flag and surrendered.

Governor Grey would have been glad now to make peace. But his advisers would not listen. So still the war went on.

At Orakau, one of the bravest defences of the war took place. Here two or three hundred badly-armed, half-starving Maori men and women bid defiance to more than fifteen thousand British soldiers.

After trying in vain to storm the fort, the British leader resolved to mine it and blow it up. But he knew that both women and children were within the pah. He wished to save them, so he sent a messenger with a flag of truce, asking them to surrender.

"We will fight to the end, for ever and ever," was the reply.

"Then send out the women and the children," said the messenger.

"Nay, the women and children, too, will fight," they cried.

So, worn with fight and watching, weary, hungry and thirsty, the Maoris still fought on. They had no food, they had no water, their shot was almost done. Yet they would not yield.

Then in their need they turned to the Christian God. He would help them. And through the crash and roar of cannon, the plaintive notes of a hymn arose. They looked to heaven, but from the once clear sky now darkened with the heavy clouds of war, no help came.

Then fiercer, wilder thoughts laid hold of the Maoris. The Christian God was the God of deceivers, they cried. He was the God of those who sought to rob them of their land. They would have no more of Him. They would turn again for help to their ancient god of War. Then fierce and loud above the clangour rose the sounds of a "Karakia," a chant of curses, a chant long unheard in Maori land.

Now the mines began to burst all around them. In noise and flame their pah was shattered. The earth shook with death. No longer could they hold the fortress.

Then, still chanting their wild and terrible song, under the eyes of the British, they marched calmly and steadily out of their fort. "As cool and steady as if going to church," said one who saw.

For some minutes all watched in wonder. No one knew what was happening. Then, "They are escaping! they are escaping!" came the cry, and the chase began.

For six long miles the way was red with blood, and strewn with dead. Yet steadily onward the Maoris pressed, now pausing to fire, now to lift a wounded comrade, until at last a broken remnant reached the wild refuge of the hills, where no white man could follow.

The war was nearly over. But at a place called the Gate Pah, the Maoris once more beat back the British troops, who fled, leaving ten officers and twenty-five men dead upon the field.

But again, in the darkness of the night, the Maoris slipped away. How they went no man knew, for the pah was surrounded by British troops. Only in the morning it was found that the pah was empty. And yet they had gone in no wild haste, for beside each wounded British soldier was a cup of water, placed there by the Maoris before they fled.

Only a few miles off the Maoris again made a stand. But here they were attacked before they had time to build a pah. After a desperate fight they fled.

Among the dead lay their leader. On his dead body was found the order for the day. It began with a prayer, and ended with the words, "If thine enemy hunger, feed him; if he thirst, give him drink."

> "Te Waru was there with the East Coast braves,
> And the chiefs famed in song and story,

Met on the spot to resist the spoilers,
Who had taken the land from the Maori
In the name of the Queen of the far land.
Only three hundred warriors were there
Entrenched within the weak unfinished pah,
Only three hundred brave men and women
To meet the Pakeha who surrounded
The sod-built fortress, with his well-drilled troops
Nearly two thousand hardy Britons.

Three hundred lion-hearted warriors
Assembled with Rewi to fan the flame
Of deadly hatred to the Pakeha
Into a vengeful blaze at Orakau,
Chanting the deeds of their ancestors,
They cried aloud, "Me mate te gangatu,
Me mate mo te whenua!" which means,
'The warrior's death is to die for the land.'

. . . . .

Then Major Mair, with flag of truce, before the Maoris stood,
And said, "O friends, be warned in time, we do not seek your blood.
Surrender, and your lives are safe." Then, through the whole redoubt,
The swarthy rebels answered, with a fierce, defiant shout,
"Ka whawkia tonu! Ake! ake! ake!"[1]

Again spake gallant Mair, "O friends, you wish for blood and strife,
With blind and stubborn bravery, preferring death to life;
But send your women and your children forth, they shall be free."
They answered back, "Our women brave will fight as well as we."

Again the fiery-throated cannon roared aloud for blood,
Again the hungry eagle swooped and shrieked aloud for food;
Again wild spirits soaring, saw their shattered shells beneath
In pools of gore, and still was heard defiance to the death.

Now, now the brave defenders in a solid body break
Right through the sod-built barricade, o'er palisade and stake,
And, leaping o'er the trenches, 'mid a storm of shot and shell,
They rushed to liberty or death, still shouting as they fell.

---

1   We will fight to the dear for ever and ever and ever.

With wild, untutored chivalry, the rebels scorned disgrace,
Oh, never in the annals of the most heroic race
Was bravery recorded more noble or more high,
Than that displayed at Orakau in Rewi's fierce reply—
Ka whawkia tonu! Ake! ake! ake!"

THOMAS BRACKEN.

CHAPTER 12

THE HAU HAUS AND TE KOOTI

NOW at last the war seemed ended. Many chiefs yielded, giving up their lands in token of submission. Sir George Grey kept one quarter of them as punishment for rebellion. The rest he returned.

But meanwhile new trouble had arisen. A wicked and wily native priest had begun to preach a new religion to the people. This new religion was called Hau Hau, because this priest told the people, that if they went into battle shouting Hau Hau, the angel Gabriel would protect them, and they would overcome all their enemies. He also said that the religion of the white people was a religion of lies, and that he had been told in a vision that in the year 1864 all the white people would be swept out of New Zealand.

Although few of the great chiefs followed the Hau Haus, many of the common people did. They did many wild and horrible deeds. Now here, now there, fighting broke out, and so although peace was proclaimed, the land was not really at rest.

The Hau Haus were not gallant and generous foes as the Maoris usually were. They were treacherous and cruel, and their own countrymen often waged war against them. They were driven about from place to place. Many were killed, and many were taken prisoner and sent to the Chatham Islands, which the government had begun to use as a sort of prison-house.

Among the friendly Maoris who helped the British was a young chief called Te Kooti. Now suddenly he was accused of being a traitor. He was seized, and without trial of any kind he was shipped off to the Chatham Islands. There was never any good reason for believing Te Kooti to be false. When Sir George Grey seized Te Rauparaha because he thought he was false, what followed proved that he was right. Only evil followed from the seizing of Te Kooti.

Upon the Chatham Islands there were about three hundred Maori prisoners, most of them Hau Haus. For two years they behaved very well, for they had been told that if they were good they would then be set free and allowed to return home. But the two years came to an end, there was no sign of freedom, and they began to grow restless.

They longed to escape, and one day a ship called the *Rifleman* came to the islands with a cargo of food. Here they saw their chance. Te Kooti was their leader, and quickly he made his plans. Two boatloads of Maoris rowed out to the ship. They swarmed on deck, and almost before any one knew what was happening, the ship was in their hands. All the guards were gagged and bound, only one man being killed in the struggle.

Then Te Kooti took command. He gathered the crew together and ordered them to steer for New Zealand. If they refused, he threatened to shoot them all.

And so the *Rifleman* sailed away, carrying every prisoner and all the guns and ammunition to be found on the islands.

Beside the helmsman stood a Maori armed with gun and sword. Night and day Maori sentries paced the deck. The crew had no choice but to obey their new masters. And so they sailed until they reached Poverty Bay.

Here the Maoris landed, took possession of all the cargo, and told the crew of the *Rifleman* that they might now go where they liked, as they had no further use for them.

Soon the news of the escape of the Chatham Island prisoners, and of their landing at Poverty Bay reached Wellington, and a force set out to retake the runaways.

But Te Kooti was a warrior. He had plenty of guns and ammunition, and again and again the British troops fell back before him. From his forest fastnesses Te Kooti flung defiance at the foe. But in the wild hills where he had taken refuge there was little food to be had. Soon the provisions taken from the *Rifleman* were all done. Te Kooti and his men were starving.

Then all the savage awoke in them, and they swept like hungry wolves down upon the peaceful settlers of Poverty Bay, and slaughtered them all unresisting in their beds. Men, women, and children, none were spared. With fire and sword they blotted out the settlement, scarce a soul escaping to tell the tale.

A thrill of horror ran through the country when the news was spread. Quickly a force was gathered and sent against the daring chieftain. But he, safe in a fastness perched upon a rock two thousand feet high, with rugged cliffs and wild gorges all around, defied every attempt to take him.

At length, however, with the help of a native chief called Ropata, who had won great renown as a soldier, the pah was one night surrounded.

The besiegers made sure that the next day they would seize their prey. But during the night Te Kooti and his band escaped, sliding down the almost sheer precipice and fleeing to the wilds.

Then in the morning, when it was found that the pah was empty, the chase began and was pitilessly pursued. Many of the Hau Haus were killed, many more were taken prisoner, and they, as soon as they were led before their conquerors, were mercilessly shot, and their bodies thrown over the steep cliffs. Many others died among the lonely mountains, but Te Kooti, wounded, half-starved, weary and desperate, escaped.

With a few faithful followers he wandered for two years a wretched exile. With the price of £5000 upon his head, he was hunted and hounded. Living on fern root, often near death from hunger, he at length gave himself up, was pardoned, and henceforth lived in peace.

All this fighting took place in North Island. In the meantime South Island was at peace, growing daily richer and greater. And in 1871 peace came to North Island too, and since then there have been no more wars.

In 1864 the Parliament had been moved from Auckland to Wellington, Wellington being nearly in the centre of the islands, and so more suitable. In 1868 an Act was passed by which Maori members sat in Parliament as well as white people, and that helped to sweep away many differences. The old days of fighting and misunderstanding are, we hope, gone for ever, and now Maori and Briton live and work side by side. For although of the eighty members of Parliament only four are Maori, every man and woman, over the age of twenty-one, whether Maori or white, has a vote.

In the last thirty-five years many things have happened in New Zealand—things which will be more interesting to you later on. New Zealand has grown and grown, and, in 1907, it was declared no longer a colony but a dominion. Like Canada it is a confederation of self-governing states. It has its own Parliament and Law Courts, yet remains a part of the British Empire.

LIST OF KINGS AND GOVENORS

Kings of Great Britain and Ireland.	Governors of New Zealand.
Queen Victoria, ... 1837	
	Captain Hobson, . . . 1840
	Lieutenant Shortland, . . 1842
	(temporary)
	Captain Robert Fitzroy, . . 1843
	Captain George Grey, . . 1845
	(Sir George Grey)
	Lieut.-Col. R. H. Wynyard, . 1854
	(temporary)
	Colonel Thomas Gore Browne, 1855
	Sir George Grey, . . . 1861
	Sir George Ferguson Bowen, . 1861
	Sir George Alfred Arney, . . 1873
	(temporary)
	Sir James Ferguson . . . 1873
	Marquess of Normanby, . . 1874
	Chief Justice James Prendergast, 1879
	(temporary)
	Sir Hercules Robinson, . . 1879
	Chief Justice James Prendergast, 1880
	(temporary)
	Sir Arthur Gordon, . . . 1880
	Chief Justice James Prendergast, 1882
	(temporary)
	Sir William Drummond Jervois, 1883
	Earl of Onslow, . . . 1889
	Earl of Glasgow, . . . 1892
	Earl of Ranfurly, . . . 1897
Edward VII., ... 1901	
	Lord Plunket, ... 1904

SOUTH AFRICA

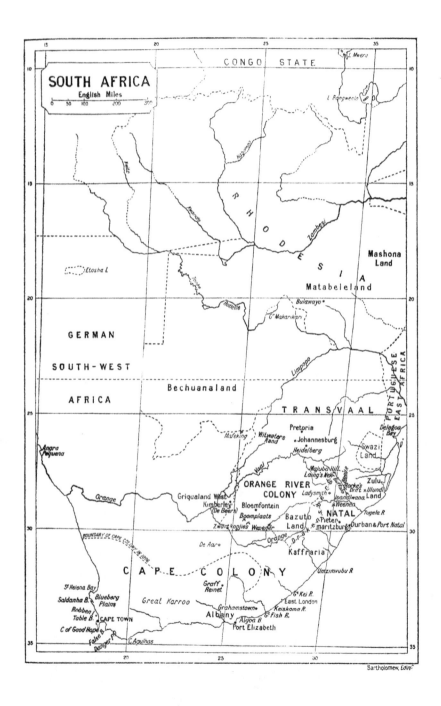

SOUTH AFRICA

English Miles

0   50   100   200   300

CONGO STATE

L. Mweru

L. Bangweolo

R H O D E S I A

Mashona Land

Etosha L.

Matabeleland

Bulawayo

G.t Makarikari

GERMAN

SOUTH-WEST

AFRICA

Bechuanaland

Limpopo

TRANSVAAL

PORTUGUESE EAST AFRICA

Angra Pequena

Pretoria

Delagoa Bay

Mafeking

Witwaters Rand

Johannesburg

Heidelberg

Swazi Land

Vaal

Majuba Hill

Laing's Nek

Zulu

Orange

Griqualand West

ORANGE RIVER COLONY

Rorke's Drift Ulundi

Land

Kimberley (De Beers)

Bloemfontein

Ladysmith

Isandlwana

Weenen

Boomplaats

Bazuto

NATAL

Tugela R.

Zwartkoplies Wepener

Land

Pieter maritzburg

Durban & Port Natal

BOUNDARY OF CAPE COLONY 26 JUNE

Orange

D.P.A

De Aar

Kaffraria

Umzimvubu R.

C A P E   C O L O N Y

St Helena Bay

Graaff Reinet

G.t Kei R.

Saldanha B.

Blueberg Plains

Great Karroo

East London

Robben I.

Grahamstown

Keiskama R.

Table B. CAPE TOWN

Albany

Fish R.

C. of Good Hope

Algoa B.

False B.

Port Elizabeth

Danger Pt

C. Agulhas

Bartholomew, Edin.r

CHAPTER 1

EARLY DAYS

LONG, long ago the Portuguese, you remember, were the great seafaring people of Europe. In those old days when America, Australia, and New Zealand were yet unknown, when no one guessed the vast extent of Africa, these fearless sailors swept the seas in their tiny vessels seeking new paths to India. And it was a Portuguese, Bartholomew Diaz, who, seeking to reach India, discovered the Cape of Storms—the Cape of Good Hope.

As on that eventful voyage he sailed southward and ever southward, he came to anchor in a bay which he called Angra Pequena or the Little Bay. He went ashore there hoping to find fresh food and water for his sick sailors. Thus he and his men were, so far as we know, the first Christian men who trod the shores of Africa, south of the equator. In memory of this landing, and to claim the land for his master, the King of Portugal, Diaz set up a marble cross, and carved some words upon it. This was in 1486, and for nearly four hundred years that marble cross stood as a remembrance of the brave old Portuguese seaman who had set it there. For nearly four hundred years it was swept by storms of wind and wave, was rained and sunned upon. The carving upon it could no longer be read, but still it stood a silent witness of days gone by. At length some one in folly and idleness cast it to the ground. There it lay neglected in the sand, until it was carried away to Lisbon, where it may now be seen in the museum, a treasured memory of the past.

If you will look on the map you will find Angra Pequena marked. It is now in German South-West Africa. But when Diaz and his men landed it was a barren and cheerless waste of sand, where they found little to eat except sea-birds' eggs. So, from Angra Pequena, Diaz sailed on again, rounded the Cape of Good Hope, and sailed as far as the great Fish River before returning with his news to Portugal.

The discovery of the Cape was, we may say, a mere accident. The Portuguese sailors had set forth, not to discover new lands, but a new way to India, and for a long time little use was made of it.

When, ten years after Diaz had made his discovery, Vasco da Gama set forth, he, too, landed on the southern African coast, not with any idea of settling there, but merely to find water and fresh food. It was he who, sailing along the shores on Christmas day, caught sight of the beautiful coasts which he named Natal, that is, the Land of the Birth, so that men might remember that it was first seen upon that Holy Day. And by that name we call it still.

Many years passed and the Portuguese trade with India grew great. Then, as you know, other peoples besides the Portuguese sought the way to India. Holland became the mistress of the seas until Britain swept her too from the path. So year by year more and more ships rounded the stormy Cape. "We ran aboard the Cape," writes Francis Drake, that old sea dog of Queen Elizabeth's time. "We found the report of the Portuguese to be most false. They affirm that it is the most dangerous cape in the world, never without intolerable storms and present dangers to travellers who come near the same. This Cape is a most stately thing, and the fairest cape we have seen in the whole circumference of the earth."

But although the Cape was calm when Sir Francis Drake passed it, it was not always so, and a Portuguese captain was heard mournfully to wonder "why God the Lord caused them, who were good Christians and Catholics with large and strong ships, always to pass the Cape with such great and violent tempest and damage; while the English, who were heretics and blasphemers, passed it so easily with weak and small vessels."

To all these ancient seamen—Portuguese, Dutch, and British—the great continent was useful only as a resting-place. Like weary land birds which, flying southward, light upon a passing vessel to rest their wings, so the seamen of long ago touched upon the shores of Africa for refreshment on the long voyage to India. Sometimes these adventurers saw the natives, and bartered with them for cattle. Generally the trade was peacefully done. But sometimes quarrels and misunderstandings would arise, and blood was shed.

These natives were very wild and ignorant, and were divided into three quite different races—the Bushmen, the Hottentots, and the Bantu.

The Bushmen were the most ignorant, although it is thought that they were the oldest of the three races. They were of a yellowish brown colour, and very small. But although they were small, they were very wiry and could run with wonderful speed. They lived in caves and holes in the ground, wore no clothes, and had no possessions at all. They roamed about hunting the wild animals with which Africa swarmed, living on them and on wild plants.

The Hottentots lived along the shores and were like the Bushmen in colour, but they were bigger and were not quite so ignorant. They built huts of woven branches and leaves, and they had herds of tame cattle and sheep. They also knew how to make use of iron and copper.

The Bantu lived north of the Bushmen, and were the most civilised of the three races. We generally speak of them now as Kaffirs, although Kaffir is not their real name. It was a kind of nickname given to them long ago by Arabian traders, and means "unbeliever," These Kaffirs are again divided into tribes, such as Zulus, Matabele, Bechuanas, Basutos, and many others.

The Bantu were big men of a dark brown colour; they built neat round houses and thatched them cleverly. Their villages were generally built in a circle with room for their cattle and sheep in the centre, and were called kraals. This word was taken from the Portuguese word for a cattle pen, "curral." Now a South African cattle pen is also called a kraal.

Besides having large flocks and herds, dogs and poultry, the Bantu tilled the ground and grew crops of millet, or what is now called Kaffir-corn. From this Kaffir-corn they made bread. They could also smelt iron and make pots of clay, and both men and women wore ornaments of copper. Otherwise they went almost naked, tattooing their bodies in strange patterns, "They cover themselves with the apparell that Adam did weare in Paradice," says an old writer, "so that when they see any white people that weare apparell on their bodies they laugh and moke at them as mobsters and ugly people."

All these three races spoke different languages, they hated each other and were constantly at war, and some of them, it was said, were cannibals.

CHAPTER 2

THE COMING OF THE DUTCH

AS ship after ship passed round the shores of Africa, the captains made rough sketches and maps, and named the bays and rivers, mountains and headlands. And so it comes about that to this day, on South African coasts, there is a mixture of Portuguese, Dutch, and British names.

But although all these nations, especially the Dutch and the British, used South Africa as a resting-place, it was the Dutch who first thought of forming a colony there.

In 1602 the Dutch East India Company had been formed, and through it Holland grew to wealth and power, until the Dutch became the carriers of the world. Fourteen years after the founding of the company a rule was made that all ships going and coming from India must call at Table Bay, and the Cape began to be used as a kind of post-office. When a ship called, the date and name were carved upon a stone, and beneath it letters were buried. When the next ship arrived the letters were dug up and carried homewards or outwards as the case might be, other letters being left for the next ship in its turn.

It was not, however, until 1652 that the first colony was founded. About two years before that a Dutch ship called the *Haarlem* had been wrecked in Table Bay. Fortunately the crew had been able to save, not only themselves, but most of the cargo and food, and to come safely to land. There, on the very spot where now the great city of Cape Town stands, they set up their tents and huts. Knowing that they might have a long time to wait for a ship to arrive, they dug the land round and sowed seed which they had saved from the wreck. Soon they had plenty of fruit and vegetables and lived very comfortably for about six months. Then a ship arrived which carried them safely home to Holland.

Two of the men who had been among the wrecked sailors were very much struck with the beautiful climate. For they had been there in spring and summer. They had been surprised to find how easy it was to make things grow, and when they got home they advised the Dutch to send out colonists and found a settlement at the Cape.

This, after a time, the Dutch East India Company decided to do. For so many of their sailors died of scurvy on the long voyage to India that they thought it would be a good plan to have a garden at the Cape, where the ships could always get fresh vegetables. They also decided to build a hospital there in which the sick men might be left until they were better.

So three little ships were sent out from Holland to carry the first settlers

"Where now the great city of Cape Town stands,
they set up their tents and huts."

to the Cape. There were about a hundred men and five women. They were grave, stern-faced men and women not unlike our own Pilgrim Fathers. But they did not flee from their country or from tyranny. They went at the command of their country to help it to grow greater in trade and wealth.

The leader of this little band was a small man with a fiery temper named Jan van Riebeck. It is worth while to remember his name as he was the first Governor of the Cape which has grown to be such a great part of our Empire.

It was in April 1652 that the first settlers anchored in Table Bay. April is, as a rule, a beautiful month, for the first rains have come and the great heat of summer is over. But this year no early rain had fallen, the earth was baked hard and dry, all the grass and herbs were withered. This was not the beautiful land, gay with flowers and greenness, that had been described to the colonists. So it was with heavy disappointed hearts that they began to build Fort Good Hope, and try to dig the hard ground.

The work went on slowly. The men were sick and feeble after their long voyage. There was no green thing to eat, and no fresh food of any kind except fish, and now and again a hippopotamus, which was looked upon as a great delicacy. The ground was hard as iron, and needed pick-axes rather than spades to break it up. It was useless to sow any seed, and there was no sign of rain. A fierce, dry, south-east wind blew, blinding the men with dust as they tried to work, and nearly blowing them from the walls which they were building.

Day by day more men fell ill. Day by day fresh graves were dug. Those who could still work grew more and more feeble, till at last the whole settlement seemed like one great hospital, and work of all kinds ceased.

Far from friends and home the little handful of white men dwindled and grew less. They saw few natives even, and these were poor, wretched Hottentots whom they called Beachrangers. They were too poor to help the colonists in any way, having no cattle, or possessions of my kind. Living a miserable life, they kept themselves from starving by eating shell-fish or such refuse as they could pick up on the shores.

At last the rain came. But matters for a time were made worse. For the tents and frail wooden houses could not keep out the rain which fell in torrents, and the misery of life grew greater than before.

But in the long-run the rain brought relief. For in a very short time, almost it seemed as if by magic, the earth was once more covered with green, the ground became soft, the gardeners planted seeds, and soon the sick men had fresh food enough. Then, as the grass grew, the Hottentots who had cattle drove them down to the Cape, and Jan van Riebeck was able to buy them for bits of copper and tobacco. So for a time the sufferings of the colonists were over.

For a little time all went well. But one drizzling wet Sunday, while all the colonists were at church in the hall of the fort, the Beachrangers attacked the herdsman, killed him, and carried off all the cattle. As soon as the theft was known the governor and his men mounted and rode after the thieves. But although they chased them for several days they could not catch them, and were obliged to return to the fort disappointed.

So again the colonists had to suffer from hunger. They had indeed plenty of vegetables now, but they had little else. And the Hottentots who had cattle would not sell them, for Riebeck had no more copper, and they would not take anything else.

But in spite of all difficulties the little colony grew. After a time some of the settlers left the service of the Company and were allowed to become farmers on their own account. They were called Free Burghers, but they had really very little freedom, for they were not allowed to buy or sell with the natives. Anything they had to sell they were obliged to sell to the Company, and the Company fixed the price. If a ship came into harbour they were not allowed to go near it for three days, so that the Company might have a chance of buying or selling all they wanted first. They were not even allowed to hunt or kill any wild animals, except lions, or leopards, or wild cats.

Those were the days of monopolies, and all these rules were made so that the trade of the Company might prosper. The settlement at the Cape had been founded merely as a garden and a hospital for the Company's servants, and they really did not care whether the Free Burghers got on well or not.

With so many rules to hamper them the Burghers found it hard to make a living, and the number of farmers did not increase quickly. Indeed some who began farming for themselves gave it up and came back to the service of the Company.

For some time the natives were quite friendly, and the Dutch had to suffer nothing more than having their cattle stolen every now and again. But when the Hottentots saw that the Dutch did not mean to leave the land again, as other white people who came in ships had done, they began to grow angry. Then when they drove their cattle to pastures which they or their fathers had used for years, and found them fenced in, or ploughed up, they were more angry still. For the Dutch had never asked for the land and had paid nothing for it. They simply took it.

Soon what is called the first Hottentot war began. But it was hardly a war, for the natives, knowing what strange and deadly weapons the Dutch carried, never met them in battle. Now and again there were little skirmishes when four or five men would be killed, but nothing more. Then after about a year of this kind of fighting an old chief, who was called the Fat Captain because he was so big and stout, came to Fort Good Hope. With him came two men who had learned to speak Dutch, and after a great deal of talking peace was agreed upon. A feast of rice and bread was then given to the Hottentots, and a dance followed which lasted two hours.

In the courtyard of the fort a tub filled with a kind of brandy was placed. Of this every man drank as much as he liked. Then the savages formed in two long rows and began to dance, while their women sat on the ground clapping their hands and singing a doleful chant. The men danced and danced until they could dance no longer, and fell to the ground exhausted. Then they were carried out and laid on the grass outside the fort to sleep. This went on until, at the end of two hours, only two men were left, and so the ceremony ended, and the governor could say that he was at peace with all the people of South Africa.

CHAPTER 3

THE COMING OF THE FRENCH

FOR a good many years nothing very important happened. The colony grew slowly, and every year became more and more useful to the Dutch as a calling station. Indeed it came to be looked upon as the outpost to India. So in 1665 war being declared between Great Britain and Holland, the Dutch began to build a stone castle to take the place of the little mud fort. For the fort, although strong enough to withstand any number of savages, would have been useless against British guns. The building got on very slowly, however, so slowly, indeed, that one day the governor and his wife and little boy, with all the chief inhabitants and their wives, set to work to help to carry earth out of the moat. The governor carried twelve basketfuls and his wife six, and after that a law was made that every one who passed the castle should do as much to help on the work. But even then peace was proclaimed before the castle was finished. It was solid enough, however, when it was finished, and still stands almost unchanged to this day, and is used as the headquarters of the British army in South Africa.

When the Dutch first came to the Cape they simply took possession of the land they wanted, and when the Hottentots objected they fought them, and kept the land. But after a time they began to think that that was perhaps not quite right, and in 1672 they made a treaty with some of the leading chiefs.

By this treaty they bought all the great tract of land from Saldanah Bay to False Bay for the value of about £10 paid in tobacco, beads, trinkets, and other trifles. They agreed to pay £1600, but all they did pay was £10. It was not perhaps a very honest bargain, but the chiefs were quite pleased. They had no idea of the value of the goods which they were given. They had no idea of the value of the land, besides which, they had already lost it, and were now being paid for what they had little hope of ever getting back again.

But the treaty did not put an end to the wars, and the very next year there was fighting with a tribe under a chief called the Black Captain. He was so called because he painted himself with soot instead of with red clay like the other warriors.

The fight was begun by the Black Captain seizing wagons and other things belonging to some farmers who had gone on a hunting expedition. Soldiers and burghers turned out to punish the Black Captain, and some friendly natives joined too. It was by no means easy, however, to catch the Hottentots, and make them fight a battle, for they moved quickly, swooping down upon the Dutch unexpectedly, and vanishing silently in the night to hide in the mountains where the Dutch could not follow them. Thus for four years the country was kept in unrest. Besides fighting with the Dutch, the Black Captain kept other tribes from bringing cattle to the Cape to trade. So the colonists had no fresh meat for the ships when they called, and sometimes little enough for themselves, and the colony suffered in every way. But at length the Black Captain grew tired of living in the mountains, and asked for peace. This was granted; Dutch and Hottentot exchanged presents, and once more agreed to live quietly together.

But still the colony grew very slowly, for the people of Holland found enough work to do at home, and it was hard to persuade them to leave all their friends behind, and go far away to live in an unknown country among savages. But about this time something happened which shows how the history of one country helps to make the history of another.

You know that long ago when people first began to be divided into Protestants and Catholics, they hated each other because of their religion, and whichever side was stronger in a country, treated the other side cruelly. In France the Protestants were called Huguenots, and they were often hardly treated, until one of their kings made a law called the Edict of Nantes. By this law the Protestants were allowed to live in peace and worship God in their own way. For more than eighty years they lived quietly, growing rich and prosperous, for the Huguenots were, for the most part, thrifty, industrious farmers and manufacturers.

Then another king recalled this law, and once more the Huguenots had to suffer terrible things. They were forbidden to worship God in their own way; they were also forbidden to leave the country to seek freedom elsewhere. But in spite of that many did flee away. They dressed up in all sorts of ways and tried to escape to England, Switzerland, and Holland. Ladies stained their faces and their hands, put on old clothes and tried to make themselves look like peasants. Children were hidden in empty wine casks, and put down into the holds of ships till they got out of sight of the shores of France. Gentlemen trudged along the road begging from door to door like tramps. And thus many escaped, but many too were caught. Then the men were sent to the galleys to work in chains beside thieves and cut-throats, and the women were put into convents, where they were often treated more cruelly than they would have been in prison.

It was perhaps easier to escape from France to Holland than to any other country, and a great many Huguenots fled there. The Dutch were kind to these refugees as they were called, but Holland was small and the Dutch did not want any more people in their little country at home. They did want them at the Cape, however, so about two hundred French Huguenots were persuaded to go out. They arrived at the Cape in April 1688, just thirty-six years after the first Dutch had settled there. They were given farms like the Free Burghers, and the place where most of them settled down came to be called Franche Hoek, or French Corner.

The Huguenots had fled from tyranny at home, but they found that the Dutch East India Company which ruled the Cape was a tyrant as great as their own king. The Dutch, it is true, were Protestants like themselves, but in everything else they were different, yet they were bent on making the French colonists live like themselves. The governor—not now van Riebeck, but another—had asked the Government to send more farmers, but he made up his mind not to have anything but Dutch farmers, and he set about turning the French into Dutch as quickly as possible.

So the new colonists were hardly allowed to speak French. The children at school learned only Dutch. Dutch ministers preached to them on Sunday, and, when the French begged to be allowed to have a church of their own, the governor flew into a rage. He called it French impertinence and talked of their rebellious conduct. So it came about that, in a few years, only the older people could speak French. The children forgot the sunny land from which they had come, and their pretty native tongue, and nothing about them remained French except their names. So, although the colony grew much larger, it remained as thoroughly Dutch as before.

But it was not the Huguenots alone who felt the tyranny of the Dutch Company. The Dutch farmers themselves felt it, for they could neither buy nor sell without the leave of the Company. Their whole life indeed was bound with rules and laws about every little thing. Some of these laws seem very funny to us now. In spite of the fact that in South Africa the sun is very hot, only a few people were allowed to use umbrellas for shade. Very few ladies were allowed to wear silk dresses, and no woman at all, high or low, was allowed to wear a train. If any person, driving, met the governor, he had to stop his carriage, get out, and stand hat in hand, until the governor had passed, or even sometimes he was expected to turn his own carriage out of the way, so that the governor might have plenty of room. Only the governor might drive a gilded coach, and few except him might have two horses.

All these laws and many besides became very tiresome to the Dutch farmers, and to get away from them they moved farther and farther from Cape Town. As the Dutch were nearly all farmers they came to be called Boers, as boer is the Dutch word for farmer. And when many years had passed, people almost forgot how the name first arose, and we talk now of the Boers as of the French or the Germans, forgetting, or perhaps not knowing, that the word really means farmer.

When the Boers moved from place to place they called it trekking, from another Dutch word trekken, to draw or remove, and they themselves were called Trek Boers. And the great plains of South Africa over which they trekked, they called the veldt, from another Dutch word meaning field.

And as they trekked away into the solitudes of the vast rolling plains a race of stern, silent, freedom-loving farmers arose—men who loved loneliness and who hated rules and restraints. These Trek Boers were very ignorant of everything but farm work, for travelling about as they did the children could not go to school, and often the only book they possessed was the Dutch Bible. Their houses were poor, and they had few goods of any kind. For, living far from their fellows, surrounded only by wild natives, they might at any time be attacked and robbed, so it was not worth while for them to have many possessions. Sometimes, indeed, the Trek Boer had no house at all, but he and his family lived in the covered wagons in which they moved about from place to place. But if the life was hard and full of dangers both from natives and wild beasts, it was at least free. And freedom to do as he liked, came to be the chief desire of the Boer.

CHAPTER 4

THE COMING OF THE BRITISH

TIME went on and many governors followed one after the other. Some were good, and some were bad, and the Cape prospered more or less. But meanwhile Holland sank from its great place among the nations of the world, and the Dutch East India Company became poorer and poorer, getting daily deeper into debt, and nearer and nearer ruin. To pay its debts the Company taxed its colonists more and more heavily, and many of the Cape Boers became very discontented.

Then in the end of the eighteenth century, the French rebelled against their king, and declared their land to be a republic. The shock of the French Revolution, as it was called, was felt by all the countries of Europe, and not only by them, but by their colonies, and many lands wished to follow the example of France.

In Holland two parties arose. One, calling itself the patriot party, wished to make the land a republic like France. The other, called the Orange party, kept true to its ruler, the Prince of Orange. War broke out between the two, Britain helping the Orangeites, and France helping the Patriots. After some fighting the Prince of Orange, finding most of his people against him, fled to England in a fishing-boat. King George III. received him kindly, but Holland meantime became a republic and declared war with Great Britain.

At the Cape, too, people took sides, some declaring for the Prince, and others for the Patriots, while yet a third party of burghers formed themselves into a republic of their own. So the whole Cape was in a great state of confusion.

By this time the British had become very anxious to get possession of the Cape, for they saw what a good half-way house it was to India. They were afraid, too, that the French might seize it, and so strengthen their power in India, and they determined to keep the French out of it at all costs.

So one day ships set sail for the Cape, the commander carrying with him an order from the Prince of Orange to the governor, telling him to allow the British to take possession of the colony. For the Prince believed that the British only meant to take possession of it for him, and give it back when there was peace once more.

But when the ships arrived the governor would not give up the Cape at once. He was an Orangeite, it is true, but the Prince was an exile and wrote from a foreign land, and the governor was afraid to obey him. News travelled slowly in those days, and he did not know what had been happening in Holland. So he tried to put off time, hoping that something would happen before long to show him what was the best thing to do. For some weeks letters passed between the British Commander and the Dutch Governor, but nothing came of it, and although the governor talked very grandly about the duty of defending the colony against the enemy, he really did nothing.

The burghers and farmers, however, gathered to arms, for most of them were Patriots, and wanted to resist the British who came in the name of the Prince. But they were not united, as some wished to be ruled neither by British nor Dutch, but to be a free republic. They did not trust their leaders either, and there was a great deal of confusion.

At last the British soldiers were landed, and after a very little fighting the governor consented to give up the colony. Many of the Dutch cursed him as a traitor, and said that he had sold his country, but with flags flying and drums beating the Dutch soldiers marched out of Cape Town castle to lay down their arms, and give themselves up as prisoners of war.

Thus on 16th September 1795 Cape Colony became a British possession, and the rule of the Dutch East India Company, which had lasted less than a hundred and fifty years, came to an end for ever.

But although the rule of the Dutch was at an end, and the colony in the hands of the British, many of the burghers were very unwilling to yield to their new rulers. The new British Governor tried hard, however, to make the colonists pleased with the change. He did away with all the petty rules and restrictions of the Company. "Every man may buy from whom he will," he proclaimed, "sell to whom he will, and come and go whenever and wherever he chooses. From this day forward there is free trade and a free market for all." No new taxes were imposed, and where it was possible the old ones were made lighter. So, finding that they were really better off, most of the colonists took the oath to be faithful to King George.

Only in a district called Graff Reinet the people would not yield. Here the colonists pulled down the Union Jack, and declared that they would never consent to be ruled by the British. But after a time, when they found themselves cut off from other people, when they found that they could only get guns and ammunition, and all the other things that they required, through the British, they yielded too, and took the oath to the King.

But at home the rulers of the new Dutch Republic were not inclined meekly to allow the rich colony to slip away from them without a struggle, and so nine Dutch ships sailed one day into Saldanha Bay. But the British admiral had heard of their coming, and a strong British fleet shut them in on the sea side, while a British army threatened them from the shore.

The Dutch were caught as in a trap. They could neither go back nor forward. Resistance was useless, and they gave in without a shot being fired on either side.

A great many of the soldiers whom the Dutch had brought with them were Germans who had been taken prisoner by the French, and forced to fight for Holland. They did not at all mind changing sides, and soon hundreds of them were wearing British uniforms ready to fight for the very men they had been sent out to fight against.

But now that the British had secured possession of the Cape, the Prince of Orange discovered that they had no intention of handing it back to him. They kept it for themselves, and Lord Macartney, an old Irishman, was sent out as governor.

Lord Macartney was a good ruler but very severe. He put an end to free trade, which made people angry. But they had to be careful how they talked, for if they so much as said that they liked the French or the Dutch, they might find themselves clapped into prison or fined a large sum of money.

After him came another governor, during whose rule nothing very important happened. There were troubles with the natives and with the colonists, but in spite of them the colony grew in wealth and greatness. It was not for long, however, as when at last peace was made in Europe by the Treaty of Amiens, the Cape was given back to the Dutch.

So one day the governor made a proclamation setting people free from the oath that they had taken to King George, and on Sunday evening the 20th February 1803, as the sun set, the Union Jack was hauled down. When the sentries were changed, Dutch soldiers once more took the place of British redcoats, and when the sun rose next morning the Dutch flag was hoisted. The Cape once more belonged to Holland, and all the British officers and soldiers went home. The Dutch, rejoicing greatly that their country had been given back to them, held a day of thanksgiving. In the churches there were services of joy, and afterwards the new Dutch Governor was set in his place with solemn ceremony.

But although the Cape again belonged to Holland, the Dutch East India Company with its petty tyranny was gone for ever. The colony was now under the direct rule of Holland, and the colonists were well pleased with the change. Hardly three months, however, had passed, before the nations of Europe were once more at war. Then the Dutch Governor, well knowing that the British would again try to take the Cape, gathered all the soldiers and ammunition he could.

But for three years nothing happened. The Cape was left in peace, for the British had enough to do fighting at home. Then one day, almost without being noticed, a British squadron set sail, and turned southwards. And while Napoleon was marching triumphantly over Europe, while the fleets of France and Spain were being shattered in Trafalgar Bay, the little squadron still sailed on southwards, and at last, one January morning in 1806, anchored in Table Bay.

Guns were fired, beacons were lit, and from hill to hill the message flashed, calling the Dutch to fight for their country. Leaving half his men to guard Cape Town, the governor marched with the other half to meet the enemy. His army was a mixed one. In it were Dutch and French and German soldiers, Boers and Hottentots, and slaves from Java. And with such an army he had to fight a well-trained British force of twice the number.

The two armies met on the plains of Blueberg, some miles north of Cape Town, in the cool, fresh, early morning. The battle was not long. From the very beginning there had been little doubt of how it would go, for many on the Dutch side were not fighting for their country. They were merely paid to fight, and when they saw the great force against them they fled. They were not paid to die. The burghers, indeed, stood their ground for a time. But when a regiment of Highlanders, uttering their fierce war-cry, charged upon them with fixed bayonets glittering in the sunshine, they too gave way, and, fleeing from the field, sought shelter in the hills.

In a few hours the contest was over, and the Cape once again became a British possession. Once more the Union Jack was hoisted, once more the burghers took the oath to be faithful to King George, and a British Governor ruled the land.

Then a few years later, after Waterloo had been fought, and the wars of Napoleon were at an end, the great powers of Europe acknowledged British rule in South Africa. And Britain for this and for some other lands, paid six million pounds to the Prince of Orange, who had returned to Holland as its ruler. Thus the Cape became a British possession by right of conquest and by right of purchase. But, although the rulers had changed, the people remained Dutch. Except in Cape Town there were few English-speaking people in the land, and the Boers did not willingly settle down under British rule. The British Governor had no easy time, for there were troubles with the Boers, troubles with the natives, and sometimes troubles between the natives and the Dutch.

CHAPTER 5

THE REBELLION OF SLACHTER'S NEK

L ONG ago it was the habit of all white races to treat dark races with cruelty. The British about this time were beginning to see that that was wrong, but the Boers, who lived a lonely life, cut off from all the world, were slow to learn, and they still looked upon the natives of South Africa as little better than troublesome animals that might be hunted from the land, and killed if they became too troublesome.

When the British took possession of the Cape, they made up their minds to protect the black man. So, when a farmer named Bezuidenhout ill-treated a black servant, he was ordered to appear before a magistrate to answer for his misdeeds. But Bezuidenhout, thinking as he did that a black man was of very little account, refused to go.

The part of the country where this farmer lived was wild and hilly, and a company of Hottentot soldiers was sent to seize him. Bezuidenhout thought it was an insult to send black soldiers against him, and when he saw them coming he fired at them from his house. Then with two other men he took refuge in a cave where he had already placed a store of food and ammunition.

The path to this cave was so hidden by bushes that for a long time the soldiers hunted about in vain to find it. At length, however, they caught sight of the shining barrels of guns, and scrambled up the narrow track. But it was so narrow that only one man could come along it at once. So for a long time Bezuidenhout kept the soldiers at bay refusing to surrender and declaring that he would fight to the death. But at length one or two of the men managed to scramble to the mouth of the cave, and in the scuffle which followed Bezuidenhout was shot dead.

Next day the dead man's friends gathered to bury him. It was a great funeral, and when all his friends and relatives had come together his brother Jan made a passionate speech, calling on all true burghers to drive the usurpers from the land. If they did not, this, he told them, was what they might expect; to be hunted from their homes and murdered by black men. He spoke such burning, glowing words that many who heard him resolved to rebel.

A plot was soon formed. The rebels met at a place called Slachter's Nek, and from that was called the Slachter Nek Rebellion. But it was one of the most hopeless rebellions ever undertaken. In all, the rebels numbered only about fifty, for most of the burghers took the side of the Government. Yet these fifty hoped to drive the great British power out of their land. They tried to make a powerful Kaffir chief called Gaika help them, promising him land and other rewards if they succeeded. But Gaika was wary. He wanted to be on the winning side, and would do nothing until he saw which was the stronger. "Before I sit by a fire I must see which way the wind blows," he said.

But with help or without it the rebels were bent on driving the "tyrants" from the land. And when the news of the rising reached Grahamstown, which was the nearest fort, soldiers were sent against them. Most of the rebels yielded almost at once, but some, taking their wives and children with them, trekked away over the borders of the colony to take refuge among the Kaffirs. Among these was Jan Bezuidenhout.

At first it was not known in which direction they had gone, for all unknown Africa was before them. But when at length it was discovered, the soldiers quickly pursued and surrounded them.

The fugitives had taken the oxen out of their wagons and placed them in a circle forming what is called in South Africa a laager, or camp. But when they were surprised by the soldiers, most of the men were outside the laager, and yielded at once. Jan alone would not yield. "Let us never be taken alive," he said.

"Let us die together," said his wife Martha.

So he, and she, and their boy of fourteen stood together behind the sheltering wagons to fight for what they thought was the right. Out in the wide veldt, with miles and miles of rolling hill and plain around, with never a friend near, these three stood to fight against a force of twenty-two burghers and two hundred Hottentots.

Jan fired gun after gun, Martha standing beside him quietly loading. But at last he fell wounded to death. So, brave, but ignorant and mistaken Jan, died, and his wife and son were made prisoner.

Besides them there were thirty-three prisoners. Some were banished, some imprisoned, some fined, and five were condemned to death. Every one hoped and expected that these last would be pardoned. But the governor was stern and hard, and would not pardon them. They met their death bravely. Singing a hymn they went to the scaffold while a great crowd of angry, sorrowing friends looked on.

The rebellion was at an end. In itself it had been no great thing. There never had been any chance that it could succeed, and as so many of the burghers sided with the rulers, it might have helped to draw the two races together. Instead of that, the bitterness was made worse. For the burghers had never thought that in helping to put down the rebellion they were bringing their fellow countrymen to death. When they saw what they had done they were angry, both with themselves and with the governor. Instead of the two races becoming more friendly they became more unfriendly, and for many years the rebellion of Slachter's Nek was remembered with soreness and grief.

CHAPTER 6

THE GREAT WITCH DOCTOR

E VER since white people first came to South Africa there had been wars with the natives, for as the farms of the white people spread themselves out more and more they forced the natives away from the land which had been theirs, and very naturally the natives were angry. As the black people were not strong enough to drive these white strangers out, they stole their cattle and ruined their houses whenever they had a chance. To prevent this, forts were built along the line which divided the land claimed by the white people from the land of the black people. But in spite of that, robbery, plunder, and destruction were frequent.

The Kaffir braves were very swift and silent. In the dead of night they would creep down from their mountains. Stealthily they would surround some farm-house, and in the darkness drive off all the cattle. So noiselessly did they come and go that often the farmer and his family slept peacefully, knowing nothing of their loss until in the morning they would find their cattle-pens empty.

Besides robbing and plundering the farmers, the Kaffirs often fought among themselves, adding thus to the unrest and confusion of the land. The British kept out of these quarrels as much as they could, but at last there came a time when that seemed no longer possible.

There were two great rival chiefs named Gaika and Ndlambe, and between them a bitter feud arose. Ndlambe defeated Gaika, and he fled to the British begging for help. Gaika had been acknowledged by the British as the head of the Kaffir tribes, and he had always seemed friendly, whereas Ndlambe had always been unfriendly. The quarrel between them had nothing whatever to do with the British, yet the governor thought that he must help Gaika.

So a British officer and some soldiers were sent to help the Kaffir chief. Ndlambe's land was overrun and many villages destroyed. Then Gaika's joy at being able so easily to punish his enemies knew no bounds. He and his men revelled in blood, and did such deeds of cruelty that the British officer, feeling that he could no longer fight for savages, marched away leaving Ndlambe only half-subdued.

As soon as Ndlambe saw his enemy deserted by his white friends he once more took courage, and, gathering his braves, utterly defeated Gaika. Then his wild hordes poured like a torrent into the colony, burning houses, plundering farms, and murdering both white men and natives. On and on they came, destroying all in their path until the dark masses swarmed round the town of Grahamstown. It was the first and only time that the Kaffirs ever dared to attack the white man in his town. But Ndlambe's men were full of a wild and boundless courage, for they were led on by a wonderful medicine man or witch doctor called Makana.

Makana had sent messages through all the land, calling on all true Kaffirs to join in sweeping the British into the sea. He promised sure victory to those who fought, and threatened those who held back with the anger and revenge of the Great Spirit. The Kaffirs believed Makana to be a mighty prophet, and so they thronged to fight for him.

The burghers too gathered to defend their town. But within the walls there were scarce three hundred men, and without there swarmed nine thousand savage warriors.

At daybreak Makana gathered his men, and spoke to them in stirring words. "The spirits of the earth, the spirits of the air will fight for us," he cried. "The fire of the white man can avail naught against us. To battle! to battle! Fight till we drive him into the sea from whence he came."

Then with awful war-cries, sure of victory, mad for blood, the dark host poured upon the town.

But the white men were ready. Their guns rang out, their cannon roared, shells ploughed their way through the dark charging masses, and laid hundreds dead upon the ground. But nothing made them pause. Leaping over their dead and dying comrades, the savages came on right up to the British guns. It became a hand-to-hand fight.

The Kaffirs were armed only with assagais, as the native spears were called. They were protected only by skin-covered shields, which against shot and shell were useless. Man after man went down, till at last their savage courage was quelled. Those in front wavered and fell back. The whole army was thrown into wild confusion and fled, leaving a thousand dead upon the field. On the British side only three were killed.

After this daring attack upon the white man a British force marched into Ndlambe's country. Thousands of cattle were seized, villages were destroyed, his followers scattered far and wide, and Ndlambe's power utterly broken.

Then seeing the misery that had come upon his people, Makana did a noble thing. One morning, unknown to his followers, he marched alone into the British camp. "I am told that it was I who caused the war," he said. "I have come to see if by giving myself up I may bring peace to my country."

And thus the war was ended.

Makana was sent a prisoner to Robben Island. In less than a year, however, he grew weary of restraint, and he tried to escape in a fishing-boat. But the boat was upset and Makana was drowned. When the people were told that their prophet was dead, they would not believe it, so great was their faith in him. "He will come again," they said; "he will surely come again to lead us to victory as he promised." So they carefully kept his spears, bracelets, and sleeping mat. But young men grew white-haired, and old men died, and still Makana did not come. Yet a few hoped always. Old men told stories to their children of the great witch doctor who had done such wonderful deeds, and who would one day appear again. But at last even the most hopeful lost hope, and little more than thirty years ago, his spears and all that belonged to him were buried.

Before the war with Makana, the boundary of the colony had been the Great Fish River. After it the Kaffirs were driven farther back beyond the Keiskama River. But an agreement was made that between the two rivers no one, either white or black, should settle. In this way it was hoped to keep a barrier of deserted land between the colony and the natives. But this was soon found to be a very bad arrangement. It became a hiding-place for wild hordes of plundering natives. After a time both natives and white people broke the agreement and settled in the "ceded country" as it was called.

MAKANA'S GATHERING

Wake! Amakosa wake!
And arm yourselves for war,
As coming winds the forests shake,
I hear a sound from far:
It is not thunder in the sky,
Nor lion's roar upon the hill,
But the voice of him who sits on high,
And bids me speak his will.

He bids me call you forth,
Bold sons of Kahabee,
To sweep the white man from the earth,
And drive them to the sea:
The sea, that heaved them up at first,
For Amakosa's curse and bane,
Howls for the progeny she nurst,
To swallow them again.

Then come, ye chieftains bold,
With war-plumes waving high;
Come every warrior, young and old,
With club and assagai.
Remember how the spoiler's host
Did through our land like locusts range.
Your herds, your wives, your comrades lost—
Remember—and revenge!

Fling your broad shields away—
Bootless against such foes;
But hand to hand we'll fight to-day
And with their bayonets close.
Grasp each man short his stabbing spear
And, when to battle's edge we come,
Rush on their ranks in full career,
And to their hearts strike home.

THOMAS PRINGLE

CHAPTER 7

ABOUT THE COMING OF BRITISH SETTLERS AND THE WARS OF THE BLACK NAPOLEON

WHEN the Cape became a British possession, the settlers were nearly all Dutch, and although a great tract of land had been claimed by them it was very thinly peopled. In places on the wide veldt as far as the eye could reach there was no sign of a dwelling. In other places only here and there might be seen the smoke of a lonely farm-house. There were really not enough settlers on the land to make the best use of it. So the British Parliament resolved to send out more colonists to people the wide plains of South Africa.

The wars which Britain had carried on against Napoleon for so many years had cost a great deal of money, and many of the people had become very poor. So when the British Government offered to take them to South Africa and give them farms there for nothing, numbers were eager to go. Indeed, so many wanted to go that the government had not money enough to send even a quarter of those who asked to be sent. So about four thousand only of the number were chosen.

The government did not only choose farmers, but all kinds of people, such as shoemakers, tailors, clerks, doctors, army officers, shopkeepers, and many others, most of whom had no idea of farming, many no idea of hard work. But somehow the government seemed to expect that all these people would become good farmers as soon as they reached South Africa.

Of course no such magic happened, and many of them failed. They did their best, however. They set to work at once to build their houses, and fence and plough their land. But fortune was against them. That year all over South Africa the crops failed, and many of the new settlers, after suffering great trials, gave up their land and wandered back to the towns. There many of them found that they could easily get work at their old trades, and so nearly all were able to begin life over again, and in the end make comfortable homes for themselves and families. About a quarter of those who had come out still held to their farms, and in spite of many troubles from blight, and drought, and floods, at length they too succeeded.

Most of these new British colonists settled farther east than the Boers, and their part of the country came to be called Albany, and it was by them that the town of Port Elizabeth was founded. It is now the second seaport, and still one of the most British of South African towns.

And now that the Cape was a British possession and that there were many British colonists settled there, the government at home thought that it was time to make English the language of the country.

You remember that when the French Huguenots came to the Cape the Dutch soon made them give up their own language and speak Dutch. They did not see that there was any hardship in that. But now that the Dutch themselves were treated in something of the same way it seemed to them very hard. They strove against the new law as much as they could, but it was of no use. They were allowed to speak Dutch in their own homes as much as they liked, but when they went to law, or wanted to speak with the Governor, or do anything in connection with the ruling of the land, they were forced to speak English. Thus English became what is called the "official" language of the country. Since then, however, in 1882, an act has been passed allowing Members of Parliament to speak either in Dutch or English.

The Boers did not like the introduction of the English language, but they soon had another and far greater grievance. A great deal of work on the Boer farms was done by slaves, but about this time the British people began to see that slavery was wrong, and in 1833 it was forbidden, not only in Britain but in all British colonies. Of course those who owned slaves lost a great deal of money, and although the British Government voted a large sum to help to repay the slave-owners, it was not nearly enough, and many people who had been well off became quite poor.

Many of the Boer farmers did not object to the slaves being freed, but they did want to be properly paid for their loss. The sum set aside for the freeing of the Cape slaves was so small, however, that many of the owners got very little. The money could only be paid in London, and as the farmers could not go to London to get it they had to trust to others, and often in the end received only a quarter of it. Of course it was right that the slaves should be freed, but the way it was done caused a great deal of bitterness among the colonists.

While these things were happening in the colony, beyond its borders the land was seething with war and bloodshed, for the native tribes were fighting terribly among themselves. There was a warlike and cruel Zulu chief named Tshaka who attacked and conquered all around him. He was so fierce and terrible that he was called the Black Napoleon of South Africa. This chief swept the land, killing and destroying without mercy until there were few left to kill. The country was strewn with bleaching bones, the villages were blackened ruins, their gardens trampled and deserted.

Those who escaped from the spears of Tshaka's terrible soldiers died of starvation, a few only taking refuge among other Kaffir tribes, who gave them the name of Fingoes or wanderers. A million people it was said died through Tshaka's wars, and thousands of miles of country were made a desert.

At last this fierce chieftain was stabbed to death by his own brother Dingaan, who then became head of the Zulus. But things were made little better, for he was almost as cruel and warlike as his brother had been.

There were other chiefs too who followed Tshaka's example, and fire and bloodshed desolated the land until all the wide tract from the borders of Cape Colony to the river Limpopo, and from the sea almost half across Africa, became a desert, in which scarcely a human being was to be found.

These wars were of course only among the natives themselves, but later on they came to have an effect on the colony.

LANDING OF BRITISH SETTLERS—1820

Upon this South-sea strand—
Unto the savage land—
Welcome, ye little band,
    Fit to brave danger.

Losses and wars will be
Fires of adversity,
Tests which ye cannot flee
    Trials and sorrows.

Yours for success to fight;
Yours to defend the right;
Striving with all your might
    For life and freedom.

Under benignant skies,
Fruits on the plains shall rise,
As labour's sacrifice
    To the Creator.

Herds, flocks, and trade shall be
Proof of your industry,
Making prosperity
    Smile upon labour.

Sons of the great and free!
Oh! let your motto be,
'God and the right for me,
    Forward for ever."

ALEX. WILMOT.

CHAPTER 8

THE GREAT TREK

THE Kaffirs had always been a great trouble to the colonists. Their farms and cattle were never safe, and between the colonists and the natives there had been many fights, and at least five wars, in spite of the fact that the government tried to keep peace. So anxious indeed were the rulers not to have war that often the Kaffirs were allowed to go unpunished for their misdeeds. This, however, only made them bolder, and the farmers more angry with the rulers.

Now, about three weeks after the freeing of the slaves a new war with the Kaffirs began. For some time they had been restless and insolent. The more they were allowed to go unpunished, the more they laughed at the colonists, scorning them for their weakness, and the bolder they became in their plunderings. Still, in spite of everything, few people believed that they meant war. But suddenly, two days before Christmas 1834, a wild horde of twelve thousand warriors poured over the border into the eastern part of the colony. The farmers, whose homes were scattered far and wide over the plains, were completely taken by surprise. They were murdered without mercy, their farms were ruined, and their cattle driven off.

Everywhere round Grahamstown the great rolling plains had been dotted with little whitewashed houses, surrounded by gardens and orchards. Now night after night the sky was lit up with flames, and day by day fresh blackened ruins showed where these peaceful homes had been.

The whole land was turned into a desert of blood and ashes. Those who escaped from the fury of the savages fled to the nearest towns, and Grahamstown was soon full of refugees. There a church was turned into a shelter for those homeless ones, most of whom had lost everything that they possessed. The streets were barricaded, and the townspeople did what they could to defend themselves. Every man walked about with his gun ready, but there were few soldiers in the colony at this time, and there was no one to take command.

But before many days had passed the news of the uprising reached Cape Town. As soon as he heard of it, Colonel Harry Smith set out for Grahamstown. He wasted no time, starting off in the middle of the night on his long ride of about six hundred miles. It was summer, and the heat was great, but in spite of that he rode on and on, hardly pausing to rest till six days later he reached Grahamstown. It was a wonderful ride.

Colonel Harry Smith at once took command. He called out every man between sixteen and sixty to fight for his country, and every man who could carry a gun came willingly. More than a thousand Hottentots were called out too, a regiment of Highlanders came from the Cape, and the war began in real earnest.

But to fight the savages was difficult. They would not come out and fight the British in the open. They lurked in wild fastnesses in the hills and valleys, and had to be driven from one strong fortress after another. As soon as they were beaten in one place, they fell back to a second, and then to a third. But the British at length swept bare all the land between the great Fish River and the Kei, Hintsa the chief was killed, and his son made peace.

By this peace the boundary of the colony was put forward to the river Kei. This was done, said the governor, because "Hintsa had, without just provocation or declaration of war, burst into His Majesty's colony of the Cape of Good Hope; laid waste the eastern province with fire and sword; and plundered and murdered the peaceful inhabitants."

Along the frontiers of this new province, the governor ordered several forts to be built. To these he sent small garrisons so that in future the farmers might be protected.

Peace being made, the farmers returned to their homes. They began to build again their ruined houses, and gather in what was left of their wasted crops, hoping that now at last they would be able to live in peace.

But to the surprise of every one, and to the rage of the farmers, news soon came that the treaty was not to be allowed. The forts were to be given up, and the boundary of the colony was to be put back to where it was before the war.

Men who believed themselves to be the true friends of the black people had gone home to England to tell the government that the war had been unjust, and that the Kaffirs were not to blame. Those in power believed what they were told. "Justice is on the side of the conquered, not of the victorious party," said the Secretary of State for the Colonies. The Kaffirs were quite right to fight, he thought, and they were not to be punished.

The Boers had never liked British rule, now they hated it. It was nothing but tyranny, they said, and they refused to live any longer under the rule of tyrants. Their slaves had been taken from them, and no just return had been given. Again and again their farms had been plundered by the Kaffirs, and the government had given them neither protection nor help. And so they made up their minds to leave the colony, and seek liberty and peace elsewhere. "We solemnly declare," they said, "that we leave this country with a desire to enjoy a quieter life than we have hitherto had. We will not molest any people or take from them the smallest thing. But if we are attacked we will defend ourselves as well as we can against every enemy. We quit this country feeling that the British Government has nothing more to ask of us, and will allow us to govern ourselves in future."

There was plenty of land to be had in Africa. For Tshaka in his cruel wars had swept bare large tracts, some of which were known to be very fertile. To this land the Boers made up their minds to go.

Having made up their minds, they made haste to be gone. They sold their farms for little or nothing, loaded up their great ox-wagons with chairs, and tables, and beds, and the few simple household goods they could not do without. Then driving their flocks and herds before them, they slowly wound their way out of British territory. The Boers generally went in companies, twenty or thirty families joining together, and from their number they chose one to be their leader. Day by day they moved slowly along, so that the sheep and cattle should not get too tired. At night they outspanned (that is, took the oxen out of the wagons), wherever they might be, forming their wagons into a laager for safety. Sometimes when the grass was fresh and green the company would encamp for a week or more at a time to rest the flocks and herds. Then on again they travelled day by day, first through grass-covered country, where rivers and streams flowed, and forest trees gave shade and shelter from the sun. Then through barren treeless wastes they went, where water was scarce and where the grass grew scant. Sometimes they climbed steep slopes, where it needed twenty or thirty oxen to draw the heavy wagons. Sometimes they crept along under the shadow of great blue hills, on and on over the seeming endless veldt. For there were no roads, and the bullock wagons wound along over the billowing plains like ships upon the sea.

But many of these stern-faced, silent farmers who set forth in search of freedom never reached their journey's end. Over and over again they were surprised by savage tribes, and murdered without mercy. Others died of fever, and those who escaped both sickness and the spear of the savage, often lost all their cattle from the bite of the deadly tse-tse fly, and became little more than homeless beggars.

The tse-tse is a South African fly with a deadly sting which kills tame animals, but does no harm to wild animals. Yet when the wild animals in a district are all killed or driven away the tse-tse vanishes too. It is still one of the enemies that the South African colonist has to fight.

But in spite of all disasters, in spite of every difficulty and danger which met them on the way, the Boers continued to stream out of the colony. In one of these slow moving caravans it is interesting to remember there was a small boy of eleven named Paul Kruger.

The governor was in despair. He saw many of the best colonists go, but he could do nothing to stop them. It seemed as if the colony would be left without people. Yet there was no law to prevent people leaving a country if they wished. The only thing to be done was to try to make them so comfortable that they would not want to go. The governor, Sir Benjamin D'Urban, had done all that he could. He could not disobey his orders from home. So the Great Trek, as it came to be called, went on.

"The bullock-wagons wound slowly over the billowy plains."

CHAPTER 9

DINGAAN'S TREACHERY

THE Boers wanted to get away from British rule, but they did not want to be shut out from the sea. So one party under a leader named Pieter Relief resolved to settle in Natal.

Natal was at this time under the power of Dingaan, the brother of the cruel chief Tshaka. It was part of the country laid waste by his wars. Retief felt that it would be well to make a treaty with this chief, and get leave from him before forming a colony in his land, and so he set out to pay a visit to Dingaan at his capital.

For about fourteen years a few British traders had been settled in Natal. They had made a kind of treaty with Tshaka. He had granted them about a hundred miles of country round Port Natal, and they had founded a little town which they called D'Urban in honour of the governor of Cape Town. But this little settlement had never been acknowledged as a British colony, for again and again the British Government had said that they wished no more land in Africa.

The British at Durban lived a wild life. The natives round about came to look upon them as chiefs, and they often helped them in their wars. When these white people heard that the Boers wanted to settle near they were quite pleased, and promised to do all that they could to help them.

Dingaan too seemed pleased, and received Retief and his comrades in the most friendly way. He treated them as honoured guests, and displayed before them all his savage splendour. There were sham fights, almost as fearful as real ones; there was dancing and singing and feasting.

When Retief told Dingaan why he had come, the chief replied that he would gladly allow the Boers to settle in his land, but first, to show their friendship, they must get back for him some cattle which had been stolen.

This seemed an easy thing to do, for the Boers knew who had taken the cattle, so Retief agreed. Then he went back to tell the other farmers how well he had succeeded. With very little trouble they got Dingaan's stolen cattle back from the chief who had taken it, and then hundreds of wagons began to cross the Drakensberg range into the fertile land of Natal.

There was plenty of room, and the farmers spread out over the plains, while Retief and about sixty of the best of the Boers, with thirty Hottentot servants, set off once more to visit Dingaan and deliver his cattle to him.

Again Dingaan pretended to be glad to receive the Boers. Again there was dancing and feasting and great display of savage greatness. Then Dingaan asked a missionary who was there to draw up a writing saying that the place called Port Natal, together with all the land from the Tugela to the Umzimvubu River, and from the sea to the north as far as might be useful, was to be given to the Boers.

The same land had already been given to the British traders at D'Urban by Tshaka. But Dingaan had no care about that, for all that he wanted was to draw the Boers into a trap.

But the Boers saw no trap. Everything continued to be as friendly as before. The paper was signed, and one morning Retief and his men prepared to leave. When all was ready, and their Hottentot servants had gone to saddle and bridle their horses, the farmers once more went to Dingaan's hut to say good-bye. Outside the kraal they piled their guns, for they had often been told that it was not proper to go into the presence of the king armed.

They found Dingaan as usual surrounded by a great number of warriors, and as usual he received them kindly. He made them sit down, and bowls of native beer were brought so that they might drink a parting toast.

Then suddenly, as the men sat laughing and talking and holding the bowls in their hands, Dingaan shouted, "Bulala matagati, bulala matagati," which means "Kill the wizards." The Zulu warriors then rushed upon the unarmed farmers, and before they could even draw their knives most of them were struck senseless by the Zulu clubs and bound. One or two managed to get out their knives, and fought bravely for their lives, but they were soon overpowered. Then, wounded and half dead, they were all dragged to a hill outside the kraal, and there cruelly put to death. The Hottentot servants, too, who were waiting with the horses, were surrounded and killed, and their bodies with those of their masters left to the wild beasts to devour.

As soon as this horrible massacre was over, a great army of Zulus marched towards Natal bent on utterly destroying every white man, woman, and child.

Swiftly and silently they crept onward through the land, till a few mornings later they reached the first encampment.

It was early morning and no one was astir. In the little encampment all were peacefully sleeping. So sure were the Boers by this time of the friendly feeling of the natives, that the wagons were not even in laager, but were spread here and there wide over the plain.

Suddenly the sleepers were awakened by the wild war-cry and terrible hiss of the Zulu warriors, the hiss as of a thousand snakes, with which they began battle. Almost in their sleep the Boers were murdered. No one was spared, neither woman nor child. Then when all were dead, the savages wreaked their wild rage on the wagons, smashing and burning them, and carrying off anything they fancied, as well as all the flocks and herds. Where the peaceful encampment had been, they left a waste of blood and ashes, a place of wailing. And when later the friends of the murdered people came there, and stood with tears in their eyes amid the wreckage

"BESIDE THEM STOOD THE WOMEN QUIETLY LOADING GUNS."

and the dead, they named the place Weenen, the place of tears. And the little town which stands there to-day is still so called.

Two men alone succeeded in escaping from the awful slaughter. They, flinging themselves on horseback, sped away over the veldt to warn other companies of farmers of the awful death that awaited them. And they, as soon as they heard the terrible news, formed their wagons into laagers and made ready to defend themselves as best they could. Scarcely were they ready, when the black hordes poured upon them.

The Zulus swarmed in yelling thousands around the barricades of wagons, showering their spears upon the men within. But these grim, stern farmers fired steadily, ready to die rather than yield. Beside them stood the women quietly loading guns. They too were ready to die rather than yield. And if a black man, braver than his fellows, reached the wagons and tried to climb the barricade, he found himself struck down by an axe swung by a woman's hand. Even the children fought. "Go and hide yourself," said a mother to her little boy of ten.

"I can"t see any place where to hide," he said, "give me a pistol and let me shoot too."

The Boers fought so well that from laager after laager the savages were driven back, until at length, disheartened, they marched away leaving many dead upon the field.

Then the farmers who were left gathered together to decide what they should do. "Let us flee from the land," said some.

But the women would not hear of that. "We will never leave Natal," they said, "until we have avenged the death of our dear ones." And so they stayed.

The news of the terrible slaughter soon spread, and other Boers, together with the British who had settled at Durban, came to help to fight Dingaan. But the white people were few, and the natives swarmed in thousands, and what was worse, the white people did not all fight together. Several wanted to be leaders, and were jealous of each other. So the war went on for months, and disaster after disaster fell upon the Boers.

But at last, in December 1838, an army of nearly five hundred marched against Dingaan. There were no real soldiers among them, they were all farmers, but perhaps they were more like Cromwell's Ironsides than any soldiers that were ever seen. They were men of little learning, the Bible had often been their only lesson book, and they had the words of it constantly on their lips. No noise of laughter or merriment was to be heard in the camp, but morning and evening rose the sound of prayer and psalm-singing. It was as if a church had come out to do battle.

On Sunday, 16th December, the great battle was fought. At five o'clock in the morning the Zulus attacked the Boer encampment, and for five hours or more the fight lasted. With savage bravery the black hordes flung themselves again and again against the barricades. As they came on they were mown down in hundreds by the deadly fire of the Boer guns. For hours they attacked, but at length they fled, and were pursued by the Boers till darkness fell. The slaughter was awful. The ground was piled with dead and dying, and sodden with blood, the very river ran so red that afterwards it was called the Blood River. More than three thousand Zulus lay upon the field, and many more perished in the chase, but not a white man was killed, and only three were wounded. In memory of this great victory, the 16th December was called Dingaan's day, and kept ever after as a holiday.

After the fight the Boers moved on, and next day came to Dingaan's town. But they found it a smoking ruin, for the chief had set it on fire and fled. On the hill outside the town the Boers found the bleaching skeletons of their friends who had been murdered so many months before. They had not been touched since the day that they were thrown there. Although it was now little more than a skeleton, Retief's body was known by the clothes he wore and by a leathern pouch which he had carried. In it was found the treaty signed by the false Dingaan.

Reverently and sadly the Boers buried the dead comrades they had come to avenge. Then having rested for a few days they set off again to fight the savages. At length, having scattered them far and wide, they returned to Natal bringing with them many thousand cattle as spoil.

The Boers now took possession of Natal and proclaimed it to be a republic. The Dutch flag was hoisted, and the town of Pietermaritzburg founded. It was so called in honour of Pieter Retief and of Gerrit Maritz, another of the Boer leaders.

But Dingaan was not yet beaten. He built himself a new town, and waited quietly for a chance to swoop down upon the Boers. Meanwhile, however, he quarrelled with his brother Panda. Panda with many of his followers fled to Natal asking the Boers to help him. They were not sure at first that this might not be a trick. But Panda proved to them that he was in earnest, and so the Boers, joining him, once more marched to attack Dingaan. Another battle took place in which Dingaan was utterly beaten, and was forced to flee with the remnant of his army to hide in the fastnesses of the north. There he was soon killed by another savage tribe.

The Boers then proclaimed Panda king. But he was only a vassal king. He was really under the Boers and had little power. So at last there was peace once more between Kaffir and white man.

CHAPTER 10

THE WAR OF THE AXE

MEANWHILE another enemy had risen against the Boers. While the fight with the natives was still going on, a British officer with a Highland regiment arrived at Durban. He took possession of the town in the name of Queen Victoria, who had just come to the throne. The Boers, however, would not admit that this officer had any right to interfere with them. There was no fighting. The British officer simply told the Boers that they were still British subjects, and they went on acting as an independent nation. At last the British officer and his soldiers sailed away and went back to the Cape. And although the governor there still kept on saying that "Her Majesty could not acknowledge the independence of her own subjects," the Boers were left alone, and they believed that they should always be left alone to rule themselves as they pleased.

So for a time the Boers did rule themselves. But they were for the most part ignorant men. They knew no history, they knew nothing of how other countries were ruled, and got most of their ideas from the Bible. So really there was very little government at all, and most men did as they chose. There was a good deal of quarrelling and jealousy, too, among them.

At last, for various reasons, of which it would take too long to tell, the British Government decided to force the Boers to own themselves British subjects once more. So again an officer and troops were sent to Durban.

When the officer arrived, the Boers told him that he must go, for they were now under the protection of Holland. This was not true, but at the time the Boers really believed that the Dutch would help them against the British. So little did they know of what was going on in Europe that they thought that Holland was still the great state it had been two hundred years before. They could not believe that it had sunk to a small state, and that the King of Holland had no power to help them even if he would.

But the British officer refused to go. "I shall not go, I shall stay," he replied, and fighting began.

At first the Boers had the best of the fighting. But more soldiers were sent from Cape Town. Then many of the farmers, already tired of fighting, went back to their farms. And at last, after a great deal of talking and trouble, the Boers owned themselves once more British subjects. This was in August 1848, nine years after the Great Trek began.

But although they had been forced to own themselves British subjects, many of the Boers were as determined as ever not to live under British rule. They trekked away again, so that by the end of 1848 there were not more than five hundred Boer families in all Natal. In spite of all the suffering that they had endured they were ready to endure as much again, rather than live under a rule they hated. Some went to the part now known as the Transvaal, and some to what is now the Orange River colony.

Meanwhile the British had begun to make treaties with the natives who lived in the country bordering on Cape Colony. By these treaties some of the native chiefs were recognised as kings over great stretches of land to which they had no claim at all. But the British seemed to think that they had some claim, and that by acknowledging them as kings they would be sure of a line of friendly states between Cape Colony and the wilder tribes of the north. It would also, they thought, help to cut off the Boers from trade, and force them to come back to the colony.

One of these chiefs claimed the Orange River district into which some of the Boers had trekked, and new trouble began. For although the British recognised the natives as a free people, living under their own chief, they still looked upon the Boers as British subjects who were now living under a black king, and bound to obey his rule. This made the Boers angry, and they refused to obey these puppet kings, who before the treaties had really been of very little importance and who never could have been powerful without the help of the British.

A quarrel soon arose in which the British sided with the natives. There was a little skirmish (for it could hardly be called a battle) at a place called Zwartkopjies, in which the Boers were beaten. After that, most of the farmers gave in, and swore again to become British subjects. But some still would not take the oath. Rather than do that, they trekked away again to join their fellows in the Transvaal, and for a little time there was peace in that part of the country.

But about this time a new war with the Kaffirs began on the eastern border of Cape Colony. This was called the War of the Axe, because of the way in which it began.

A Kaffir stole an axe, and with some other prisoners he was sent to Grahamstown to be tried. But on the way, Kaffirs swooped down upon the party, killed one of the guards, and carried off the man who had stolen the axe.

The governor then sent to the head of the tribe ordering him to give up the thief and the murderers. But the chief refused. Upon that the governor decided that he must force the chief to obey. The guard who had been killed, although a Hottentot, was a British subject, and the crime had been committed within the borders of the British colony. The chief must be made to see that such things could not be done in British territory. Year by year, too, the raids of the Kaffirs upon the farms of the colonists had been growing worse and worse, for each time that they were left unpunished they grew bolder. The governor hoped to put an end to that too, and so war began.

But at first the war was badly managed. An enormous train of baggage and stores fell into the hands of the Kaffirs. Then they, exulting in their success, poured in swarms into the colony. There, as was their custom, they drove off the cattle, burned the houses and destroyed everything that they could not carry away. But this time the farmers were not unprepared. They gathered together into fortified posts, and few were killed, though many lost all they had, for they were obliged to leave their farms to the mercy of the savages.

On and on over the colony the black hordes swept, leaving a track of ruin and desolation behind them. But against them gathered a far larger army than had ever been seen in South Africa before, both of regular soldiers and of farmers. The great difficulty, however, was not so much finding people to fight as finding means of feeding and clothing them. For there were few roads and no trains at all. It was difficult to carry inland all the food that was needed for a great host when there were only bullock wagons in which to carry it, and at times the army came near being starved.

For nearly two years the war dragged on. Then the Kaffirs grew tired of the fight, and peace was made, but the savages were not by any means subdued.

Sir Harry Smith now became governor of the Cape. He was that Captain Smith who had ridden so far and so fast at the time of the sixth Kaffir war. He soon saw that the British treaties with the black peoples along the borders of Cape Colony had proved worse than useless, and he made up his mind to do away with them.

Part of the land from the eastern boundary of the colony to the sea he proclaimed to be British Kaffraria. This land was not annexed to the Cape, it was, he said, to be kept entirely for the blacks, but it was declared to be under the rule of Queen Victoria, and the governor of Cape Colony was to be the Great Chief, whom all the other chiefs were bound to obey.

Next Sir Harry made a proclamation adding all the land between the Orange and the Vaal rivers to the British dominion. This he called the Orange River Sovereignty, and all the white people living in that part were declared to be British subjects.

But the Boers who lived there resolved not to give up their independence without a struggle. They had suffered a great deal in order to be free, so as soon as Sir Harry went back to the Cape they rose in rebellion, under Andries Pretorius. The British officer who had been left to govern the new Sovereignty could do nothing. He had only a few Hottentot soldiers and about a dozen raw recruits. He gave in at once, and Pretorius and his men marched the British officers out of the country and set them across the river into Cape Colony. But as soon as Sir Harry Smith heard the news he gathered an army and came marching against Pretorius with about eight hundred men.

At a place called Boomplaatz the two armies met and fought. For three hours the battle lasted, both sides fighting bravely, but at length the Boers were beaten. They were not strong enough or united enough to fight longer, so Sir Harry again proclaimed Queen Victoria's rule over the land. Many of the farmers then settled down quietly once more, but others trekked away and joined their comrades across the Vaal beyond British territory. Pretorius was among these. He was made an outlaw with the price of £2000 upon his head. But across the Vaal he lived freely and openly, no one trying to attack or take him prisoner.

CHAPTER 11

THE WRECK OF THE "BIRKENHEAD"

B UT while the governor was claiming great lands and adding them to
British rule, the colonists had another trouble to face and fight. For
about this time the British Government began to find it more and more
difficult to know what to do with their convicts. Australia wanted no more,
Tasmania wanted no more. So at last they decided to found a convict colony
at the Cape. There, roads and harbours and many other public works were
needed, all of which could be built by convicts.

But when the Cape colonists heard of what the British Government
meant to do, they all, Boer and British alike, began to object. They would
not have convicts in the colony, and they wrote home telling the British
that they would not have them. They had great meetings, they protested
and petitioned, but the British Government took no notice of all that the
colonists said and did. They had made up their minds, and on the 19th
of September 1849 a ship with a number of convicts on board anchored
opposite Cape Town.

As soon as it became known that the ship was there, a kind of terror
and dismay seized the people. Hither and thither through the streets they
hurried, anxious and excited. The church bells were tolled, meetings were
held. The colonists solemnly swore that they would have nothing to do
with the ship and her crew, and they wrote to the governor telling him
that it must be sent away. "The convicts must not, cannot, and shall not
be landed," they said.

Sir Harry Smith was on the side of the colonists, and he would not
let the convicts land. But he had no power to order them to go anywhere
else. So the ship remained anchored in the bay, while the captain sent to
England asking what he was to do. There were no telegraphs to Africa in
those days, so for five months the ship lay there, waiting orders. During
all that time the people on board found it hard to get enough to eat. For
the colonists were so bitter against them that they would not even sell
them food. And when it was discovered that the commanding officer of
the garrison was sending food to the convict ship, the farmers and traders
refused to sell to him, so that the soldiers came near starving too. At last,
to the joy of every one, a letter came from home telling the ship to go on
to Tasmania, and land the convicts there. Thus ended the attempt to make
the Cape a convict station.

Hardly was this trouble over when another war with the Kaffirs broke
out. Ever since British Kaffraria had been made a state and brought under

213

British rule, many of the chiefs there had been restless. For the British rulers had tried to put down some of their old savage customs, and the Kaffirs did not like that at all.

The Kaffirs believed that all kinds of misfortunes came upon them through wizards and witches, and every tribe had a "witch-finder," whose duty it was to "smell out" these witches. When any misfortune came upon them, the tribe was called together. Then the witch doctor, fearfully painted and adorned with all kinds of terrible savage grandeur, rushed about among them. Trembling and anxious, the people stood waiting, each man knowing that his life was unsafe, until the witch doctor, pointing to one among them, accused him of being the cause of all the trouble. Then the poor wretch, who had no more to do with it than you or I, was seized, tortured, and killed without more ado.

The British forbade this "smelling out" of witches, much to the wrath of the Kaffirs, and they became so angry that it needed very little to make them fight again. So when a witch doctor began to tell the people that he could give them a charm that would make the white man's bullets turn to water and do no harm, they thronged in hundreds to him. Then believing that guns had no power against them, they became more bold in their attacks.

At first, however, the governor would not believe that the Kaffirs meant war. But at last there could be no doubt about it, the savages attacked and destroyed three villages just within the border of the colony, and a terrible war was begun which lasted two years.

The Kaffirs were not easily beaten, and many new soldiers were sent from home to help in the fight. Some of those never landed in South Africa, yet we remember them as heroes who kept their Colours without spot or stain. For it was while on its way to Africa that the Birkenhead went down.

Sailing through the dark night on its way to Algoa Bay, the ship struck on a rock near a point called Danger Point. It struck with such force that the whole ship was shivered from stem to stern, and in a moment the water rushed in on every side.

So fast did the water rush in that many of the men who were sleeping on the lower deck were drowned before they could leap from their beds. Every one who could scrambled on deck as quickly as possible, while a terrible strange cry of fear rose in the darkness, for there were many women and children on board. It was seen at once that there was no hope of saving the ship, that indeed great speed must be used to save the women and children, for there were not boats enough for all. But although the decks were crowded there was no confusion. The soldiers quietly formed in companies, and stood waiting, as cool and calm as upon a parade ground, while the women and children were being put into the boats.

While this was being done, some of the soldiers let loose the horses and threw them into the water. For though the bay was swarming with sharks, and the shore too far off for even the strongest swimmer to reach it, it was hoped that some of the poor animals might be able to swim as far, and so save themselves.

Amid the sobs of women, some of whom were leaving their husbands and their sons behind, and the cries of frightened children who knew not what was happening, the boats were filled. But the ship was sinking fast. There was not the slightest hope that the boats could reach the shore and return in time to save the men. Yet not a soldier stirred. Calmly and quietly they awaited certain death. It was harder, this, than facing cannon, harder than charging a savage foe. To die fighting, that were easy! But to have this courage to be still, to stand shoulder to shoulder, in the cold grey light of dawn, to feel beneath their feet the boards heave and sink, to see the cruel waves creep upward, and the black hideous monsters await their prey—that was hard.

And so four hundred heroes stood to meet their death. The boats with the women and children were scarcely at a safe distance when the ship went to pieces and every man went down. A few only, clinging to floating spars and bits of wreckage, reached the shore.

> The brave who died,
> Died without flinching in the bloody surf,
> They sleep as well beneath that purple tide
> As others under turf.
>
> They sleep as well! and, roused from their wild grave,
> Wearing their wounds like stars, shall rise again,
> Joint-heirs with Christ, because they bled to save
> His weak ones, not in vain.
>
> If that day's work no clasp or medal mark;
> If each proud heart no cross of bronze may press,
> Nor cannon thunder loud from Tower or Park,
> This feel we none the less:—
>
> That those whom God's high grace there saved from ill,
> Those also left His martyrs in the bay,
> Though not by siege, though not in battle, still
> Full well had earned their pay.

CHAPTER 12

THE FOUNDING OF TWO REPUBLICS

WHILE the eighth Kaffir war was being fought there was trouble in the Orange River Sovereignty too. Moshesh, a great Basuto chief, claimed part of the Sovereignty. He was one of those chiefs with whom the British had made treaties, and thus from being a petty chief he had risen to great power. But now that those treaties had been done away with, Moshesh saw his power again grow less and less. Then, although still pretending to be friendly with the British, he began to quarrel and fight with some other chiefs, hoping in the long-run to be able to throw off British rule. Major Warden, who had been left to govern the Sovereignty, tried at first by peaceful means to quiet Moshesh. But when that failed he marched against him with an army.

But in a battle at Viervoet Moshesh defeated Major Warden, and after that he gave up all pretence of friendship for the British and became an open enemy. There were still some farmers in the Sovereignty who did not like the British, although most of these had crossed the Vaal after the battle of Boomplaatz. Now these farmers made a treaty with Moshesh. They promised not to fight against him, and he on his side promised not to attack them. And this promise Moshesh kept, for although he wasted and destroyed the British settlers' farms, he left the Boers alone.

After a little Moshesh and the Boers wrote to Pretorius and asked him to come with his farmers from beyond the Vaal and help them to fight the British. Pretorius, however, did not come. Instead he wrote to Major Warden telling him that he had been asked to come to help the people of the Orange River Sovereignty to revolt, but that he would rather make peace with the British Government, if the British would acknowledge that the Boers beyond the Vaal were a free people.

Major Warden sent this letter on to the governor, for he had no power to answer it. The governor did not want to acknowledge the independence of the Boers, but he could not help himself. He must either yield to the demand or fight. He could not fight, for he had not a man to spare from the Kaffir war which was still raging on the eastern borders of Cape Colony. If the Boers from beyond the Vaal joined with those who were already discontented in the Sovereignty, there would be an end of British rule there.

So seeing nothing else for it, the governor made up his mind to acknowledge the independence of the Boers beyond the Vaal. And on 17th January 1852, a treaty known as the Sand River Convention was signed. By this treaty the British gave up all rule over the Boers north of the Vaal and acknowledged their right to manage their own affairs. Then those of the Orange River farmers who still disliked British rule trekked over the border to join their comrades. And thus at last after years of wandering and struggle the Boers gained their end, and the South African Republic was founded. Pretorius became the first president of the new republic, and gave his name to the capital Pretoria.

Moshesh had now no more help from the Boers, but he still continued to fight, and although the British officials remained in the Sovereignty the savages did very much as they liked. But as soon as the governor could spare soldiers from the war in Kaffraria, he sent them to fight Moshesh.

The wily chief, however, by this time was growing anxious for peace. He saw that now that the Boers had got what they wanted, there was no longer any hope of help from them. As the war in Kaffraria was over, he knew that more and more soldiers would be sent against him. At present he was the real conqueror. If he fought more he might be beaten. So thinking of all these things, he went to a missionary and asked him to write a letter begging for peace.

"Your Excellency," he said, "this day you have fought against my people and have taken much cattle. I beg you will be satisfied with what you have taken. I entreat peace from you—you have shown your power —you have chastised. Let it be enough, I pray you. Let me no longer be considered an enemy of the Queen. I will try all I can to keep my people in order in the future."

So wrote the wily Moshesh, pretending to be very humble, but not really humble in the least. At first, however, no one could be found willing to carry the letter to the British camp. But at last a man was found who, waving a white flag, took it to the governor.

The governor on his side was very glad to have a good excuse for making peace. The Basutos were far stronger and better drilled than he had expected. To beat them would take a long time, and he did not want to begin another long war. For although Moshesh wrote so humbly the governor knew quite well that he was not really beaten. But that he should pretend was enough, and the governor resolved to make peace.

Many of the officers, however, were very angry. So were the white people and the natives who had helped the British. They all wanted to fight Moshesh until he was really beaten. But the governor would listen to none of them. He proclaimed peace, and marched back to Cape Colony as fast as he could, leaving only a garrison of three hundred men at Bloemfontein, the capital of the Sovereignty.

By this time the people at home had become thoroughly tired of all the wars in South Africa. And they made up their minds that the Orange River Sovereignty was not worth all the blood and money that it had cost, and was likely still to cost. So now a message came from home saying that

"Her Majesty's Government had decided to withdraw from the Orange River Sovereignty." And on the 23rd of February 1854, by the Convention of Bloemfontein the Orange River Sovereignty was changed into the Orange Free State, and the people were declared to be free to manage their own country and rule themselves.

About this time too, a change was made in the Cape government. The colonists were no longer ruled by the British Parliament, but chose their own rulers. In June 1854, the first Cape Parliament met.

So now there were five states in South Africa. These were Cape Colony, Natal and British Kaffraria under British rule, and the South African Republic and the Orange Free State, independent countries.

CHAPTER 13

THE STORY OF A FALSE PROPHET

AFTER the eighth Kaffir war was over the governor hoped that he had made a lasting peace with the natives. But they were really ready to fight again as soon as they saw a chance, although Sir George Grey, who was now governor, did his best to prevent war and make the people happier.

Among many other things Sir George built a large hospital where black people might come when they were ill. He did this hoping to stop the belief in witch doctors and the terrible cruel habit of "smelling out" witches. Many Kafis did come to the hospital, and some of them were so pleased and grateful that they wrote to Queen Victoria to thank her.

"I am very thankful to you, dearest Queen Victoria," wrote one, "because you have sent for me a good doctor and a clever man. I was sixteen years blind, Mother and Queen, and now I see. I see everything. I can see the stars, and the moon, and the sun. I used to be led before, but now, Mother, O Queen! I am able to walk myself. Let God bless you as long as you live on earth. Let God bless Mother. Thou must not be tired to bear our weaknesses, O Queen Victoria!"

But although the hospital did much good, a great witch doctor had meanwhile arisen who did much harm. He was so powerful and so clever that the people believed in him more than ever, for he told them that he had seen and talked with strange beings who were the everlasting enemies of the White Man. They had come, he said, from battlefields far across the ocean to help the Kaffirs. They were very powerful spirits, against whom none could stand, and if the Kaffirs only obeyed them, the White Men would soon all be driven into the sea.

But, said the prophet, if the Kaffirs wished to be free they must obey the commands of these great spirits. They must kill and eat all their cattle, they must destroy all the grain they had, they must leave their fields and gardens untilled. And when all this was done at a day appointed, a new world would begin. The gardens would then spring to fresh and undreamt-of beauty; corn would suddenly start from the ground, waving, golden, ripe for harvest; herds of cattle, such as never before had been seen, would come thundering over the plains. Never more would the Kaffirs know pain, or sorrow, or suffering. Every joy that they could imagine would be theirs. As for the White Man, he would be swept into the sea, and go down for ever into darkness.

All Kaffirland went mad with joy and excitement. With such a fairyland in promise they made haste to kill and eat as they had been commanded.

Everywhere there was feasting and revelling. And as they feasted and grew fat the Kaffir pride grew great. They looked upon the White Man with haughty hate mingled with savage joy, for soon these pale faces were to be swept into the sea, and the Kaffir was once more to be lord in the land, a land made glorious.

As the days passed and the destruction of cattle went on, the excitement grew wilder and wilder. Many Kaffir's spent their time making huge skin bags from the hides of the slaughtered animals. These bags were to hold the immense quantities of milk which they expected from the fabled herds. Others built great kraals in which to pen the flocks and herds which were to swarm upon the earth in numbers greater than the stars of heaven. But even before the work was done and the great day came, hundreds were starving. The herds were all slain, the corn all eaten or destroyed, and the fields and gardens lay barren, and so, with hunger and excitement, many went mad.

At length the long-looked-for day was near. The night before the great dawn, the Kaffirs shut themselves into their huts, and spent the hours of darkness in trembling, impatient watching. When morning was near they came forth in wild excitement, expecting to see not one, but two, blood-red suns rise glorious in the east.

But the dawn was dim and misty. Breathlessly the people waited and watched. Slowly, slowly the sun rose above the hills, casting a pale yellow light around. Slowly there mounted into the sky one pale yellow ball, not two, nor blood-red.

Then there was heard a cry of agony, "We are deceived! we are deceived!"

"Nay," said some, "have patience, at midday we shall see the marvel."

But midday came, and passed, and the golden sun sank to evening in the west, and not in the east as had been foretold. Still there was no sound of hoof, no thunder of coming cattle, no rustle on the earth of yellow corn ripe for harvest, no darkness and death for the hated White Man. Then wild exultation was followed by wilder wailing, and the madness of despair.

A whole nation was starving, and they had themselves destroyed their food. By their own act they had brought famine and barrenness upon the land. From end to end the country was filled with hopeless agony and clamour, it was one wild cry for food. Men killed each other for a handful of roots, a mouthful of bread, mothers snatched the food from their children's mouths. The great milk sacks so joyfully prepared were torn to pieces and fought for. Father and son, mother and daughter, strove with eah other for scraps; mercy and kindness were forgotten.

Hundreds of starving wretches poured into Cape Colony, imploring help from the very white men that they had hoped to see driven forth with fearful slaughter. It was said that this was what Kaffir chiefs wanted, that they had spread wonderful tales on purpose, thinking that when the people were mad with hunger they would swarm over the colony destroying all that came in their way. But if this was so the plan failed utterly. For the people were too weak to do more than crawl and beg.

The British had known how the dream must end, and they had prepared for it. Great stores of food had been gathered, and now they were able to help many of the famishing wretches, sending them, when they were fit, to work on the farms. But thousands died of hunger and of the terrible diseases that hunger brings, before they reached even the borders of the colony. They fell by the wayside as they staggered along, they lay down to rest and never rose, till the plains of Kaffraria were whitened with the bones of thirty thousand skeletons.

By this slaughter of hunger, great tracts of land were left desolate, and Sir George Grey sent white settlers to take the place of the dead Kaffirs, so that the bounds of the colony were extended. Among these new settlers were a great many Germans. During the Crimean War Great Britain had raised some German regiments to help them, and when the war was over these soldiers were given farms in South Africa. Other Germans came too, and proved very good colonists. And as British Kaffraria had thus become full of white people, it was thought better to add it to Cap Colony. This was done in 1865.

CHAPTER 14

A STORY ABOUT A PRETTY STONE

AS years went on South Africa became more and more important for its trade and commerce. First wool-bearing sheep had been brought to the country, and the trade in wool had grown large. Then the strip of land along the eastern coast of Natal had been found to be so warm and fertile that sugar-cane, tea, coffee, arrowroot, and all kinds of tropical plants would grow easily there. So there a trade grew up especially in sugar. There was also a great deal of trade done in ostrich feathers. But as more and more colonists came, and more and more land was cultivated, the wild ostriches disappeared, and the trade was almost lost. Then it was found possible to tame ostriches, so ostrich farms sprang up in South Africa just as sheep farms might elsewhere. And now, added to all these a new and wonderful industry arose, one that we have grown to think of as belonging more than any other to the Cape. I mean diamond mining.

One day in 1867 a farmer paid a visit to another farmer who lived near where the rivers Vaal and Orange join. There the children were playing with some pretty stones that they had found along the river banks. The farmer was very much taken with these stones. One of them especially he admired, for it seemed to him to shine in a wonderful way. As he liked this stone so much the children's mother gave it to him. The farmer took the stone home, and a little while after he showed it to another friend who was a trader. The trader at once said that he was sure the pretty stone was a diamond, and asked to be allowed to take it to Grahamstown. So the stone was taken first to Grahamstown and then to Cape Town to be shown to people who knew about such things. They said that it was a very good diamond, and soon this stone which the children had played with and tossed about in fun was sold for £500. Half of this money you, will be glad to know was given to the children's mother.

The story about the pretty stone soon became known, but at first few people came to look for diamonds, for no one really believed that there were diamond mines in South Africa. They thought that an ostrich, which swallows all kinds of things, had brought the stone from far away, or that it had come there by some accident or another. But soon other diamonds were found. One man found one sticking in the mud of which the walls of his house were made. The farmer who had got the stone the children were playing with heard that a native witch doctor had a curious stone which he used as a charm. The farmer went to this witch doctor and bought the stone for some herds of sheep and cattle, and it turned out to be a splendid diamond. This diamond became known as the Star of South Africa, and was sold for £11,000.

Then as the news of diamond finding spread, people came from all parts of Africa, and then from all parts of the world, eager to share in the search.

The place where the diamonds were found had always been looked upon as rather a desert, and hardly any one had lived there. Now day by day more and more people thronged the district. Towns sprang up as if by magic, towns of tents and wagons. Along the river banks, where a few months before there had been no sign of man, where there had been no sound except the cry of wild beasts and birds, was now heard all day long the sound of pick and shovel and the rattle of cradles, as the pans in which the diamonds were washed were called.

The tented towns moved from place to place. As soon as it was known that diamonds had been found in one spot men rushed there, leaving their last camping ground a desert once more. For a time the workings were only along the river banks. Then came news that far richer mines had been found some way from the river, and men rushed in thousands to the dry diggings, as they were called.

Here four mines were found, all within two miles of each other. The names of two have become familiar to every one—Kimberley and De Beers.

At Kimberley a town soon sprang up, first a town of tents and then of ugly corrugated iron houses. Streets and squares were laid out, shops, schools, hotels, churches, theatres, all appeared one after the other, until in three years Kimberley was the second largest town in South Africa. It was a town, too, very different from any of the others. The people in South Africa were for the most part farmers, rising early, going to bed early, leading a simple country life. Now at Kimberley were gathered all manner of people, clerks, labourers, students, shop-keepers, broken-down gentlemen, soldiers, sailors, all eager for diamonds and wealth. So the life there was very different from the life on the farms. In the country a man's nearest neighbour would be three or four miles away at least. For months at a time he would see no one except his own family, perhaps twice a year he would make a journey to the nearest town to go to church and buy some clothes. But at the diamond mines a man worked all day long with hundreds beside him, and when the day's work was over the evenings were spent in merriment and laughter, such as the grave farmers knew nothing of. Had it not been for the diamond fields perhaps no town would have stood where Kimberley now stands, for it is one of the most desolate parts of South Africa. The land round it was treeless and barren. It was badly watered. At first even water to drink had to be brought in carts long distances. Then when the town grew large, wells were sunk, but for a long time no good water could be found. But besides the want of water the miners had to endure many hardships. Kimberley is hot and wind-swept. Fine yellow dust seemed to fill the air, making it difficult to breathe. At times there would be terrible dust storms, for the wind caught up the sandy dust which was always being thrown out of the mines, whirling and scattering it till the sky grew dark and it became impossible to work in the dust-laden air. The flies, too, were a torment, everywhere they swarmed thickly.

There were hardly any railways in Africa at this time, so everything had to be carried to Kimberley in bullock carts, and as Kimberley is five hundred miles from the sea everything was very dear. Green vegetables were hardly to be had, and sugar was two and sixpence a pound. Many people fell ill from the heat, and dust, and dirt, but yet in spite of all discomfort the diggers worked on cheerfully, some making fortunes, others losing all that they had.

Among those who came to try their fortunes in the mines was a young man named Cecil Rhodes. He was a very clever man, and it was through him that nearly all the diamond mines were joined into one great company, now known as the De Beers Consolidated Mines, which has become one of the most powerful companies in the world.

But while hundreds of men were working, digging and sifting all day long for diamonds, the rulers of the various states round began to quarrel as to which of them the diamond mines really belonged.

The South African Republic claimed them, the Orange Free State claimed them, and Andries Waterboer, a Griqua, also claimed them. The Griquas were a kind of half-cast tribe, and as Andries Waterboer saw little chance of making people listen to his claim, he gave up his rights to the British Government.

The three governments could not agree, so it was decided that Mr. Keate, the Lieutenant-Governor of Natal, should be asked to decide as to who had the best right to the land upon which the mines were. He decided that Waterboer had the best claim, and so, in 1871, the diamond mines were declared to be British. This decision is known as the Keate Award.

The Keate Award made the people both of the Orange Free State and of the South African Republic very angry. But they had to submit, and the British took possession of the mines, and of the land claimed by Waterboer. This land was not at first added to Cape Colony, but was kept as a separate state and called Griqualand West.

A short time after this a British judge was sent to settle some quarrels about farms, and while he was settling this he found out that Waterboer had had no real right to Griqualand West, but that it had really belonged to the Orange Free State.

When this became known, Mr. Brand, the President of the Orange Free State, went to England to put his claim before the British Parliament. "You took this land with the diamond fields from us," he said, "because it had belonged to Waterboer. Now your own judge has decided that Waterboer had no right to it. Surely in justice you must return it to us."

The British, however, found that this would be very difficult to do, for various reasons. So they offered President Brand £90,000 to make up for the loss of the mines. This President Brand and the Volksraad, as the Parliament of the Orange Free State was called, accepted, and both sides were pleased. For although the Orange Free State had lost the mines, the fact that they were so near the border of the state brought a great deal of trade. And in Kimberley the Free-Staters found a good market for everything that they could produce. Besides this, the £90,000 gave them money with which to build roads and bridges and make many improvements in their country. So the Orange Free State became more prosperous than it had ever been before.

CHAPTER 15

FACING FEARFUL ODDS

BUT while the Orange Free State was prospering, the South African Republic was full of strife and trouble. The country was badly ruled. The Boers quarrelled among themselves, and were often at war with the natives. They had no money, they had no trade. The farmers, indeed, had enough to live on, but the government had no money to spend on the country. They had nothing with which to make roads or railways or bridges, for no one paid their taxes, some because they could not, others because they would not. The country became a refuge, too, for wild, bad men who wanted to live without law or restraint, and they made the confusion worse.

News of the wild turmoil of the South African Republic at last reached England. There it was said that the Boers had shown that they could not govern themselves, that they ill-treated the natives, that slavery was allowed. All sorts of stories were told, until people began to believe that the Republic was not only a disgrace to civilised people, but a danger to peaceful neighbours. It was also said that the Republic was trying to get a port on Delagoa Bay. That, of course, might hurt British trade.

So Sir Theophilus Shepstone was sent to talk to the Boer people and see what could be done. Many of the Boers were very tired of misrule, and Sir Theophilus was received with great rejoicing, although the people did not know what he had come to say or do. After a little time, however, he told the President that if he did not govern his country better he would be obliged to declare it a British possession.

To this, of course, most of the Boers objected. They wanted to have nothing to do with British rule. But they were weak, they were not united, and so on 12th April 1877 the South African Republic was declared to be at an end. The Union Jack was hoisted at Pretoria, and the name of the country was changed to the Transvaal, which means across the Vaal. Then at once British troops poured into the country, and took possession of the chief towns.

The state of the Transvaal had been bad enough, but in spite of that the farmers would not have British rule. They wanted to be left alone to govern their own country well or ill as they liked. Twice they sent messengers to England begging that Sir Theophilus Shepstone's proclamation might be recalled and their freedom given back to them. But the British Government would not listen, and the Union Jack continued to float over Pretoria.

One of the reasons that Sir Theophilus had given for annexing the Transvaal was that the Zulus were ready to fight the Boers—that indeed

226

they were only kept in check by British power. The Boers did not believe that, but very soon a Zulu war did break out. It was, however, more against Natal than against the Transvaal.

Panda, you remember, had been recognised as king of the Zulus by the Boers after Dingaan's death. He too was now dead, and his son Cetywayo ruled. Cetywayo was a clever and warlike savage, more like Tshaka and Dingaan than like Panda, and under him the Zulu army grew great and well disciplined. It was more dangerous, too, than Tshaka's army had ever been, for by this time many of the natives had succeeded in getting guns.

For some time, however, Cetywayo lived quietly at peace with the British. But as time went on it became more and more plain that he wanted to fight. His young braves were anxious to "wash their assagais in blood," and as Zululand was shut in between the sea, the Transvaal, and Natal, it was only against white people that he could fight.

For a long time Sir Bartle Frere, who was now Governor of the Cape, tried to keep peace. But at last Cetywayo became so daring and insolent that it was no longer possible. Sir Bartle then gathered an army of soldiers, colonists, and friendly blacks, and sent them to fight the Zulu king.

The Transvaal Boers were asked to help too; but they were still too angry about the loss of their freedom, and only a very few joined. But even without their help, it was believed that the army was quite strong enough to crush the savages. Unfortunately, however, Sir Bartle did not know how strong Cetywayo's army was.

About ten days after the war began, the British were encamped at the foot of a hill called Isandlwana, which means the Little Hand. Here part of the army was left while the commander-in-chief with another part went forward a few miles to examine a native fortress.

The British had been warned by the Boers to be careful how they trusted themselves in the land of the Zulus. But no one listened to the warning. The camp was not fortified in any way, the baggage-wagons even were not laagered in the usual Boer fashion, for the British did not believe that there were any Zulus near.

But meanwhile a great army of twenty thousand savages was swiftly and silently closing round the camp. Too late the British awoke to their danger. They were surrounded by black, exulting hordes. It was a fearful fight. The British stood to their posts and fought till they could fight no more. They fought till they had no powder or shot left, and it became a hand-to-hand struggle with bayonets and clubbed rifles against the short stabbing assagais of the savages. Hundreds had fallen beneath the British fire, but hundreds more came on. In wave after wave the Zulus broke upon the British camp, and above the crash of guns rose their fearful war hiss, their shouts of triumph.

To a man the foot-soldiers fell where they stood. A few mounted men made a dash through the swarming savages. But most of them were shot down even as they fled. In an hour all was over, and the camp of Isandlwana was in the hands of the plundering, rejoicing Zulus, and eight hundred white men lay still and silent on the ground, with at least six hundred friendly blacks. In an hour the camp at Isandlwana had been wiped out.

Meanwhile two horsemen who had escaped galloped madly back to carry the awful news to Rorke's Drift, where another part of the army was stationed with the stores and a hospital for the sick. Drift means ford, and Rorke's Drift was a crossing or ford over the Buffalo River.

The men rode hard, but it was after three o'clock in the afternoon before they reached the camp. Then as soon as they heard the news the soldiers there began to fortify the position as best they could. There was little time and little material, but they used what they had. Wagons were lashed together, bags of grain, biscuit-boxes, packing-cases, were piled so as to make a breastwork. The store-house and the hospital were loop-holed. Everything was done that could be done in the short time; but before the preparations were finished the Zulus were upon the camp.

With the knowledge of Isandlwana in their hearts, the soldiers set their teeth and fought with desperate courage. Again and again the black waves of savages surged up to the frail ramparts, again and again they were beaten back. Hour after hour the fight lasted. The hospital was set on fire and charged by the savages, but while one party defended the burning building, another dragged the sick men out, and the Zulus were again beaten back. In the gathering darkness the flames leaped and roared and still the fight went on. The flames died down and darkness fell, but still the fight lasted. Not till midnight did the firing slacken, and at last towards daybreak the disheartened enemy fell back to the hills around, and the fight was over.

Thus did a hundred men keep three thousand savage warriors at bay, and save Natal from being overrun by a heathen horde, mad with blood and victory.

And while at Rorke's Drift a handful of men were fighting for their lives and for the life of the colony, the commander-in-chief had turned slowly back to Isandlwana. He was still some miles off when he met a horseman spurring wildly towards him with the news of the disaster. Then he hurried towards the camp, but night had fallen before he reached the spot.

What a sight was there! As the men stood upon the terrible field and saw their comrades, from whom they had parted only a few hours before, lying dead around them, they sobbed aloud. And there among the dead, amid the ruin of their camp, they waited till dawn, with hearts full of grief and anger.

As soon as day dawned they left the ghastly field and hurried on to Rorke's Drift, not knowing what news might await them there. Anxiously they marched, but as they neared the British camp they saw that the Union

"THUS DID A HUNDRED MEN KEEP THREE THOUSAND SAVAGES AT BAY."

Jack still waved over it. And when they heard of the gallant fight that had been fought, a British cheer rent the air.

But splendid though it was, the defence of Rorke's Drift did not end the war, nor was Isandlwana the only loss. Troops, however, came from England as fast as steamers could bring them, and at last, after months of fighting, the Zulus were defeated at the battle of Ulundi, Cetywayo was taken prisoner, and the war was at an end.

After a little Cetywayo was allowed to return to his kingdom. But he found that all his people were not glad to welcome him back, for already some of them had chosen another king. So there was civil war in Zululand, and a year later Cetywayo died, it is thought now by poison. He was succeeded by his son Dinizulu. Under him the state of Zululand grew worse and worse, till in 1887 it was taken under British rule, and later annexed to Natal.

Dinizulu was sent as a prisoner to St. Helena. He remained there nine years, at the end of which time he was allowed to return to his own land. But the troubles with Dinizulu are not quite over yet.

The Defense Of Rorke's Drift

Come listen for a moment,
All ye, whose peaceful life
In even flow is ne'er disturbed
By scenes of blood and strife;
Who sit around your hearth fires,
Secure from war's alarms;
This humble lay sets forth to-day
A British deed of arms.

Left on the wild, lone border
A small but fearless band,
Guarding the watery entrance
To savage Zululand;
On the warm midday breezes,
Like thunder's distant sound,
Came the long roll of cannon
Far o'er the hostile ground,
And we wondered that our column
So soon the foe had found.

Then came two flying horsemen
Riding with loosened rein,
And the powdery dust like a whirlwind rose

As they scoured across the plain;
A few more rapid hoof strokes,
And we heard the news they bore—
"In yonder glen nigh half our men
Lie weltering in their gore.

"Our men, too soon surrounded,
Were slaughtered as they stood,
Facing their slayers to the last,
Dying as soldiers should.
How we escaped we know not,
From that fierce whirlwind's frown,
But on this post a conquering host
E'en now is marching down."

We set to work undaunted
To raise a barricade,
With mealie bags and scattered stores
A breastwork soon was made;
And scarcely was it finished,
When burst upon our sight,
Dark as the lowering storm-cloud
Sweeps the blue vaulted height,
Moving along the fair hill-side,
In vast black lines extending wide.
Rank upon rank of warriors tried,
In panoply of savage pride
Advancing to the fight.

Yes, on they came in thousands—
One hundred strong we stand,
Against the very pick and flower
Of warrior Zululand:
And how may we resist them,
Or hope to hold our own,
Flushed as they be with victory—
The greatest e'er they've known?

And eyes with lust of carnage,
Like coals through the darkness gleamed,
And bayonets crashed with stabbing spear,
Thick the red torrent streamed:

Drowning the roar of battle—
Drowning the deafening clang—
Each demon yell like a blast of hell,
Fiercer and higher rang.

Again and again we met them
Through the long fearful night,
We fought as ne'er we fought before
And ne'er again may fight,
To 'venge our slaughtered comrades,
To guard our solemn trust,
And to reclaim our country's name
Trampled in savage dust.

Piled high against our breastwork,
And scattered o'er the plain,
Four hundred of their warrior strength
Lay stark amid the slain
Lay where their fierce hot life-blood
The greedy earth had wet
Still terrible, in threatening scowl,
Each grim dead face was set.

And twelve from out our number
Their brave career had run,
Their final muster-roll had passed,
And their last duty done;
So carefully we laid them
Deep in the green earth's breast,
An alien sod above them trod;
Peace with their ashes rest!

Yes, for old England's honour
And for her perilled might,
We strove with vast and whelming odds,
From eve till morning light;
And thus with front unflinching,
One hundred strong we stood,
And held the post 'gainst a maddened host
Drunken with British blood.

Her sons in gallant story,
Shall sound old England's fame,

And by fresh deeds of glory
Shall keep alive her name;
And when, above her triumphs,
The golden curtains lift
Be treasured long, in page and song,
The memory of Rorke's Drift.

BERTRAM MITFORD.

CHAPTER 16

UPON MAJUBA'S HEIGHT

AFTER the Transvaal was annexed to Britain, many British colonists went to make their homes there, and the country grew much more prosperous. But in spite of that most of the Boers were still discontented. As months and years went on and they saw no chance of regaining their freedom quietly they made up their minds to fight for it. As their leaders they chose three men, Kruger, Joubert, and Pretorius, the son of that Andries Pretorius who had been first President. Then as Pretoria was in the hands of the British they chose the town of Heidelberg as their capital. And there on Dingaan's day, 16th December 1880, the flag of the Republic was once more hoisted, and that very day fighting began.

The Boers set out to fight in the spirit of the old Puritans. To the God of battles they committed their cause, sure that He would fight for them. When the Boers won a battle the British said it was because they knew the country and could shoot well, but the Boer said that it was God's will, and from the rejoicing camp arose the sound of prayer and psalm-singing.

In the first skirmish the British were beaten, and afterwards many misfortunes fell upon them. On January 1881 there was a battle fought at a place called Laing's Nek, a ridge between Majuba Hill and some other hills running along the banks of the Buffalo River. Here the Boers were encamped in a very strong position, and when the British attacked they were driven back with great loss.

It seemed then to the commander-in-chief that there was but one way of dislodging the Boers from their strong position. That was by taking possession of Majuba Hill, and from there firing down upon their camp until they were obliged to march away. This the British leader resolved to do.

So one dark, moonless night the commander-in-chief with about six hundred men, led by Kaffir guides, began the steep ascent. On and on up the rugged slopes the men scrambled in silence. Breathless and panting they stumbled on over boulders and stones, now hanging on to shrubs and bushes, now crawling on hands and knees. They crept round rocks and clambered along sheer precipices where one false step would have sent them headlong.

Every few yards the leaders whistled softly and the men paused to gather breath. Then on again they struggled, laden with guns and ammunition, picks and shovels, and food for three days. Up and up they went, until after a climb of five hours the first men reached the top. Panting and exhausted they flung themselves down to rest. Then in the darkness each man sought his own regiment.

There was not much time for rest, for already the darkness was fading, and as early dawn streaked the sky point after point of light shone out in the Boer camp two thousand feet below. One by one the lights shone, grew bright, and faded again in the growing sunlight. The Boer camp was all astir, and above them the British soldiers were already rejoicing in the thoughts of victory. But although they had gained a point of vantage they had brought no rockets up with them with which to shell the Boer camp. It seems difficult to understand what good the position was without cannon.

Very soon the Boers, looking up at the hill, saw the British there. At first they were filled with dismay, and thought that they must abandon their camp. Then they took courage again, and resolved to storm the hill. And so from bush to bush, from boulder to boulder, they crept up. They went carefully and fearfully at first, but when they found that the British bullets which whizzed and whistled around them passed over their heads, doing no harm, they gained courage. Faster and faster up the hill they came, firing all the time with deadly aim. At last they reached the summit and charged, and the British, suddenly seized with panic, fled down the way that they had come. And now the path up which they had toiled so painfully the night before was strewn with dead. And upon the hill-top, fighting foremost among his men, fell the commander, Sir George Colley. "He fought well," said the Boers as they stood beside his dead body. "He did not think that we were wrong, but he was a soldier and he must obey orders."

> He needs no tears who, in the van
> And foremost of the fight,
> Met death as should an Englishman
> Upon Majuba's height.

The rout was complete. Two hundred or more of the British lay dead or wounded, while only one of the Boers was killed. "They fought like true heroes," said their general, "but our God who gave us the true victory and protected us, exceeded gloriously all acts of courage."

Majuba was a great disaster for the British, but it by no means ended the war. Pretoria and other towns were besieged, but the Boers were not strong enough to take them, and now many more troops came from home to help the British. But when the news of Majuba reached England a message was sent out to the new general, Sir Evelyn Wood, telling him to make a truce. The truce became a peace, and the Transvaal was once more acknowledged to be a free state. But although the Transvaal was really free again, Queen Victoria was acknowledged as Overlord or suzerain.

This treaty of peace was called the Convention of Pretoria, and was signed on August 8, 1881. Three years later another agreement was made giving back to the Transvaal every freedom except the right to make treaties with foreign states, so that the overlordship of Queen Victoria was little more than a mere form.

Once more the Transvaal took its old name of South African Republic, and Mr Kruger became President. The flag of the Republic was hoisted, and the Union Jack, which had been run up so light-heartedly four years before, was hauled down and solemnly buried by those who grieved that British rule in the Transvaal was over. For although the Boers were pleased with the change, many of the British settlers who had come into the land since 1877 were very angry, and declared that they would never rest until British rule was restored. Many others, indeed, who thought that to annex the Transvaal had been a blunder, thought that it was a still greater blunder to restore it after the disaster of Majuba. To them it seemed a disgrace to British arms.

CHAPTER 17

THE GOLD CITY

ABOUT a year after freedom had been given back to the South African Republic a discovery was made which has perhaps changed the fortunes of South Africa more than any other. This was the discovery in the Republic of the richest gold mines in the world.

For many years gold had been found and worked in South Africa, but it was in such small quantities and so hard to get at that few people went to these gold-fields. But when the Witwatersrand mines were discovered, about forty miles from Pretoria, people from all parts of the world flocked to them.

The mines there could not be worked like those of Australia or California, for machinery was needed to dig out and crush the rock in which the gold was embedded. This machinery cost far too much money for one man to buy. So men joined together, and many companies were formed. It was a time of great excitement, for some companies succeeded and the men grew rich, others failed and the men who had spent all that they had in the hope of making more became beggars.

And meanwhile a new and great town arose in the Transvaal, a town which grew as if by magic to be the largest in all South Africa. This new town of Johannesburg was at first only a huge camp. Everywhere white tents and ugly corrugated iron houses sprang up. But soon these were swept away, and beautiful buildings, laid out in streets and squares, with parks and gardens, took their place.

This beautiful city, with glittering palaces, with theatres, schools, hospitals, and churches, with telephones and electric light, and everything that a great city needs, grew up as if by enchantment in a country where all around there were only simple farmers, living in two-roomed cottages. It grew up hundreds of miles from a railway, for in all the Orange Free State and the South African Republic there was no railroad. The machinery for the mines, the stone and wood, iron and bricks for the building of the city had all to be dragged hundreds of miles in ox-carts. But no difficulty stopped the growth of the city, and in the solitudes of Africa one of the brightest and gayest cities in the world sprang to life. Soon railways were laid down, and in a few years Johannesburg was connected with Natal, Cape Colony, and Portuguese East Africa, and from the mines a constant stream of gold flowed out to all the world.

This discovery of gold brought a great deal of money to the Republic. In Johannesburg the farmers found a great market for their produce, and in many ways the country grew prosperous. But with new prosperity new troubles arose. Until now the President had been the ruler of simple farmer folk. He or they knew little of books or business, cared little for the outside world and its fierce struggle for wealth.

But now, suddenly, the President found himself called upon to rule a new people, a people keen for business, eager for "progress," impatient of his slow farmer ways. Most of these men who had rushed to Johannesburg were British subjects, and the Boers looked upon them with distrust. They began to fear again for the liberty of their country. So they called these people Uitlanders, that is, Outlanders or strangers, and made it very difficult for them to get any share in the ruling of the country. This made the Outlanders angry, for they wanted to have a share in the governing, and to manage things better than the slow, old-fashioned Boers.

But the Boers said, "No, it is our country. We did not ask you to come, we do not want you to stay, and if you don't like it, you can go away again." But of course the Outlanders did not want to go. They wanted to stay and make money out of the gold mines.

Many things in the South African republic were really badly managed. The Outlanders had some grievances, but the more they complained the more suspicious did the Boers grow. Boer and Briton did not understand each other, and as the years went on anger and bitterness deepened and darkened on both sides.

CHAPTER 18

WAR AND PEACE

MEANWHILE the rule of Britain was spreading rapidly over South Africa. A great tract of land called Bechuanaland had become a British Protectorate. Mr. Cecil Rhodes had helped greatly in this, and now another great tract, named after him Rhodesia, was added.

By Lobengula, the King of Matabeleland, Mr. Rhodes and some others were given the right to look for gold and other minerals in his land. Then in 1889 Mr. Rhodes started the British South African Company. It was a company like the old East India or the Hudson Bay Company, and is generally known as the Chartered Company.

It received from the Crown a Royal Charter or writing by right of which the Company might use the British flag, be under British protection, yet make its own laws, appoint its rulers, and make war against or treaties with the native tribes. Mr. Rhodes was manager of the Company and his friend Dr. Jameson became ruler of Rhodesia.

After the Company was formed its officers began to take possession of the best positions in the country and to build forts. But Lobengula did not like that. He had supposed that a few white men would come to look for gold and go away again. But instead of that they came in hundreds and seemed as if they meant to stay. So he began to fight. In various ways there was a good deal of fighting and trouble. Then the Matabeles made war on another tribe, the Mashonas. The Mashonas fled to the British for protection, and there was more trouble. But at length Bulawayo, Lobengula's capital, was taken and he fled beyond the Zambesi. There he died, and there was peace for a time in Rhodesia.

A few years later, however, the natives again rose and many white people were killed. But after a good deal of fighting, first the Matabele and then the Mashonas gave in. Since then there has been peace in Rhodesia, but as yet there are not many white people there, for the British do not care to go so far away to farm. The land is, however, rich in coal and other minerals, and will doubtless one day become a prosperous colony.

Meanwhile, the Outlanders in Johannesburg were growing more and more discontented, and at last they resolved to rise in rebellion and force the government to grant them what they wanted. Mr. Rhodes, who was now Premier of the Cape, felt with them, and Dr. Jameson, the ruler of Rhodesia, agreed to help them too.

It was arranged that Dr. Jameson with five hundred horse was to march into the Transvaal, and at the same time the discontented Outlanders were to rise. But things went wrong. The people of Johannesburg and Dr. Jameson did not act together. The Boers found out about the intended revolt, and Dr. Jameson and all his force fell into their hands. And so the Jameson Raid, as it is now called, came to nothing.

Mr. Kruger gave his prisoners up to the British, and no very heavy punishment fell upon them. Some of them were sentenced to be imprisoned for longer or shorter times, and some were fined. Dr. Jameson was no longer allowed to be ruler of Rhodesia, and Mr. Rhodes had to give up being manager of the Company and Premier of the Cape.

The Jameson Raid came to nothing, indeed, but it made matters in the Transvaal much worse. The Boers had now grown more suspicious, and they began to gather guns and ammunition, and to build fortresses and batteries. That they should arm themselves in this way made the British angry, and so the quarrels and misunderstandings grew until they ended in war.

A great many reasons have been given for this war, and the one which most people believed to be the true one was that the Outlanders were taxed and yet were not allowed to vote for members of the Raad, and so had no voice in the ruling of the land. That was doubtless very hard. Yet looking back on all the horror and the pain of the war, which seems so near us still, we ask ourselves if indeed all the reasons taken together were worth fighting about. Could the granting of all our demands, could the winning of all our desires, repay us for the loss of so many gallant men? Yet it was freedom we fought for, or so it seemed, and freedom has ever been a Briton's watchword. The Boers, too, thought they fought for freedom.

Many books have been written about this war, and I do not mean to write much about it here. In October 1899 it began. The Orange Free State joined with the Republic, and instead of being a matter of only a few weeks or a few months at most, as most Britishers believed, the war lasted for two and a half years. But when at last peace was signed, both the Orange Free State and the South African Republic had lost their freedom, and had become British possessions.

The South African war wrought much sorrow both in South Africa and in Britain. But it wrought some good, for one thing it proved to all the world was that Great Britain was no mere name. Britons from all over the world gathered to help the Mother Country in her struggle, and right or wrong, we stood together and fought and died for Our Empire.

LIST OF KINGS AND GOVENORS

Kings of Great Britain and Ireland.		Rulers of Cape Colony.	
		GOVERNORS.	
George III., ...	1760	Earl Macartney, . . .	1797
		Major-General F. Dundas, .	1798
		Sir George Yonge, . . .	1799
		Major-General F. Dundas, .	1801
		Lieut.-General Jan Willem Janssens, ...	1803
		Major-General David Baird (temporary), ...	1806
		Lieut.-General Henry George Grey (temporary), . .	1807
		Earl of Caledon, . . .	1807
		Lieut.-General Henry George Grey (temporary), .	1811
		Sir John Francis Cradock, .	1811
		Lord Charles Henry Somerset,	1814
George IV., ...	1820	Major-General Sir Rufane S. Donkin (temporary), .	1820
		Lord Charles Henry Somerset,	1821
		Major-General Richard Bourke,	1826
		Sir Galbraith Lowry Cole, .	1828
William IV., ...	1830	Lieut.-Colonel T. Francis Wade (temporary), ...	1833
		Sir Benjamin d'Urban, . .	1834
Victoria, ...	1837	Sir George Thomas Napier, .	1838
		Sir Peregrine Maitland, . .	1844
		Sir Henry Pottinger, . .	1847
		Sir Henry Smith, . . .	1847
		Sir George Cathcart, . .	1852
		C. H. Darling, Esq. (temporary)	1854
		Sir George Grey, . . .	1854
		Lieut.-General R. W. Wynyard (temporary), . . .	1861
		Sir Philip Wodehouse, . .	1862
		Lieut.-General Hay (temporary)	1868
		Sir Henry Barkly, . . .	1870
		Sir Bartle Frere, . . .	1877
		Major-General Clifford (temporary), ...	1880
		Sir G. C. Strachan, . . .	1880
		Sir Hercules Robinson, . .	1881
		Sir Henry Loch, . . .	1889
		Lord Rosmead (Sir H. Robinson)	1895
		Sir Alfred Milner, . . .	1897
		Sir W. F. Hely-Hutchinson, .	1901

KINGS OF GREAT BRITAIN AND IRELAND.	RULERS OF CAPE COLONY.
	COMMANDERS.
Oliver Cromwell, . . . 1653	Jan van Riebeck, . . . 1652
Richard Cromwell, . . 1658	
Charles II., ... 1660	
	Zacharias Wagenaar, . . 1662
	Cornelis van Quaelberg, . . 1666
	Jacob Borghorst, . . . 1668
	Pieter Hackius, . . . 1670
	Albert van Breugel (temporary), 1672
	Isbrand Goske, . . . 1672
	Johan Bax, ... 1676
	Hendrik Crudop (temporary), . 1678
	Simon van der Stel, . . 1679
James II., ... 1685	
William and Mary, . . 1689	**GOVERNORS.**
William III. (alone), . . 1694	
	Wilhem Adriaan van der Stel, 1699
Anne, ... 1702	Johan Cornelis d'Ableing (temporary), ... 1707
	Louis van Assenburgh, . . 1708
	Wilhem Helot, . . . 1711
George I., ... 1714	Maurits Pasques de Chavonnes, 1714
	Jan de la Fontaine (temporary), 1724
George II., ... 1727	Pieter Gysbert Noodt, . . 1727
	Jan de la Fontaine, . . . 1729
	Adriaan van Kervel, . . 1737
	Daniel van der Henghel (temporary), ... 1737
	Hendrik Swellengrebel, . . 1739
	Ryk Tulbagh, ... 1751
George III., ... 1760	
	Joachim van Plettenberg, . 1771
	Cornelis Jacob van de Graaff, . 1785
	Johan Isaac Rhenius, . . 1791
	COMMISSIONERS-GENERAL.
	Sebastian Cornelis Nederburgh } Simon Hendrik Frykenius } 1792
	Abraham Josias Sluysken, . 1793
	Council of British Officers, . 1795
	Major-General James H. Craig, 1795

INDIA

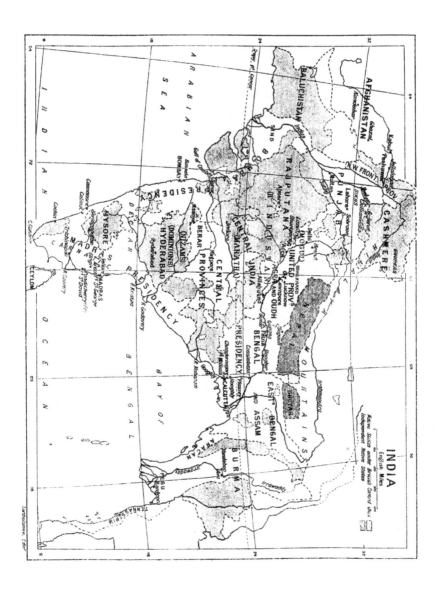

INDIA

English Miles

Native States under British Control
Independent Native States

Bartholomew, Edin.

CHAPTER 1

ALEXANDER THE GREAT INVADES INDIA

UNLIKE the other countries of Greater Britain, India is no new-discovered land. At a time when our little island was still unknown, still lost in the cold grey mists of the ocean, ships sailed from India's sunny shores, and caravans wound through the sandy deserts laden with silks and muslins, with gold and jewels and spices.

For through long ages India has been a place of trade. The splendours of King Solomon came from out the East. He must have traded with India when he built great ships and sent "his shipmen that had knowledge of the sea" to sail to the far land of Ophir, which perhaps may have been in Africa or equally perhaps the island of Ceylon. From there these ship-men fetched such "great plenty" of gold and precious stones, that "silver was nothing accounted of in the days of Solomon."

The court, too, of many an ancient heathen king and queen was made rich and beautiful by the treasures of the East. Yet little was known of the land of gold and spice, of gems and peacocks. For beside the merchants, who grew rich with their traffickings, few journeyed to India.

But at length, in 327 B.C., the great Greek conqueror Alexander found his way there. Having subdued Syria, Egypt, and Persia, he next marched to invade the unknown land of gold.

The part of India which Alexander invaded is called the Punjab, or land of the five rivers. At that time it was ruled by a king called Porus. He was overlord of the Punjab, and under him were many other princes. Some of these princes were ready to rebel against Porus, and they welcomed Alexander gladly. But Porus gathered a great army and came marching against the Greek invader.

On one side of a wide river lay the Greeks, on the other side lay the Indians. It seemed impossible for either to cross. But in the darkness of a stormy night Alexander and his men passed over, wading part of the way breast high.

A great battle was fought. For the first time the Greeks met elephants in war. The huge beasts were very terrible to look upon. Their awful trumpetings made the Greek horses shiver and tremble. But Alexander's soldiers were far better drilled and far stronger than the Indians. His horsemen charged the elephants in flank, and they, stung to madness by the Greek darts, turned to flee, trampling many of the soldiers of Porus to death in their fright. The Indian war-chariots stuck fast in the mud. Porus himself was wounded. At length he yielded to the conqueror.

But now that Porus was defeated Alexander was gracious to him, and treated him as one great king and warrior should treat another. Henceforth they became friends.

As Alexander marched through India he fought battles, built altars, and founded cities. One city he called Boukephala in honour of his favourite horse Bucephalus, which died and was buried there. Other cities he called Alexandreia in honour of his own name.

As they journeyed, Alexander and his soldiers saw many new and strange sights. They passed through boundless forests of mighty trees beneath whose branches roosted flocks of wild peacocks. They saw serpents, glittering with golden scales, glide swiftly through the underwood. They stared in wonder at fearful combats of beasts, and told strange stories when they returned home, of dogs that were not afraid to fight with lions, and of ants that dug for gold.

At length Alexander reached the city of Lahore and marched on to the banks of the river Sutlej beyond. He was eager to reach the holy river Ganges and conquer the people there. But his men had grown weary of the hardships of the way, weary of fighting under the burning suns or torrent rains of India, and they begged him to go no further. So, greatly against his will, Alexander turned back.

The Greeks did not return as they had come. They sailed down the rivers Jhelum and Indus. And so little was known of India in those days, that they believed at first that they were upon the Nile and that they would return home by way of Egypt. But they soon discovered their mistake, and after long journeyings reached Macedonia again.

It was only the north of India through which Alex- ander had marched. He had not really conquered the people, although he left Greek garrisons and Greek rulers behind him, and when he died the people quickly revolted against the rule of Macedonia. So all trace of Alexander and his conquests soon disappeared from India. His altars have vanished and the names of the cities which he founded have been changed. But for long ages the deeds of the great "Secunder," as they called him, lived in the memory of the Indians.

And it is since the time of Alexander that the people of the West have known something of the wonderful land in the East with which they had traded through many centuries.

CHAPTER 2

HOW BRAVE MEN WENT SAILING UPON UNKNOWN SEAS

CENTURIES passed. India suffered many changes. It was overrun and conquered by Mohammedans and Turks. Its temples were destroyed, its people slain or carried away captive.

But through all the changes, through battle and war, revolt and massacre, the trade of India continued, and merchants vied with each other for the possession of it. Nearly all of it, however, was in the hands of Arabs and Moors, and, except for the merchants of Venice, few Christians had a share in it The Moors brought the goods from India in their ships to Suez. There camels were laden, and by them the merchandise was carried through Egypt to Alexandria. And at Alexandria the Venetian merchants took it in their ships to the ports of the Mediterranean.

The old trade-routes to India and the East were by the Red Sea and the Persian Gulf. These being in the hands of heathen peoples, Christian sailors and adventurers turned their thoughts ever more and more to the finding of a new way to the East.

In the fifteenth century the Portuguese were a great and powerful people. Among the bold adventurers who sailed the unknown seas their sailors were the most daring. And one of their greatest sailors and explorers was Prince Henry the Navigator, the fifth son of King John I. He did much to make his country great in trade, and was called the "Father of Discovery."

Prince Henry sent out many expeditions, and although the new way to India was not discovered, many new lands and islands were, and were added to Portugal. The Pope, too, who was very powerful in those days, issued a Bull, as it was called, saying that all lands and islands which might be discovered between Cape Bojador on the west coast of Africa and the shores of India should belong to Portugal for ever.

After Prince Henry died, the people of Portugal still eagerly sought for the new way to India. But for many a long year they sought in vain. It was in 1486 that a sailor called Bartholomew Diaz set out. Southward and southward he sailed down the coast of Africa until, driven by storms, he and his sailors lost sight of land. For thirteen days they sailed they knew not whither, battered by wind and waves, fleeing with furled sails before the storm. At length the sea grew calm again, the wind sank. Then Diaz turned eastward, hoping soon to come in sight of the coast of Africa, from which he had been driven.

For many days he sailed along and saw no land. So he turned northward, and at length came in sight of what is now known as Flesh Bay.

Without knowing it Diaz had rounded the Cape of Good Hope. He had passed it so far to the south as to be out of sight of laud. The adventurous sailor still sailed on, not knowing where he was, for now land lay west of him instead of east. After many days he reached the mouth of a great river. It is now known as the Great Fish River. Here he was obliged to turn back, for his sailors, fearful of the unknown regions into which they were drifting, were unwilling to go further.

Once again the Cape was safely rounded, and Diaz, mindful of the dangers through which he had passed there, called it the Cape of Storms.

But when they at length reached home and King John II heard the tale, he named it the Cape of Good Hope, for now he had good hope that the long-looked-for road to India was indeed discovered.

For some years after this King John was unable to send out any more expeditions. And meanwhile Christopher Columbus, sailing westward, discovered what he believed to be the further shore of India, and claimed it for the King of Spain. Then the King of Spain asked the Pope to grant to him all lands which might be discovered by sailing westward even as he had granted to the King of Portugal all lands which might be discovered by sailing eastward. This being done, the King of Spain and the King of Portugal agreed to share between them all the world which might be still unknown.

After the discovery of Columbus, the Portuguese became more eager than ever to find the way to India. King John ordered three ships to be built, tall and strong such as should be able to withstand the storms of the Cape of Good Hope. Bartholomew Diaz himself made the plans, for none knew better what stout ships were needful, for only he and his men in all the world had passed that stormy cape.

Before the ships were ready to sail, King John died. His cousin Manuel, however, who succeeded him, was as eager as his uncle had been that Portugal should be great and prosperous, so he ordered that the ships should be finished.

A noble called Vasco da Gama was chosen to be leader of the expedition, and one bright spring day in 1497 the King and courtiers, monks and priests, and a great crowd of people followed Vasco da Gama and his sailors to the shore, and there took leave of them with prayers and cheers and thunder of guns. But the rejoicings were mingled with such tears and sobs of those who thought never to see their dear ones again, that the place was afterwards called the Shore of Tears.

When the last farewell had been said, these brave men sailed out into unknown seas, there to meet many dangers and perils, danger from wind and waves, from fierce dark savage peoples, from strange and terrible beasts.

Nor were the dangers all from without. Within the ships were dangers too. For the men grew weary of the long struggle with storms, fearful of what might lie before them, and prayed their leader to return. "But nay," he cried sternly, "if I saw an hundred deaths before mine eyes, yet would I sail right on. To India we shall go, or die."

Then, seeing that they could not move their commander to return, the sailors mutinied. But Vasco da Gama was both bold and quick. Seizing the ringleaders, he loaded them with fetters on hands and feet, and thrust them prisoner into the darkness of the hold. Then taking the chart and all the instruments which helped him to find his way across the pathless ocean, he cast them overboard. "I need neither pilot nor guide, but God alone," he cried. "If so we merit it, He will lead us safely to our journey's end."

Thus the fearless leader crushed the mutiny, and continued his voyage.

CHAPTER 3

SUCCESS AT LAST

HAVING escaped many dangers, having suffered many misfortunes, having lost two of his ships, Vasco da Gama did at length, after a voyage of eleven months, reach India. The joy was great when at last the long-looked-for shore appeared, and the dream of years was realised.

Vasco da Gama landed some little distance from the town of Calicut, which was well known in Europe as the place from which calico came. But until that day no European had set foot there.

But even now that India was reached, the dangers were not over. The Arab merchants, who had grown rich through their Indian trade, were jealous of the newcomers. So they tried to make mischief between the Zamorin or King of Calicut and the Portuguese. They told him that these white-faced people had come not to trade, but to conquer his land.

By treachery the Arabs succeeded in taking Vasco prisoner. The Indians who helped them, however, did not dare to put him to death, and he was at length set free. But he never forgave the Moors and Arabs for their treachery, and swore to be avenged upon them.

Meanwhile, however, they had so set the people of Calicut against the Portuguese, that it was only with great difficulty that Vasco could gather a small cargo of spices and drugs. With this he was forced to be content, and set sail for home.

But, as the wind was against them, the Portuguese, instead of sailing straight across the Indian Ocean, sailed northward along the Indian coast until they came to Cannanore. Here the King received them with great honour. For it had been foretold long ago by one of his wise men that the whole of India should one day be ruled by a distant King whose people should be white, and who would do great harm to those who were not their friends. So the King of Cannanore and his counsellors, making sure that these were the white men who were one day to rule India, made haste to be friendly.

To Vasco da Gama the King sent such great presents of pepper and cinnamon, clove, mace. ginger, and all kinds of spice, that the ships could not hold it, and Vasco was obliged at last to refuse to take more.

Thus at length, well rewarded for their troubles and toil, Vasco and his men sailed home. And after more adventures and dangers they reached Lisbon in safety.

Great were the rejoicings when the ships arrived. For they had been gone two and a half years, and both King and people had given up all hope of their return.

Now that at length the route to India was found, Portugal was raised to great importance. Her kings took the proud title of "Lords of the Conquest, Navigation and Commerce of Ethiopia, Arabia, Persia, and China," and for a hundred years the flag of Portugal was honoured on every sea.

Vasco da Gama was richly rewarded. He was given the title of Dom or lord. And when every one was paid, and the widows and children of those who had lost their lives in the adventure had been cared for, it was found that the Portuguese had still made sixty times as much as they had spent on fitting out the expedition.

The way to India once found, the Portuguese were not slow to make use of it. Again and again expeditions set out, and soon not only traders went, but soldiers also, to guard them from the hatred and spite of the Moors and Arabs.

The Portuguese made friendly treaties with the Kings of Cannanore and Cochin. They built factories and left factors and clerks there, and thus the commerce of Europe with India was begun. These factories were not what we mean now by factories. They were not places where goods were made, but simply trading stations, houses where the natives brought their goods and exchanged them for other goods. A factor means really one who does trade for another.

With the King of Calicut and with the Moors there was war. Whenever the Portuguese met a Calicut vessel they attacked it, took what they wanted of the cargo, sunk or burned the ship, and killed all the sailors.

Those were terrible times, and trade was not the peaceful thing that it is now. It was almost as dangerous and quite as exciting as war, and traders were often little better than pirates.

When Vasco da Gama made his second voyage to India he avenged himself terribly on the Moors, as he had vowed to do. Coming upon a fleet of twenty-four of their vessels he captured them all. After having taken as much of the cargo as he wanted, he cut off the hands, noses, and ears of the sailors. He then tied their feet together, and so that they might not untie the knots with their teeth, he ordered his men to knock them out. Lastly he set fire to the ships, and with sails set to the shore, he let them drift homeward with their ghastly crew.

That a wise brave man like Vasco da Gama should be so brutal seems terrible now, but in those fierce times he seemed only to be taking a just revenge.

In a very short time the little Portuguese trading stations grew into forts, the forts grew into towns, where Christian churches rose beside Moslem mosques and Hindu temples; Portuguese vessels cruised along the coasts attacking any ship, no matter of what country, which might dare to enter Indian waters; Portuguese viceroys held sway on Indian shores from the

Gulf of Cambay to what is now Madras; and the trade with Burma and Bengal, with China and Japan and all the East was in their hands. All this was not brought about without much fighting and many wars. But Portugal in those days was strong and powerful, and all over the world her merchants were as much feared for their might as envied for their wealth.

CHAPTER 4

HOW THE DUTCH AND THE ENGLISH SET FORTH TO INDIA

THE Dutch, like the Portuguese, were a sea-going people. For many years they had been the carriers of Europe. Every year their ships came to Lisbon, there to buy the goods which the Portuguese brought from India, and from Lisbon they carried them to every port in Europe.

At that time the Dutch were under the rule of Spain, but in 1572 they revolted, and in 1580 they declared themselves free. In the same year King Philip II. of Spain made himself King of Portugal too, and soon afterwards he ordered that all Dutch ships found in Spanish waters should be seized, and that all Spanish and Portugese ports should be closed to them. In this way he hoped to ruin the trade of the rebellious Dutchmen. But they, finding that they could no longer trade with Lisbon, resolved to seek the way to India for themselves and trade direct.

Just as the Moors had tried to keep the Portuguese out of India, so now the Portuguese tried to keep out the Dutch, and there was much fighting both by land and sea. Even after the Dutch reached India the Portuguese tried to make mischief between them and the natives. These were no true traders, they said, but spies come to view the land, and later they would return in force to conquer it.

But the Dutch were hardy and brave, and not easily discouraged. In 1588 the Spanish Armada was defeated by the English, and after that Spain had few ships and men to spare for fighting in distant seas. So by degrees the Dutch drove the Portuguese out of their colonies and took them for themselves. They founded a Dutch East India Company, which grew wealthy and powerful, and soon all the trade of the East was in their hands. Holland had more ships than all the kingdoms of Europe put together. The Dutch ruled the sea. Dutch harbours and colonies were scattered over all the globe, and Holland became the market of the world.

The spice trade especially, the Dutch were determined to keep in their own hands. And in order to make this easier, they destroyed whole plantations of spice and pepper trees. For that and other reasons the price of pepper was soon doubled. At one bound it rose from three shillings to six and eight shillings.

Up to this time the English merchants had been content to buy from the Dutch as the Dutch had before been content to buy from the Portuguese. But now they were angry, and resolved in their turn to go to India direct for what they wanted.

So it was in a tiny matter like the price of pepper that the seeds of our great Indian Empire were sown.

On the 22nd September 1599 the Lord Mayor of London with the aldermen and merchants met together and resolved to form an East India Company. "Induced thereto," the old paper says, "by the successe of the viage performed by the Duche nation," they to resolved "to venter in the pretended voyage to the Easte Indias, the whiche it maie pleased the Lord to prosper."

But although meantime there were several meetings "annent the said viage," it was not until about a year and a half later that the first ships set out. For there were many preparations to make, the Queen's consent (it was Queen Elizabeth who ruled England in those days) had to be given, money had to be found, ships had to be bought and fitted out, and even the fact that we might be going to make peace with Spain had to be thought about.

But at last, on the 13th of February 1601, five ships set sail from Woolwich. They were named the *Red Dragon*, the *Hector*, the *Ascension*, the *Susan*, and the *Guest*. Although they set sail in February, there was so little wind that they did not reach Dartmouth until Easter. But at length a fair wind blew, and the bold adventurers sailed out into the ocean and were soon beyond sight of land.

Many adventures befell them; storms and calms, sea-fights and sickness they endured. At last so many of the men were ill with scurvy, that on reaching Table Bay they resolved to land. Scurvy is brought on by eating salt meat and no fresh vegetables. It was a new disease, having never been heard of until Vasco de Gama took his first voyage to India. In those days they had not found out how to carry fresh food on ships. The men had to live for the most part on salted meat and biscuits, and they nearly always fell ill.

So now Captain James Lancaster, who was in charge of the expedition, thought that if he could land and find fresh food for his men, they would soon be better. The people who lived in Africa were all black savages. When they saw these strange ships come into the bay they gathered round to look and wonder. Then James Lancaster made signs to them to bring him sheep and oxen. "He spake to them in the Cattels Language, which was never changed at the confusion of Babell, which was Moathe for Oken and Kine, and Baa for Sheepe. Which language the people understood very well without an Interpreter," says an old writer. "The third day after our coming into this Bay the people brought downe Beefes and Muttons, which we bought of them for pieces of old Iron hoopes, as two pieces of eight inches a piece for an Oxe, and one piece of eight inches for a Sheepe, with which they seemed to be well contented."

For seven weeks the Englishmen stayed in Table Bay. By the end of that time nearly every one was well again, and they sailed on their way once more. After passing through more adventures and dangers, and seeing many strange and wonderful sights, they at length came to Achin in the island of Sumatra.

Queen Elizabeth had sent a letter to the King of Achin, and now Captain James Lancaster went on shore to deliver it. He was received with great honour and was led to the King's court riding upon an elephant, while a band marched in front of him making a fearful noise with drums and trumpets.

After Lancaster had presented his letter there were banquets and cockfights in his honour, with much present giving, without which no Eastern could do any business. Then after a great deal of talking the King wrote an answer to the Queen, and a treaty of peace and agreement to trade was made.

Although the Eastern kings were heathen, they were not wild savages like the people of Africa. This king was a Mohammedan, and when the Englishmen came to take leave of him, he turned to Captain Lancaster and asked, "Do you know the Psalms of David?"

"Yes," replied Lancaster, greatly astonished, "we say them every day."

"Then," said the King, "I and these nobles about me will sing a psalm to God for your prosperity."

So very solemnly this heathen king and his nobles sang a psalm. It was a curious sight. There in the gorgeous heathen palace stood the few rough English sailors. Around them singing crowded the dark-faced Indians, clad in brilliant dresses of red and yellow, glittering with jewels and gold.

When the psalm was ended, the King again turned to Lancaster. "Now," he said, "I would hear you too sing a psalm in your own language."

So in turn the Englishmen sang. And the psalm being finished, they took their leave.

From Achin Lancaster sailed on to other places, for he had not enough goods yet to carry home. And he felt that it would be little to his credit did he sail back with empty ships, when all the Indies lay before him from which to gather precious stores.

Like the Dutch, the English had to deal with the Portuguese, for they "had a deligent eye over every steppe we trode," and by force and treachery they tried to keep the English from trading with the Indians.

The Englishmen, however, got the better of the Portuguese, and at last, well laden with spices, they sailed homeward. But on the way they met with great and terrible storms, so that "the ship drave up and downe in the sea like a wrake" and "Hayle and snow and sleetie cold weather" took the heart out of them, until the master and crew were in despair, and gave up hope of ever returning home.

But at length the sea grew calmer, and after months of toil and peril they reached the safe shelter of the Downs, and gave thanks to God for all the perils and dangers passed.

Such were the beginnings of British trade with India. And although some of the ships and many of the men had been lost on the voyage, the Company had made much money. King James of Scotland was now upon the throne. He made Captain Lancaster a knight as a reward for the brave way in which he had steered his ships and led his men through storms and dangers.

CHAPTER 5

THE FIRST BRITISH AMBASSADOR GOES TO THE COURT OF THE EMPEROR OF INDIA

WHEN the first English adventurers sailed to India, the Dutch treated them kindly. But very soon the struggle between English and Dutch became as fierce as the struggle between Portuguese and Dutch had been. For a long time Bantam, in the island of Java, was the only town where the English had a factory, and in some places the natives were so afraid of the Dutch that they would not trade at all with the English. Yet the English trade grew, and almost every year the East India Company sent out new ships. Now, instead of giving the vessels names like the *Red Dragon* or the *Roebuck*, they called them the *Peppercorn*, the *Clove, Trades Increase*, or *Merchant's Hope*.

Finding it difficult to found factories in the East India Islands, the English next tried to do so on the mainland. The first factory which they succeeded in founding was at Surat. Sir John Hawkins, one of our great English "sea-dogs", was the first to land there. But he found it very hard to trade, for the Portuguese were still in power. There he met "a proud Portugal" who "tearmed King James King of Fishermen and of an Island of no import. And a fig for his commission!" There, he says, "I could not peepe out of doores for fear of the Portugals, who in troops lay lurking in the byways to give me assault to murther me."

The kings of India were not like the savages of Africa and America. They were great potentates living in splendour, although the people over whom they ruled were miserably poor. They sat upon golden thrones studded with jewels, they bathed in golden baths and ate and drank from golden vessels. Their clothes glittered with gems and were fringed with pearls.

The Great Mogul was the chief of these kings. He was Emperor of all India, and the other kings paid him money or tribute, and acknowledged him as "overlord." Over those states which lay near his capital at Delhi he ruled like a tyrant, but over distant states he had little power. There the kings did very much as they liked.

It was often very difficult for the English to get leave to trade in the dominions of these proud tyrants. For the curious thing was that in those days they thought little of Europeans. The King of Great Britain was to them merely the ruler of a tiny, barbarous and poor island somewhere far away in the cold bleak seas. It seemed to them that they were being very kind, and that they stooped from their high state in listening at all to the wishes of such a petty prince.

The Great Mogul was haughtiest of all. He was quite willing to take presents from the King, but he was not willing to do anything in return. So at last it was decided to send an ambassador from England to live at the court of the Great Mogul to see what he could do for British trade.

Sir Thomas Roe was the first ambassador who went from Great Britain to India. He was also the first gentleman who had to do with the East India Company. For at the beginning they had said, "We purpose not to emploie anie gent in any place of charge, but to sort our business with men of our own quality." Even now, although many of them thought that it was a good idea to send an ambassador to the court of the Great Mogul, they were very fearful lest the King should send some gay favourite of his own who would cost them much and do but little good. "A mere merchaunt" would do just as well and cost them far less they thought. But in the end the choice fell on Sir Thomas, who was both courtly and wise. He was used to kings and courts, he was courteous and polite, but he made up his mind that the dusky Eastern kings should treat him with honour, as became a messenger from a ruler greater than themselves.

So from the beginning Sir Thomas held himself proudly. "If it seeme to any," he says, "that shall heare of my first carriadge that I was eyther too stiff, to Punctuall, too high, or to Prodigall, lett them Consider I was to repayre a ruynd house and to make streight that which was crooked."

When Sir Thomas Roe landed at Surat he did so in great state. The ships in the harbour were decked with flags and streamers, cannon fired, and before him went a boat in which a band played, and when he reached the shore eighty soldiers marched around him as a bodyguard.

Roe's troubles soon began. The Mogul was not at Surat, but at Ajmere, about six hundred miles away. To get there the ambassador needed men and horses. But the Mogul's servants and the governor of Surat delayed and delayed. They said one thing and did another. They promised easily and broke their promises just as easily. "In all their dealinges ther was new falshood," says Sir Thomas, and in every way they tried to hinder him.

At last he overcame all the difficulties and started on his long journey. The country through which he passed he found miserable and barren. The towns and villages were all built of mud, and the houses were so miserable and dirty that there was hardly one fit to rest in. To-day that same region is rich and fertile. Green fields and gardens are everywhere to be seen, and well-built prosperous towns and villages are dotted about.

The journey was long and difficult, and Sir Thomas fell ill on the way and did not reach Ajmere until Christmas. A few days later he went to see the Great Mogul.

Sir Thomas kept a diary and wrote many letters when he was in India. In them he tells of much that he did and saw, and of the troubles he had to bear.

Among other things he tells us exactly how the Great Mogul spent his days. Every morning as soon as he rose he showed himself at a window called the Jharukha" or interview window. Here the people came to do honour to him. While he worshipped the sun they cried out, "Live, O great king! O great king, life and health!" Here too the Great Mogul gave and received presents, letting them down and pulling them up with silken cords, From this window he reviewed his troops and gave judgments, never refusing the poorest man's complaint, says Roe. At nine he went away, and at midday he came back to the window again to watch elephants and other wild beasts fight. After watching for an hour or two he went away to sleep. At four he appeared at the Durbar or audience, when he received the great men who came to visit him, and did the business of the state. Then after supper he went into another room which was very private, and where only the most honoured guests were allowed to come.

Every day was exactly the same as another, so that Sir Thomas said it seemed to him that the Great Mogul was as much a slave as the poorest in the land. For had he failed to show himself for one day the people would have broken out into riots.

It was at the Durbar that Roe first saw the Mogul. When eastern princes came to visit the Mogul they bowed themselves to the earth and fell upon their faces. But Sir Thomas refused to do any such thing. He was a stiff-necked Englishman with a very good idea of the importance of the King and of himself. He was quite willing to be as polite and courteous to the Great Mogul as he would have been to a European prince, but no more.

Sir Thomas found the Mogul seated upon his throne, and surrounded by his nobles who stood in three rows, one below the other. As Sir Thomas passed each row he bowed, and at last stood before the Mogul.

The Mogul was very gracious to Sir Thomas and seemed pleased with the presents which he had brought. What pleased him most was an English sword and scarf, although, pretending to be very grand and dignified, he did not pay much attention to them at the time. But at ten o'clock that night he sent for one of Roe's servants to come to show him how to wear the sword in English fashion. Then he strutted up and down the hall, drawing it and flourishing it like a child with a new toy, and for a month he was never seen without it.

But although the Great Mogul continued to be very friendly, Sir Thomas could get little out of him but empty promises. Neither he, nor his sons, nor his counsellors were willing to bind themselves to any treaty.

For nearly three years Sir Thomas remained in India. He followed the court about from place to place, seeing many wonderful and some dreadful sights. At last, finding that he could do but little good, he begged to be allowed to go home. This he soon did, carrying with him a letter from the Great Mogul to King James full of flowery language but little more.

"SIR THOMAS STOOD BEFORE THE MOGUL."

It almost seemed as if Sir Thomas had failed in what he had been sent to do. But this was not so. He failed indeed to get any real treaty signed, but when he left India the position of the British there was far better than it had been. They were allowed to trade much more freely, and Sir Thomas had shown that Britons must be treated with dignity and that they were not to be trampled upon. Above all, danger from Portuguese rivals was over.

CHAPTER 6

THE HATRED OF THE DUTCH

YEAR by year the jealousy of the Dutch grew, until in 1622 it burst out in bitter hatred.

At Ambonia in the Molucca Islands the Dutch had built a large factory and a strong fort where they had two hundred soldiers.

The British too, had a factory there. But it was only an ordinary house without fortifications or defences of any kind. They had no soldiers, and they numbered only eighteen traders.

Suddenly one day the Dutch seized all the British, loaded them with fetters, and threw them into dark and horrible dungeons. They did this pretending to have discovered a plot to take the fort.

Next day the prisoners were brought out of their dungeons one by one, and were told to confess their share in the plot. But there had been no plot, so the Englishmen could confess nothing. Then in the horrible manner of the time, the Dutch tortured them to make them confess. With the rack, with fire and with water, the poor wretches were tortured, until at last, in order to free themselves from the torment, they were willing to confess to anything, and to say any words which might be put into their mouths.

But although they confessed to a plot, and accused each other of taking part in it, that did not save them. They were all condemned to death. Once more, heavily laden with fetters, they were thrown into the dungeons there to await death.

Now some courage came back to the poor men. They were not afraid to die, but they wanted their fellow-countrymen to know that they died innocent of any plot against the Dutch. One of them had a Prayer Book, and in that he wrote a few pitiful words. "We be judged to death," he wrote, "this 5th of March Anno 1622. We through torment, were constrained to speak that which we never meant nor once imagined. They tortured us with that extreme torture of fire and water that flesh and blood could not endure it. But this we take upon our deaths, that they have put us to death guiltless of that we are accused. And so farewell. Written in the dark."

Through the long sad night the prisoners comforted each other. They asked pardon, and freely forgave each other for the false things they had said, then praying and singing psalms they waited for the morning.

When day came they were led out to die. Guarded by soldiers they were marched through the town so that all might see the triumph of the Dutch. Then they were led to the place of execution and their heads were cut off.

When the news of this cruelty reached England, the people were filled with horror and anger. But the matter was hushed and the Dutch were never punished for what they had done.

The rivalry between the two nations now became even more bitter than before. For a time the Dutch were the more successful, and instead of making money the English East India Company began to lose it. As they had been driven from Java, they became very anxious to set up a factory on the east coast of India. But from place to place they were hunted about by the jealousy of the Dutch and the dislike of the Indian rulers.

At last a trader called Day bought a piece of land from one of the native princes. This was the first land owned by the British in India. It was only a narrow strip of sandy beach about five miles long and one wide, but it was a foothold. Here in 1639, the British built a fort which they called Fort St. George. This was the beginning of the town of Madras.

Day had many difficulties to fight. Both the Portuguese and the Dutch had factories near Fort St. George, and the Dutch especially tried to make the Indian prince forbid the British to build a fort. The East India Company too had at this time little money to spare, and some of the Council were not well pleased at the thought of all that would be spent on a fort, which they thought of as unnecessary.

But at last every difficulty was overcome. The little British fortress was finished. Brass cannon shone at the loopholes and the Union Jack floated from the walls.

Within the walls were houses for all the company's staff. And here they lived very much like a large family. In the morning they went to chapel and heard prayers read by the chaplain; they all dined and supped together in the great hall, and when work was over for the day they met in their pleasant gardens and amused themselves with shooting, archery and bowls. But in those days no ladies were allowed to go to India, and if any of the men were married they had to leave their wives at home.

Outside the walls of Madras a native town grew up quickly. For the Hindu people soon heard of the new town, and, as they were not allowed to live within its walls, they built their little mud and bamboo huts without. Under the trees which grew near they set up their looms, and wove and printed in the open air the cottons and muslins which the British were so eager to buy. So the fort where the British lived came to be called "white town" and the native village without the walls was called "black town."

By degrees the British got leave in various ways to build other factories. One day the daughter of the Great Mogul set herself on fire and was very badly burned. The native doctors did not know what to do. So the British doctor from Surat was sent for. He cured the Princess very quickly, and the mogul was so delighted that he told the doctor to ask for whatever reward he liked. He asked that the Company might be allowed to build a factory at the town of Hooghly on the Hooghly river. This they were allowed to do, but they were forbidden to build a fort or to land a cannon.

Then when Charles II. of England married Princess Catherine of Portugal, he received the Island of Bombay as part of her dowry. But Charles did not care for a possession which was so far away, and which was said, too, to be damp and unhealthy. So he gave it to the Company for £10 a year. The Portuguese, who had already settled there, were not very pleased at being handed over to the British. But they soon found that they were free, or freer than they had been under their own king, and they settled down quietly. The Company strengthened the castle which the Portuguese had already built. And although the climate was so unhealthy that no European could live there for more than three years at a time, the harbour was so good that in about sixteen years it became the chief trading port on the west coast. Now it is the second city in the Empire, and one of the healthiest towns in India. For the marshes have been drained and the forests of cocoa-nut trees, which kept off the fresh sea breezes and made the town unhealthy, have been removed.

About this time the Great Mogul tried to make every one in India Mohammedan, as he was. He persecuted those who would not become Mohammedan, and among other things he made them pay a heavy tax. The Nawab, as a native prince who ruled for the Mogul was called, now insisted that the British at Hooghly should pay the tax too. This, and other oppressions of the Nawab, at last became so unbearable that the British left Hooghly and went back to Madras.

Soon after this the Nawab of Bengal was changed, and the new ruler asked the British to return. They did go back, but not to Hooghly. Instead they built their factory at a little village twenty miles nearer the sea, but it was still without any fortifications. A few years later the persecutions of the Mogul became so bad that the Hindus rebelled. Then the Nawab gave the British leave to fortify their factory against the rebels. So they built a fort called Fort William. They also bought three small native villages. And this was the beginning of the beautiful city of Calcutta which is now the capital of British India.

Thus at the beginning of the eighteenth century the British had a firm footing in India. They had three fortresses—Bombay castle on the west, Fort St. George at Madras on the south-east coast, and Fort William at Calcutta in the north-east—in this way commanding trade from all directions.

Soon, from these three towns as head-quarters, other factories began to be dotted all along the coast and far inland. These three towns were called Presidency towns as a head or president of the Company lived in each. Under the president there were merchants, factors, writers and apprentices. Every week the president and four or five of the chief men met in council to arrange the business of the Company. Within the walls of the factory or fort the president was as powerful as the Viceroy of India is to-day. Every

British factory was ruled by British law as if it had been a town at home. And out of such small beginnings our great Indian Empire has grown. To-day a large part of the west coast is still called the Bombay Presidency, and in the north is the Bengal Presidency. They take their names from those far-off days when the Company first began to trade.

CHAPTER 7

THE FRENCH IN INDIA

WHILE year by year British trade in India had been growing greater, another European country had begun to try and gain a footing there too. This country was France. And in India, as in Canada, the French and British were to struggle for power.

Almost at the same time as the British founded their East India Company, the French founded one too. But for one reason or another they were not fortunate, and it was not until many years later, in 1688, that the first French factory was set up in India. This, like the first of the British, was at Surat.

But besides having all the usual difficulties with native princes to get over, the French had to fight the British and also the Dutch. Both by land and sea the Dutch beat the French, and drove them again and again out of the factories which they tried to found.

At length the French bought a piece of ground from a native prince about a hundred miles south of Madras. Here they built a fort and town, which they called Pondicherry, and at last began to prosper.

The French settlement was very small, and they were everywhere surrounded by enemies. So the leader, whose name was Martin, asked the native prince to allow him to have some native soldiers. The native prince was very friendly, so he gladly agreed to give him three hundred men. Martin was the first white man who had thought of making use of the Indians as soldiers, and it was found that when they were properly drilled and had European officers they made splendid soldiers.

Besides drilling these men and teaching them order and obedience, Martin made use of them as colonists. He gave each man a piece of land and encouraged him to till it, and to set up looms and weave muslins and other stuffs which he wanted for his trade.

For nineteen years the French colony prospered. But the Dutch were determined to hunt them out. At home they were fighting with the French, and one day they appeared before Pondicherry with a fleet and an army large enough to conquer a whole state.

The French were helpless. Against this great army there were thirty-four Frenchmen, three hundred native soldiers and only six guns. Yet, few though they were, Martin and his brave men held out for twelve days. But the Dutch surrounded them both by land and sea. They were starving, and gave in.

The French, having promised that they would all go back to France, were allowed to march out of their well-defended little fort with all the honours of war, The native soldiers were allowed to go where they liked.

This seemed to be the end of French power in India. But four years later peace was signed between the Dutch and the French, and one of the conditions of the treaty was that Pondicherry should be given back to the French. This was done, and once more the French returned.

For some years after this the British, Dutch and French traders lived almost in peace. But all around them, among the native princes, there was constant war. Kingdoms rose and fell, rulers mounted thrones and were hurled again from them, "The country being all in warrs and broyles."

Then in 1744 the French and British went to war at home. This was the war of the Austrian succession. And not content with fighting at home, they carried the war into their colonies.

At this time a very clever Frenchman named Dupleix was governor of Pondicherry. He did not want to fight, and he tried to make the British president at Madras agree to keep peace, even though their kings at home were fighting.

But the British president knew that ships and men were being sent from home to help him to fight the French, and he would not agree to be at peace. Dupleix was in despair. He had begun to fortify Pondicherry, but the walls were not even finished. He had only a garrison of about four hundred men and one little warship. He knew that when the British ships with their heavy guns arrived, his town would be pounded to bits in a very short time.

The French had always kept on very good terms with the native rulers. So now in his need Dupleix asked the Nawab Anwaru-Din to help him. Dupleix had more than once helped the Nawab when he had been in trouble, and now he sent him handsome presents. Anwaru-Din was so pleased that he at once sent a message to the governor of Madras saying that he would not allow the French to be hurt, and that he would allow no fighting within his dominions.

The British thought they were not strong enough to fight the French and the Nawab too, so they left Pondicherry alone. The British fleet, when it arrived, sailed away again, and, instead of taking the town, the Admiral contented himself with attacking French trading ships on the sea, in that way doing a great deal of damage to the French trade.

Meanwhile another Frenchman named La Bourdonnais had, with great difficulty, got together a little fleet of ships, and he came sailing to help Dupleix.

One July day the French and the British fleets met. From four o'clock until the sun went down, they fought. But although the French lost most men, it was neither a defeat nor a victory for either side. Yet next day, in spite of the fact that they had the best of the position, the British sailed away and left Madras to its fate, Had they but known it, La Bourdonnais, although he was making such a brave show, had food left for only one day, and nearly all his powder and shot was done.

The news of the battle reached Madras together with the news that the British fleet had sailed away, and that soon the French might be expected to appear before the town.

Madras was almost as unprotected as Pondicherry. The walls were weak and there were scarcely three hundred men to protect them. So the British president, in his turn, sent to the Nawab for help. But, forgetting that it was useless to ask anything of a native without giving him something, the president sent him no present. This the Nawab looked upon as almost an insult, and he did nothing.

It was not long before the French ships appeared before Madras, and after three days' fighting the president gave in. Everything became the property of the French, the town, the fort, and all that they contained, gold, silver and merchandise. But La Bourdonnais agreed that the British should be allowed to buy back their town for a large sum of money. Meanwhile they became prisoners of war. The Union Jack was hauled down and the French lilies floated in its place.

But now, as soon as he heard of what had happened, Anwaru-Din was angry. Although he had done nothing to help the British, he had not meant that they should be driven away altogether. So the very day that Madras surrendered he sent an angry message to Dupleix saying that if he did not stop fighting at once he would send an army against Pondicherry.

Dupleix knew very well how to manage the Indians. So he told Anwaru-Din that if the town were taken it should be given to him. With this the Nawab was quite satisfied.

Thus Madras was promised to two people. La Bourdonnais had promised to sell it back to the British, and Dupleix had promised it to the Nawab.

Neither Dupleix nor La Bourdonnais would give way, and these two men who had worked so well for their country, quarrelled.

And while they quarrelled a great storm shattered the French fleet, and much of the spoil taken from Madras was lost. At last, with such of his ships as remained to him, La Bourdonnais sailed home. "My part is taken regarding Madras," he wrote. "I give it up to you. I have signed the treaty. It is for you to keep my word. I am so disgusted with this wretched Madras, that I would give an arm never to have set foot in it."

Meanwhile the Nawab had been growing more and more angry as week after week went past, and he saw no sign of Dupleix keeping his promise and handing Madras over to him. Dupleix did really mean to keep his promise, but he wanted to destroy the walls first. He wanted to drive the British out of India altogether, and he saw that unless the fortifications were destroyed, it would be easy for the Nawab to give the town back to the British, if he liked, and the French would be no better off than before.

While the quarrel with La Bourdonnais went on, Dupleix could do nothing. Now it was too late, for the angry Nawab had gathered his troops and was marching against Madras, which was by this time garrisoned with French soldiers.

Anwaru-Din made no doubt of crushing these impudent, faithless Europeans, as with ten thousand soldiers, with horses and elephants, and all the glitter and splendour of an eastern army, he closed round Madras.

To meet this host, four hundred men, bringing with them two cannon, marched out of the town.

The white turbaned, brilliant, Indian horsemen dashed upon this handful of men. But suddenly the French ranks divided. There was a roar of cannon and the foremost Indian horsemen lay dead.

The Indians were startled and confused, and before they could recover, the Frenchmen had fired again and yet again.

Such warfare as this was new to the Indian warriors. They indeed had cannon, but they were so old and clumsy that they were more dangerous to those who fired them than to anyone else. And if they were fired once in a quarter of an hour, that seemed to them very quick work. They had never dreamed that it was possible to fire a cannon four or five times in a minute.

Panic seized upon the Indian horsemen. They turned and fled. Soon the whole army was fleeing in utter rout, leaving their tents and baggage in the hands of the French.

For the first time the Indians had found out how powerful the white-faced traders were, and as they fled they told their tale of wonder, and spread their terror everywhere around.

Dupleix now took complete possession of Madras. It was neither given to the Nawab nor sold back to the British. Many of the British were taken prisoner to Pondicherry. Others fled in the night and took refuge at Fort St. David, another British station about twelve miles south of Pondicherry. Among these was a young man named Robert Clive.

CHAPTER 8

THE SIEGE OF ARCOT

IT seemed now as if Dupleix would sweep all before him and that France should be supreme in India. Against him were only a few hundred Britons in Fort St. David, but the little fort held out against attack after attack. At last came the news that at home peace had been signed between France and Britain, that fighting must cease, and that by the treaty of Aix-la-Chapelle Madras was given back to Britain.

Thus after five years of fighting things seemed to be exactly as they had been at the beginning. But there was this difference, the French and the British, instead of trading peacefully side by side, had now become deadly enemies. Each was eager to banish the other from India. And from now too, the Europeans were no longer merely traders. They had begun to make their power felt by the Indian princes. Now, instead of being somewhat despised and looked down upon, the Europeans were looked up to, and in their quarrels with each other, the native princes became eager to have European help. They had learned what European soldiers could do. The native princes were nearly always fighting. Now a very bitter quarrel began and as the French and the British took different sides, they were soon fighting as badly as before, although France and Britain were at peace. They were therefore not supposed to be fighting against each other, but only helping the native princes.

The part of India over which Anwaru-Din ruled was called the Carnatic, and his capital was Arcot. The Lord of the Deccan, another part of India, was Anwaru-Din's overlord. In 1748 the Lord of the Deccan died. At once his sons and relatives began to fight for the crown, and Dupleix resolved to help one of these relatives called Muzaffar Jang and his friend Chanda Sahib. Anwaru-Din was on the other side, and in a great battle he was killed, his army was scattered and his son, Mohammed Ali, fled to the British for protection.

With the help of the French, Muzaffar Jang was at length proclaimed Lord of the Deccan, and Chanda Sahib Nawab of the Carnatic. A great durbar or meeting was held, to which all the nobles of the Deccan gathered to honour their new lord. And amid the brilliant throng was Dupleix, dressed in a gorgeous Mohammedan robe. It was he who sat in the place of greatest honour. It was upon him that the honours and powers were heaped. He was made governor of all the land south of the river Kristna, he was given the title of Commander of Seven Thousand Horses, he was allowed to carry the ensign of the fish among his standards, this being

considered one of the greatest honours in India, it was he indeed who was
the true ruler of Deccan. Near the town of Gingi a monument was raised
in his honour. Upon it in French, Persian, Malabar, and Hindustani was
written the story of his greatness. And round it grew up a town called
Dupleix-Fathabad, or the place of the victory of Dupleix.

In a few months the French, from being simple traders, had become
the greatest power in the land, and the British looked on helplessly. In all
that wide land they possessed only Madras and Fort St. David. Mohammed Ali was their only friend, and he was now besieged by the French
and by the army of Chanda Sahib. For Dupleix had made up his mind to
destroy Mohammed Ali. He felt that French rule in the Deccan was not
safe or sure so long as he lived. The British, on the other hand, had made
up their minds to protect him as their only hope of checking French power.

So to the help of Mohammed Ali they sent all the soldiers they could.
Among them went Robert Clive.

Robert Clive had come out to India as a clerk or writer in the service
of the Company. He did not like his work and he was very unhappy in it.
He was never meant to be a clerk, but was a born soldier. Since the taking
of Madras by La Bourdonnais, Clive has seen some fighting. He had been
made an ensign, but when the fighting was over he had to go back to his
hated desk. Now again officers were needed, and Clive was given the rank
of captain and sent to Trichinopoli where Mohammed Ali was besieged.

But Clive had no sooner arrived at Trichinopoli than he saw that there
was little to be done there. He saw that it would be far better to attack the
capital, Arcot, which had been left almost unguarded. So he hurried back
to Madras, told the president what he thought, and begged for soldiers.

The president saw that Clive's plan was worth trying, and he gave him
all the soldiers that he could spare, keeping only a hundred men to guard
Madras and fifty for Fort St. David. So with two hundred British and three
hundred Sepoys, as the native soldiers were now called, the young captain
was soon hurrying along the road to Arcot.

He had need of haste he knew, if his going was to be of any use. So
when a fearful storm of thunder and lightning and rain overtook them,
he still marched on. When the Indian spies who were watching saw this,
they were filled with terror and admiration for the leader who was not
afraid even of the "voice of heaven." They fled to Arcot with the tale, and
so frightened the garrison there that they rushed from the fort leaving guns
and ammunition behind them. Thus without needing to fire a shot, clive
and his men marched into the town between lines of admiring, wondering
Indians, and took possession of the fort.

But Clive knew that he could not hope to be long left in possession
undisturbed. So he gathered food, strengthened the fort, and made ready
in every way he could to stand a siege. Hearing, too, that the runaway

garrison were still lurking near, he marched out one night and attacked them, killing many and scattering the rest to the hills beyond, without losing a single man himself.

Soon the news of the taking of Arcot reached Trichinopoli. And, just as Clive had hoped and expected, Chanda Sahib sent back many of his soldiers to recover his capital from the British. In this way he weakened his chance of taking Trichinopoli, for he had not enough soldiers to besiege both places properly at once.

Soon an army of ten thousand men, French and Indian, came marching to surround the handful of daring Britons. They made no doubt of crushing them very quickly. The town of Arcot had neither walls nor moat to protect it. Round the fort itself the moat had been long neglected. In places it was dried up or bridged over, and the handful of British soldiers shut up there were led by a clerk of twenty-five.

But the fort held out week after week. Side by side Briton and Indian fought, catching something of the spirit of splendid daring and patient courage which filled their leader. Food grew scarce. There was little but rice left, and not enough of that. And now the sepoys showed the stuff they were made of. They came to Clive, not to grumble, but to tell him that they could live on the water that the rice was boiled in, and that the British soldiers might have all the rice itself.

So week by week the little garrison, Indian and Briton, stood shoulder to shoulder, and worked and fought together. At length the enemy made a breach in the wall, and their leader sent a message asking him to surrender. But Clive replied with scorn. He had no thought of giving in.

The Indian leader then determined to make a last grand attack on the fort. He chose the 24th of November, which is a great Mohammedan feast day. It is said that the soul of any good Mohammedan who dies fighting on that day will be carried straight to paradise. All night riotous sounds came from the Indian camp where the men were working themselves into a fury of religious zeal. They prepared for battle by making themselves mad with a kind of drug called bhang. And when morning came they were reckless of death, eager for the joys of paradise. With wild prayers and feasting they had become so frantic that they knew not what they did.

But Clive had been warned by spies, and he, too, made ready for the attack. All night he worked, and at last, towards morning, utterly worn out, he threw himself upon his bed, dressed as he was, to try and snatch a few hours' rest.

With the first streak of dawn the alarm was given. Clive started from his bed. All was in readiness. Every man was at his post.

The stars had faded in the pale sky, and in the cool, dim light a sea of dark-faced fanatics surged and howled round the fort, their white turbans tossing like foaming crested waves on dark water. Armoured elephants, wearing iron plates upon their foreheads, with which to batter down the gates, led the way. On came the seething mass with mad, triumphant yells.

Suddenly, from the walls, the sharp crack of musketry rang out. It was unexpected; it was sharp and hot. For every spare musket in the fort was ready loaded, and men lay behind the shooters handing loaded guns to them as quickly as might be. The oncoming wave reeled. Stung to madness the elephants turned. In wild terror they broke through the crowding ranks behind them, trampling many to death.

It was not only the gates which were attacked. Where the moat was dry, the besiegers swarmed thick and fast. But the fire from the fort was sharp and steady, and man after man went down. Part of the half-ruined moat was still full of water, and here the besiegers launched a heavily laden raft. The defenders fired upon it again and again, but each time they missed it. It had nearly crossed the ditch when Clive, noticing how badly the gunners were aiming, took one of the guns himself. He aimed coolly and well, hit the raft and overturned it. In a minute the water was full of wounded, struggling, drowning men. The few who could swim made for the bank and escaped.

For an hour the fight lasted. Then the enemy fled, leaving four hundred dead and dying round the walls. Of the defenders, four only were killed and two wounded.

Now and again during the day the firing was renewed, but at last it ceased. The night passed in silence, and when the next morning dawned the enemy's camp was empty. They had fled in the darkness leaving their guns and ammunition behind. The siege, which had lasted seven weeks, was at an end.

The siege of Arcot was the turning point of British fortunes in India. From there Clive marched out to win battle after battle. Many a time he led his men with reckless almost careless daring. But he seemed to bear a charmed life. Again and again by daring he won. Again and again his genius and his bravery carried him through the greatest of dangers.

All this time the French and the British were only supposed to be helping the native rulers. But the real struggle was not between two Indian princes, but between France and Britain, between Clive and Dupleix. They were both great men, but Dupleix was a statesman, not a soldier. He had to trust to others to carry out his plans and orders. And the French generals were old and stupid, while against them they had a "heaven born general" young and eager.

Soon it was the British, not the French, who were all-powerful in the Carnatic. The French nawab, Chanda Sahib, was killed, and the British nawab, Mohammed Ali, was put in his place.

Then Clive, weary of war, and much in need of rest, sailed home. He had set out for India a poor and rather despised boy. He came home a

"Clive fired one of the guns himself."

hero and conqueror of world-wide fame. Wherever he went he was fêted and cheered. The directors of the Company called him "General" Clive although he was really only a captain. They loaded him with thanks, and presented him with a sword, the hilt of which was set with diamonds.

Meanwhile Dupleix, Clive's great rival, struggled on trying to win back for France what had been lost. But he got little help or encouragement from home. His king did not care and did not understand what a great kingdom Dupleix had won, and with proper help might have been able to keep for him,—a kingdom larger than the whole of France itself. So at last Dupleix was called home in disgrace. For a few years he lived miserably, and at last died forsaken. Three days before he died he wrote, "I have given my youth, my fortune, my life, to enrich my country in Asia. My services are treated as fables, and I as the vilest of mankind." La Bourdonnais too had been disgraced and imprisoned, and died in misery.

They were not the last men who were to earn world-wide fame in India, and disgrace at home.

CHAPTER 9

THE BLACK HOLE

WHILE these things were passing in the Carnatic the British at Calcutta had been trading quietly, growing rich and prosperous, at peace with their Nawab. But in 1959 the Nawab died. He was succeeded by his adopted grandson, Suraj-ud-Daula, or, as the British soldiers and sailors called him, "Sir Roger Dowler."

Suraj-ud-Daula was bad and cruel. He hated the British and soon managed to pick a quarrel with them. He had several make-believe reasons for quarrelling with them. One was that they had sheltered some of his enemies. Another was that they had begun to strengthen their fortifications without leave. The real reason was that he believed that the British were very wealthy and that vast treasure was gathered in Calcutta. He was greedy as well as cruel, and he wanted this treasure for himself.

He now suddenly seized a factory at Cossimbazar which was near his capital. He plundered it and took all the British prisoner. Among his prisoners was a young man named Warren Hastings. Of him we shall hear again.

Having plundered and destroyed Cossimbazar, Suraj-ud-Daula marched in haste against Calcutta with fifty thousand men.

The walls of Calcutta were weak, the guns on Fort William old and very nearly useless. Around the town was a half-dug ditch, begun years before but never finished. Of the garrison not two hundred were British soldiers and not ten of them had ever been in battle in their lives. Among them was no man with knowledge or courage enough to be a leader.

When the news that the Nawab and his army were coming reached Calcutta, everything was thrown into wild disorder. Batteries and earthworks were built in haste, but without any real knowledge of how best to defend the fort. Messages were sent to the Dutch and French factories near, begging for help. It was refused.

On Wednesday, the 16th June, the Nawab's army swarmed into the native town around the fort, and fighting began. It was a fight at fearful odds. There were less than two hundred white men against a rabble of fifty thousand dark-faced heathen, mad with hate and greed.

On Friday night the women and children, of whom there were many in the fort, were all taken safely to the ships which lay in the river. With them, to their shame be it said, went the president and the captain of the garrison. Then they sailed away leaving their comrades in the fort to their fate. In vain those left behind made signs to the ships to stop and wait. It would be dangerous the captain said, and he sailed on. Had they waited another tide every man in the fort might have been saved.

Forsaken by their leader, the garrison chose a Mr. Holwell to be their head, and for two days longer the fort held out. But although Mr. Holwell did his best he was neither a soldier nor a leader of men. He could not keep the men in order, or make them fight and hope when all was hopeless. They became unruly, broke into the store, and were soon helplessly drunk. The Nawab's soldiers swarmed everywhere. Resistance was useless, and on Sunday afternoon the British yielded.

There were one hundred and forty-six prisoners, among them on lady who had refused to leave her husband. For a short time they were gathered in the square of the barracks. There they stood and talked together, watching the flames from the burning town leap and flicker against the fast darkening sky, listening to the wild cries which reached them from without, and wondering what would be their fate.

Then suddenly they were all ordered to march into a small prison house at the end of the barracks. This was a room about eighteen feet square with only two tiny barred windows. It was known as the Black Hole.

At first the prisoners refused to believe the order. But striking them with their clubs, driving them at the sword's point, the Indians forced them in. Then the door was shut.

In the tiny space there was no room to move. The prisoners were packed tightly against each other. The evening was hot and still. The breathless heat of an Indian summer night was made worse by the flames and smoke from the burning buildings all around. In a few minutes the heat became intolerable. Gasping for breath, raging with thirst, the wretched prisoners beat upon the door and shouted to their jailers to let them out. They threatened, they implored, all in vain.

Instead of opening the door the natives brought lighted torches to the windows, so that they might the better see the agonies of their victims.

"Water, water," gasped the stifling wretches. Water at last was brought, but the skins in which it was carried could not be passed through the bars of the windows. It was poured into hats, it was spilled upon the ground, men fought for it like beasts, trampling each other down in their eagerness for a few drops which in the end only made their thirst the more unbearable.

Then came the bitter cry for "Air, air." Those who were far from the windows struggled and fought like demons to get near. Some fainted and slipping to the ground were trampled to death. Many went mad with horror and pain, and in the morning when at last the long agony was over, only twenty-three moaning, stricken spectres crept out. Among them was the lady who would not leave her husband. But she was alone, for he lay among the dead.

CHAPTER 10

THE BATTLE OF PLASSEY

CLIVE did not stay long in England. He soon returned to India with the rank of Lieutenant-Colonel, and upon the terrible day of the Black Hole he landed again at Fort St. David. But in those days news travelled slowly, and it was not until August that the people of Madras heard of the cruel deed. Then, gathering an army of fifteen thousand sepoys and nine hundred British soldiers, Clive set out to avenge the death of his fellow-countrymen. The little army went by sea, with Admiral Watson in command of the ships. Madras is a long way from Calcutta, and sailing in those days was a slow business, for the ships were often at the mercy of the winds. And although Clive set out in October, it was December before he reached Bengal.

Clive lost no time in attacking the Nawab, and very soon Calcutta was in his hands. The Nawab marched to meet Clive with thousands of soldiers, with elephants, and horses, and cannon, which were both great and many. But Clive, with his little army, beat the Nawab so thoroughly that he was soon suing for peace.

This Clive granted, the Nawab promising to restore all that he had stolen from Calcutta and to give more privileges to the British than they had had before. This was not a great triumph, and it hardly seemed as if Suraj-ud-Daula was punished enough for his cruel treatment of the British. But perhaps Clive thought that it would be difficult to force him to do more as he was so powerful.

But Suraj-ud-Daula was treacherous as well as cruel. He had made promises, which he never meant to keep, merely in order to gain peace. Now he tried in every way that he could to wriggle out of these promises. He secretly wrote to the French and asked them to help him against the British. He did all manner of things, changing his mind again and again.

Clive at last grew tired of the Nawab's lying and wriggling, and made up his mind to put an end to it.

Britain and France were again at war, for the Seven Years' War had begun. So Clive now besieged the French factory at Chandranagor. The French fought bravely, but Clive was more than a match for them, and after ten days they gave in.

With the loss of Chandranagor French power in the north of India was at an end. For more than eighty years they had struggled with their rivals, the British, in trade. Now that struggle was over. Clive, having thus put an end to Suraj-ud-Daula's hope of help from the French, next turned to crush him.

Suraj-ud-Daula, who was wicked and treacherous, was hated by all, and many even of his own followers were ready to betray him. Now, although it does not seem a very fine thing to do, Clive joined with these traitors in order to bring about the downfall of the Nawab.

Mir Jafar, the commander-in-chief of Suraj-ud-Daula's army, was one of the discontented. Now Clive promised to make him Nawab if he would betray his master.

Another of the traitors was Omi Chand, a very wealthy and very greedy Indian banker.

Clive plotted with these men, and all was nearly arranged when Omi Chand threatened to tell the Nawab all about it, unless the British promised him an immense sum of money for himself.

Omi Chand was as wicked and as treacherous as Suraj-ud-Daula, "The greatest villain upon earth," Clive calls him, and he thought that the best way to meet his lying was by lying. Clive had two treaties drawn up. One was written upon red paper and one on white. The one on red paper was only a sham treaty and in it Omi Chand was promised all that he wanted. In the other, which was the real treaty, his name was not mentioned. All the council signed both treaties except Admiral Watson. He would have nothing to do with the deceit. But Clive was not to be stopped, and some one else signed Admiral Watson's name for him.

Of course this was wrong, and this deed shows like a black blot among all the splendid and brave acts of Clive's life. But the position of the British in India was full of danger. They were but a handful of white men in the midst of millions of dark foes, and Clive thought that it was only by meeting treachery with treachery that he could save them all from death. And he was never ashamed of it.

Long afterward, when his enemies accused him of this deed, he said that he would do it again if the need came, "Yes, a hundred times!"

When Clive was ready to fight he sent a letter to Suraj-ud-Daula which made him see that he could no longer trifle. Then he gathered his army and marched to Plassey to meet the foe.

But now Mir Jafar, who had quarrelled with the Nawab, made friends or seemed to make friends with him again. Clive knew not what to do. Was Mir Jafar going to keep his word and help him, or was he not? Without his help the risk of a battle was almost too great. If the British lost, it would mean an end to their power in Bengal. In this difficulty Clive called a council of war, and asked his officers what they would advise. "Shall we attack or shall we wait for more help?" he asked. Seven officers voted to attack, thirteen, Clive himself among them, voted to wait.

So it was settled. There was to be no battle.

After the council was over, Clive went away by himself and walked about for an hour thinking it all out again. As he was sitting under some trees still in doubt, a letter from Mir Jafar was brought to him. In this letter Mir Jafar swore that he was still faithful to Clive. This might be true or it might be false, but Clive had made up his mind. He would fight, come what would. Returning to the camp he gave orders to march.

At six o'clock in the morning of 23rd June 1757, the battle of Plassey began, and by five in the afternoon the huge Indian army with elephants and camels, horses and clumsy ox-drawn cannon, was fleeing from the field. Mir Jafar had not helped Clive, neither, however, had he helped the Nawab. He had stood aloof waiting to see which side would win. And when the Nawab's most trusty general was killed and the Nawab himself in despair threw his turban on the ground at Mir Jafar's feet, begging for help, Mir Jafar soothed him with soft words. But instead of helping him he sent more messages to Clive.

Plassey is one of the most important of Indian battles. It is not important because of the number killed—on Clive's side there were only twenty-two and on the Nawab's five or six hundred. It is important because at one blow it gave to Britain the whole of Bengal, for Mir Jafar was merely a tool in the hands of the British.

When the battle was over Mir Jafar was not sure how Clive would receive him. But Clive had got all that he wanted, so he greeted him as the new Nawab, and with the usual great ceremonies he was seated upon the throne.

But when Omi Chand appeared to receive his reward it was very different. Clive, although he was many years in India, never learned to speak any of the Indian tongues. So now he turned to his secretary, "It is time to undeceive Omi Chand," he said.

"Omi Chand," said the secretary, "the red treaty is a trick. You are to have nothing."

The greedy banker could hardly believe his ears. Already he had been gloating over his ill-gotten gains. The shock of disappointment was too great. He fell back fainting in the arms of his servants. He never recovered from the bitter blow. His mind was so shattered that he became quite foolish and childish and died some months later.

Suraj-ud-Daula fell into the hands of Mir Jafar who put his late master cruelly to death. In this the British had no hand.

But Mir Jafar, although he had got what he wanted, and was Nawab, soon found that it was not all a bed of roses. He had to pay immense sums of money to the British as a reward for having made him Nawab. To get this money he ground his people cruelly. Used as they were to tyranny, the oppression of Mir Jafar was more than even they could bear, and they rebelled. Outside enemies threatened him too, and to put the rebellion down and drive out these enemies, Mir Jafar was obliged to ask help from Clive.

Clive gave the help but demanded still more money. So the Nawab was little better off than before.

Mir Jafar raged with wrath. He felt that he was a mere puppet and that the British were the real rulers and he longed to be rid of them. So now he began to plot with the Dutch, who still had a factory in Bengal. But in a fight both by land and sea the British beat the Dutch. The power of Holland in India was destroyed for ever, and the British were supreme in Bengal.

CHAPTER 11

TIMES OF MISRULE

IN 1760 Clive again sailed home. He was only thirty-five but he was
now enormously rich, a great soldier and conqueror, and perhaps the
most famous man of his day. In England he was received with joy. Honours were heaped upon him. He was made a peer and became Lord Clive,
Baron Plassey.

But while Clive was being fêted and feasted at home, Bengal was
quickly sinking into a state of fearful confusion.

Many of the British hated Mir Jafar, as he had been leader of the troops
at the time of the Black Hole. They made up their minds to depose him
and to set his son-in-law, Mir Cossim, in his place. This they very quickly
did. But they soon found that the new Nawab was not so easily dealt with
as the old, and quarrels began.

Mir Jafar had been old and feeble and a mere tool in the hands of the
British. Mir Cossim was young and clever, and anxious to free himself
from their power. They, it was true, had put him on the throne, but he
had paid them for that, and now he tried to show that he meant to rule
without their help or their interference.

The officers of the Company were very badly paid, some of them indeed
receiving only a few pounds a year. It was quite impossible to live in India
on such small sums. So, instead of attending to the work of the Company
only, every officer became a merchant on his own account, and bought
and sold to the natives. This was called private trading and was forbidden
by the directors of the Company, but in spite of that it was still continued.

Soon all the trade of Bengal was in the hands of the white people, and
the native traders were ruined. For they had to pay duty while the British
were allowed to trade everywhere without paying duty. If a boat hoisted a
British flag, or a trader showed a Company's passport, he could buy and
sell as he pleased. The Company's officers made a great deal of money by
selling passes to people who had nothing to do with the Company. They
forced the natives to sell their goods cheaply, and made them pay dear for
what they bought. In fact, they did as they liked. The whole land was filled
with misery, and these years have been called the darkest in the history of
British rule in India.

The native people were utterly miserable, and the Nawab, too, became
poor, for a great deal of his money came from customs and duties. And
now all the money from them went into the pockets of the Company's
servants. Mir Cossim tried his best to make the British stop this inland

trade and keep to the trade between India and Europe. This made the British traders angry, and both sides prepared for war.

Mir Cossim gathered his army at his capital, Monghyr, on the Ganges. He thus lay between the British at Calcutta and at Patna, where they had another factory.

The factory at Patna had no defences, and seeing themselves cut off from their friends, the British attacked and took the town of Patna, hoping to be able to defend themselves there. But they were not strong enough to keep the town, and the soldiers of the Nawab attacked and took it again from them. Many of the British were killed, and all the rest were taken prisoner.

Mir Cossim rejoiced greatly at this victory, but when the British at Calcutta heard of it they were very wrathful, and, to punish Mir Cossim, they dethroned him, and again made Mir Jafar Nawab.

Mir Jafar was by this time not only old, but ill and foolish. The traders, however, did not want a real ruler, they only wanted a figure-head, and he did as well as any other.

The British now sent an army against Mir Cossim, and as they marched towards Patna, they beat his soldiers again and again. Then a massacre, quite as bad as that of the Black Hole, took place. For the Nawab, mad with anger, ordered his men to kill all the British prisoners.

They had been shut up in a large house built round a square. Now three of the chief of them were brought out into this square, and there cruelly put to death. The Indians were then ordered to fire upon the rest who were quite unarmed. Against their fierce, dark fores, the white men defended themselves as best they could with bottles, sticks, bits of furniture, anything that they could find. But it was all useless, and soon the last man fell dead and their bodies were thrown into a well.

So the war began, and soon the whole country was ablaze, for the Nawab of Oudh and the Great Mogul both joined with Mir Cossim against the British. But they, when they heard of the massacre of Patna, swept with an avenging army over the land. For months the war lasted, and ended with the battle of Buxar. This was a victory as important as Plassey, for it made the British secure as the greatest power in India.

The Nawab of Oudh and the Great Mogul made Peace. Utterly vanquished, Mir Cossim fled, to die a few years later in wretched exile. Yet Mir Cossim, with all his cruelty, had been a clever ruler. He had tried to do the best for his own people, and much of the trouble and war was no doubt due to the misrule of the Company's officers, which was such "as to make the very name of Briton a shame."

In those days it took a long time for news to travel home. But now every ship brought news of battles, revolutions, loss. At length the directors began to be alarmed. Filled with grief at the awful news of Patna, wearied with constant tidings of disaster and war, they begged Lord Clive to go back to India again and try to bring order once more into the terrible confusion there. And in 1764 Clive sailed again for Bengal.

When Clive arrived he found that poor old Mir Jafar was dead, and that the Company had enthroned another Nawab. He found, too, everything in such confusion that he wept "for the lost fame of the British nation."

For eighteen months Clive stayed in India working hard. He had immense difficulties to fight—difficulties with the directors at home, with the Council in India, with the British soldiers and officers, with the natives and their rulers. But Clive had a will of iron, and all that one man could do, he did. He sent away the men who had done the worst deeds, he put down mutinies, he made treaties with the native rulers, and at last brought some sort of order out of wild disorder. But he made many enemies and wore his health out, and after eighteen months he again went home.

At first he was received with honour as before, and thanked for all that he had done. But soon his enemies began to attack him. They recalled again the deceit he had used against Omi Chand, they accused him of taking bribes, and of many other wicked deeds. Against these accusations Clive had to defend himself before the House of Commons. And he defended himself so well that the Commons, after much stormy debate, passed a resolution, "That Robert, Lord Clive, did render great and meritorious services to his country."

So Clive won the victory over his enemies. But the struggle had left him sad. He could not forget it. He suffered much, too, from a painful disease brought on by his hard life in India. And one day his friends found him dead, killed by his own hand. He was only forty-eight.

CHAPTER 12

WARREN HASTINGS, FIRST GOVERNOR-GENERAL

WHEN Clive left India, the British were really the rulers of all Bengal. There was still a Nawab, who lived in state, but he had really no power. He was a mere pretence. There was still a great Mogul, but he had neither land nor people, having been driven from his throne by the Afghans. He was even a greater pretence than the Nawab. But to him Clive agreed to pay £260,000 a year for the province in Bengal, thus still owning him as over-lord.

The revenues of Bengal, that is, all the money coming from taxes and customs, which are, as a rule, paid to the king or government, were now paid to the Company. But of this revenue they allowed the Nawab a salary, and paid the "tribute" to the Mogul.

But although the British were now, it might be said, the owners of the land, they did not trouble themselves about the happiness of the people. They took the money, but with it they took none of the duties of rulers, and soon the misery and poverty of the people became greater than before. The old Nawabs had perhaps spent their money badly, but they had at least spent it in the country. Now, that money was sent to China to buy tea and silks for the Company, or the officers of the Company took it home to spend in England. Thus, much of the wealth of India, instead of being "circulated," that is, passed from hand to hand among the people of India, was taken right out of the country, and the natives grew daily poorer and poorer.

A few only made money. These were the rent collectors. Now that the Nawab and his officers had no power, there was no one who could keep these native collectors in check. For the British did not know how much the land was worth, or how much rent the farmers paid, or ought to pay. They had to believe what the native collectors told them, and they, knowing this, ground the poor to the last farthing, paying what they chose to the Company, and growing rich themselves. In a few years the state of Bengal was again one of hopeless misery and confusion.

To make matters worse, in 1770 a fearful famine swept the land. Since then many famines have desolated India, but this was the first which had happened under British rule. Those in power were quite unprepared for it and knew not what to do.

The misery was awful. The people, worn to skeletons, died by thousands. They fell by the wayside, many lay unburied, poisoning the air, many were thrown into the rivers, until the waters became so foul that people dared not even eat the fish. The farmers sold their cattle and their tools to buy food. They even sold their children, until no one could be found to buy any more. They ate the leaves of the trees and the grass of the field, until there was no green thing left. Horrible diseases followed in the train of famine, and when at last the misery was over, a third of the people had died.

Many of those who still remained alive were ruined. It was impossible to gather rent from the starving and the penniless, and the Company received little or no money.

Now, at last, the directors at home saw that there must be a change. They had ceased from being mere merchants to become rulers, and they must take up the duties of rulers. Some one, with a mind beyond buying and selling, must be at the head of the government. So it was that in 1772, Warren Hastings was made Governor of Bengal and first Governor-General of India. As Governor-General he ruled not only over Bengal, but over Madras, Bombay, and all British possessions in India.

Warren Hastings had, you remember, been taken prisoner at Cossimbazar before the Black Hole tragedy. He had escaped from there, had fought at Plassey, and after a time gone home. He was now forty, and had been in the Company's service since the age of eighteen. He was not a soldier like Clive, he was a statesman. But, like Clive, who became a soldier without any training, he had become a statesman in the same way.

Clive, by the sword, had won a great empire. It was Hastings who kept it and made British rule in India sure.

When the new Governor came to Bengal he found a hard task before him. Everywhere there was confusion and oppression, and into this confusion he brought some rough order and justice. But in the doing of it he made many bitter enemies, enemies more bitter even than those Clive had made for himself. They hindered his work and made his life hard and difficult at the time, and they so blackened his name, that for a hundred years or more, people believed that Warren Hastings was a cruel, hard, unjust ruler. Now it has been shown that at a very difficult time he tried to do his best for the people of India and for the Company. And if he made mistakes, we may well believe that most men of his time would have made more.

One of the first things which Warren Hastings did was to place British collectors over the native collectors in order to try to find out how much rent the farmers really paid. And although, for want of money and proper helpers, he could not make things quite right, still he made them better.

He appointed judges to go round to the different towns and try those who had been thrown into prison, and often left there until they were almost forgotten. And although there were still Indian judges, a British judge, or collector, was always there to see that no cruel, barbarous punishment was carried out. In these, and other ways, Warren Hastings laid the foundations of British rule in India.

CHAPTER 13

WARREN HASTINGS—WAR

A LTHOUGH Hastings was no soldier he had battles to fight.
The Máráthas were a tribe of warlike Indians who every year swept over the land plundering and destroying. At first they were little more than mounted robbers, burning villages, wasting harvests, leaving a track of death and desolation behind them. But, as years went on, their power grew greater and greater. From a band of raiders they had grown to be a wealthy nation with a great army of well-drilled soldiers, and now they declared that they would conquer all India.

Another people, called the Rohillas, lived in Northern India. Rohilla means mountaineer. These mountaineers were a wild and warlike set of raiders who had come from the hills of Afghanistan and settled in Northern India. The land of which they had taken possession they called Rohilkhand, or the land of the Rohillas.

The Máráthas now made war on the Rohillas, and they, in their need, begged the Nawab of Oudh to help them. The Nawab promised to do this if they would pay him a large sum of money. This the Rohillas gladly said they would do, but when, with the Nawab's help, the Máráthas had been driven back, the Rohillas refused to pay.

For this the Nawab of Oudh resolved to punish them, and he asked Hastings to help him.

Hastings did not want to fight the Rohillas. Neither did he want to offend the Nawab of Oudh, who was now friendly. For Oudh lies next to Bengal, and Hastings was anxious to keep a friendly state between British India and the states around, where the princes were always fighting with each other. He wanted a "buffer state" in fact—a state to soften the blows which might be aimed at him.

He was also in need of money, for the directors kept writing letters saying, "Be just, govern well, but send us money." It was very hard to do both as things then were. So now Hastings decided that, although the British had no quarrel with the Rohillas, it would be well to help the people of Oudh to fight them if the Nawab would pay for the help. The Nawab readily promised a large sum of money, and the Company's soldiers were sent to help him against his enemies.

In a battle, which the British leader called the battle of St. George because it was fought on St. George's day, the Rohillas were utterly defeated and their leader slain.

The most of the fighting had as usual fallen to the share of the British.

But when the Rohillas had been beaten, when they broke and scattered, when before the glitterimg bayonets of the redcoats they swept forward in mad flight, then the men of Oudh dashed after them and began a fearful slaughter and pillage. The Rohillas left all their camp baggage behind, and while the men of Oudh plundered it, the British soldiers looked on somewhat scornful and discontented. "We have the honour of the day, these robbers the profit," they said as they saw the piles of gold and gems and rich stuffs laden upon camels and elephants to be carried back to Oudh.

But the Nawab paid the money he had promised, and the British had still a friendly state upon their borders.

Soon after this, three new councillors were sent out from England to Calcutta. These three men knew nothing of India or of the Indian people. They were jealous of Hastings and angry at the things he did. On the council there were now five—Hastings, and one friend, and these three. But as the three always voted together, and against the Governor and his friend, for some years they did very much as they liked, and although he was Governor-General, Hastings had really little power.

The natives soon began to see that Sahib Warren Hostein, as they called him, was no longer all powerful, and now one of them, who hated him, thought that the time was come when he might be overthrown.

This man was called Nuncomar. He was one of the most important among the natives, but he was a bad old man. Yet, although he was bad, he was clever and useful. So the directors told Hastings to employ him. Hastings did, but he disliked the old villain so much that he would rather have had nothing to do with him. Nuncomar knew this very well, and he became the Governor-General's deadly enemy.

Now, knowing that the three English gentlemen on the council were also the enemies of Hastings, Nuncomar wrote a letter to them, accusing Hastings of taking bribes and of other wickedness.

The letter was read at the council, and the three wished to bring Nuncomar in to hear what he had to say. The idea that these Englishmen should take the word of a wicked old Indian against one of themselves was more than Hastings could bear. He was very angry. "I will not suffer Nuncomar to appear before the board as my accuser," he said. "I know what belongs to my dignity as head of it. I will not sit at this board as a criminal, nor do I acknowledge the members as my judges." The Hastings left the room.

But the council would not be stopped, for they intended to ruin Hastings. When he had gone they made one of themselves chairman. Nuncomar was called in and questioned, and without more ado, and without any proof, they decided that Hastings had been guilty of bribery, and ordered him to repay the money he had taken.

Hastings of course refused. He did not admit that the three had any right to try or condemn him. And now other natives, terrified by the threats of Nuncomar, or bribed by his gold, made bold to accuse Hastings of all manner of cruelty and injustice. It seemed as if the authority of the Governor-General was at an end, and that there was nothing left for him but to give up his post and go home.

Then suddenly bad old Nuncomar was accused in his turn of forgery. To forge, in this sense, means to make something false, meaning, for some wicked reason, to pretend that it is real. Nuncomar had written out a paper making believe that it was written by someone else, and by this means had got a large sum of money to which he had no right.

This was only one of the many bad things which Nuncomar had done in his life. But it was enough. He was seized, put in prison, and tried before four British judges. They, finding that he was guilty, condemned him to death. Nowadays no man would be hanged for forgery, but in those days it was the law of Britain. It was not, however, the law among the Indians. Indeed lying and cheating did not seem to them to be very wicked.

Besides, Nuncomar was a Brahmin. The people of India were divided into castes or classes. Of the four chief castes, the highest and sacred class was the Brahmin. Next came the Royal caste, then the Merchant, and last, the Sudras or slave or servant caste. Each caste kept strictly to itself, and no man might marry any one who was not of his own caste, so they never became mixed. There are still castes in India, but the two middle classes have almost passed away, and the Sudras are split up into many sub-castes.

Brahmins were looked upon as sacred. If any one killed one even by mistake, the deed was looked upon with horror. Now the people of India found it hard to believe that their terrible white masters really meant, of set purpose, to put a Brahmin to death. They shuddered at the thought. But Nuncomar was hated by all, and no man, either British or Indian, not even his friends the three councillors, tried to save him.

And so one August morning a great crowd, brown-faced, bright-eyed, eager and wondering, gathered to see the end of the mighty Brahmin. Nuncomar marched to death in a calm and stately manner. His white head was bowed to a dishonoured grave, but he showed neither fear nor shame. Around him his friends wept and howled in an agony of farewell. But he stood unmoved. It was God's will, he said. And so with unshaken, eastern calm he died.

Breathless, wide eyed, the swaying crowd watched. Then when all was over, they fled shrieking with fear and horror, many in their terror plunging into the waters of the Hooghly. So great was the shock of this deed to the Indian mind that not a few Brahmin families fled from the town altogether, and for years it was looked upon as a place accursed.

The death of Nuncomar removed Hastings' greatest enemy, and because he was Hastings' enemy, and because one of the judges was Hastings' friend, it was said that the Governor-General had tried to have Nuncomar hanged.

But there was never any real reason for believing that. Nuncomar was hanged, not because he was Hastings' enemy, but because he was found guilty of forgery, and, according to the ideas of the time, was deserving of death.

One enemy was thus removed, yet Hastings had still to fight his councillors, who hated him as much or even more than before. But first one died, and then another, and the third and bitterest went home, leaving Hastings at last free to rule as he thought best.

Meantime, while Hastings was struggling to hold and rule British India, the government at home was flinging away the colonies on the other side of the world, for the war of American Independence had begun. The French helped the Americans, and war between Great Britain and France was declared. In India, too, there was war—in Bombay, Madras, and Bengal. There was war with the Máráthas; there was a war with a fierce Mohammedan leader called Hyder Ali, who, after deposing the rightful ruler of Mysore, swept the Carnatic with his terrible host, and swore to conquer all Southern India; there was war with the French who still possessed Pondicherry and some other towns. They helped the Máráthas, and still more they helped Hyder Ali. There were battles and sieges, defeats and victories.

But in 1782 Hyder Ali died, weary of warring against a powerful nation who might have been his friends and begging his son to make peace. The Máráthas, too, made peace, promising no more to help the enemies of the British, and in 1783, the news of the Peace of Versailles reached India and put an end to the war between French and British. So everywhere there was peace.

Then in 1785, after sixteen years of toil, Warren Hastings sailed home, leaving all India at rest.

At first Hastings was received with honour even as Clive had been. But his enemies had been at work, and before many months had passed, he was called to account for many of his deeds in India.

Hastings was impeached. In Great Britain to impeach means the process by which any man may be called upon by the Commons to defend himself before the house of Lords, for treason or other high crimes against the state.

Hastings was accused of cruelty, bribery, and misrule in many ways. He knew that the charges brought against him were for the most part untrue, or so twisted by hate as to seem much worse than they were, and he defended himself well. "Every department of the government which now exists in Bengal," he said, "is of my making. The office formed for the service of the revenue, the courts of civil and criminal justice were created by me. To sum up all, I kept these provinces in a state of peace, plenty, and safety, when every other member of the British Empire was full of wars and tumults. The valour of others won; I enlarged and gave shape to the dominion you hold there. I preserved it. I maintained the wars which were of your making or that of others, not of mine. I am accused of desolating the provinces in India which are the most flourishing of all the states in India. It was I who made them so. I gave you all; and you reward me with confiscation, disgrace, and a life of impeachment."

But in spite of all that Hastings might say, the trial dragged on for seven long years, filling his life with anxiety and trouble. But at last it came to an end, and the Lords declared Hastings "not guilty."

So the little, bald old man, who yet looked every inch a great man, went away to live quietly in his beautiful house, there to forget in a simple country life the glories and the troubles of the first Governor-General of India.

Once, many years later, when Parliament wished to know something about India, Hastings was called upon to attend. As he entered, the Commons received him with cheers. They listened respectfully to what he had to say, and, when he had finished, they rose to a man and stood bareheaded until he had passed from the hall. The Lords, too, treated him with like honour. So it seemed that even in his own day, his name was cleared. Yet there were many people who still believed that Hastings had been a cruel ruler. There are many who believe so to this day. Of course many things were done in those first years of British rule in India which would seem very terrible to us now. But we cannot judge those times as we would our own. And the people of Bengal did not think of Hastings as cruel. To them he was a deliverer rather than a tyrant. The men admired him, and the women sang their children to sleep with songs of the wealth and the might of the great Sahib Warren Hostein.

At last, at the great age of eighty-seven, Hastings died. To the end he was a kindly, cheerful, brave old man, taking an interest in all around him, and ruling his estate with as great care as he had ruled the broad lands of India.

CHAPTER 14

TIPPOO SULTAN

IN 1786, the year after Hastings came home, Lord Cornwallis went out to India as Governor-General and Commander-in-Chief. Unlike Hastings or the Governors before him, Lord Cornwallis was not in the service of the Company. He was the first Governor who had had nothing to do with the Company, and he was the first British peer to rule in India.

When Lord Cornwallis was first asked to go to India he refused. "I have no wish," he said, "to forsake my children and every comfort on this side of the grave to quarrel with the Supreme Government of India whatever it may be ; and finally to run the risk of being beaten by some Nawab and disgraced to all eternity." But at length, "with grief of heart," he consented to go.

Lord Cornwallis tried to keep the peace in India which Hastings had left. But he soon found himself forced into war with Tippoo Sultan the "tiger of Mysore," the son of the fierce Hyder Ali. At first Tippoo got the best of things, but in the end he was defeated. He was made to pay a large sum of money, and to give his two sons into the keeping of Lord Cornwallis as surety that he would keep the peace.

Cornwallis improved what Hastings had begun both as to the collecting of rents and the courts of justice. In this he helped by Mr. John Shore, who, when Lord Cornwallis went home, became for a short time Governor-General. He was made a baronet and later became Lord Teignmouth.

He was the first British ruler to put down one of the terrible Indian customs. This was called "sitting in dharna."

The life of a Brahmin was, as you remember, sacred, and any man who killed a Brahmin, or even caused his death without meaning it, was accursed. If a Brahmin therefore hated a Hindu for any cause, he simply sat down on his doorstep and refused to move, to eat, to drink, or to sleep. This was sitting in dharna.

The poor Hindu dared not go out or in, for fear of injuring the Brahmin. He dared not eat or drink, while the Brahmin fasted. He was caught like an animal in a trap. There was no escape, and he stayed there until he died of hunger and fear.

Lord Teignmouth made sitting in dharna a crime, and so one horrible custom was done away with.

The next Governor-General was Lord Wellesley, the elder brother of Arthur Wellesley who was later the great Duke of Wellington.

At this time Napoleon was conquering Egypt. To him was merely the first step towards India. He meant to conquer that too, and drive the British out. So the French became very busy in India. Tippoo Sultan, who had already been beaten by Lord Cornwallis, made a secret treaty with the French against the British. And both the Nizam of the Deccan and the Máráthas had large armies which were officered by Frenchmen. He quite expected any day to see French ships arrive to help to help Tippoo, or the Nizam, or the Máráthas.

Lord Wellesley, like nearly all the British of his day, hated the French and doubly hated Napoleon. And he was as full of dreams of driving the French out of India as Napoleon was of driving the British out. Lord Wellesley's thoughts were not at all turned to trade. He thought only of Empire, so his first desire was to get rid of the French officers and sepoys, and try to persuade the native rulers to make friends with the British, instead of with the French.

The Nizam was quite willing to be friends with the British, for he thought that they would protect him from the Máráthas, who were were now the strongest native power in all India, and who were eager to be still greater. So some British troops were sent to the Nizam's capital, Hyderabad. Then the French Sepoys were drawn up and told that they were no longer needed, and might go. But the sepoys had not been paid for months, and when they realised that they were being sent away without being paid, murmurs and then yells of discontent broke from the ranks. At the best of times they were a wild undisciplined army. Now they turned upon their French officers with such fury, that they fled to the British camp for refuge.

When the British heard what the riot was about, they paid the men. Greatly delighted at their unexpected good fortune, the sepoys scattered to their homes, and in a few hours the Nizam's French army had vanished. The officers were sent home to France. Wellesley promised to help the Nizam with British soldiers, should he be attacked, and the Nizam, on his side, promised not to go to war without first asking British consent. Thus one enemy was got rid of, and soon all fear of invasion by the French was over, for the news that Nelson had shattered their fleet in the Nile was brought to India.

Lord Wellesley next tried to make peace with the Máráthas. But the Máráthas were not at all anxious to make friends with the British. They were great and powerful, and feared no one. They were willing enough to help the British in battle if they were paid. But they were just as willing to help their enemies. They would fight for those who paid most.

With Tippoo there was no making friends at all. He hated the British too thoroughly, and in 1799 war with him began. Among the British leaders in this war was Colonel Arthur Wellesley.

Battles were fought in which Tippoo was beaten again and again, and at last he was shut up in his capital, Seringapatam.

"Tippoo Sultan's body was found buried beneath those of his followers."

Now Tippoo asked for peace. "Half your land and two million pounds," were Lord Wellesley's terms.

Beaten though he was, these terms were too hard for Tippoo. "Better," he cried, "to die like a soldier than to live a pensioned Nawab."

For a month the siege of Seringapatam lasted. Food was growing scarce in the British camp, when at last the town was stormed and taken.

The defenders fought bravely. Among them might be seen the short, stout figure of Tippoo clad in a dress of white and crimson. But at last, wounded in four places, he fell dead. Still his soldiers fought on, and when at last Seringapatam was taken, and the British flag floated upon the walls, his body was found buried beneath those of his followers.

Tippoo, being dead, and his capital taken, the whole of his land, called Mysore, fell into the hands of the British. Lord Wellesley divided it into three. Part he put under the rule of the Company, adding it to the Madras Presidency. Part he gave to the Nizam, who had helped him in the war, and part he formed into a new kingdom, and upon the throne he placed a little boy, a descendant of the king whom Hyder Ali had driven out. But this kingdom was really under British rule also.

Tippoo had been such a cruel ruler, that all over India there was rejoicing at his downfall, and the people made songs about it which were remembered and sung for long after.

> Fill the wine-cup fast for the storm is past,
> The tyrant Tippoo is slain at last,
> And victory smiles
> To reward the toils
> Of Britons once again.

> Let the trumpet sound, and the sound go round
> Along the bound of Eastern ground;
> Let the Cymbals clang
> With a merry merry bang,
> To the joys of the next campaign.

CHAPTER 15

WARRIOR CHIEFTAINS

WHEN Seringapatam was taken, letters from the Nawab of the Carnatic were found in Tippoo's palace. These letters showed that the Nawab had been plotting with Tippoo against the British. The Nawab was by this time very ill, almost dying indeed. So Lord Wellesley let him die in peace, then he told his family that their treachery had been found out, and that they could no longer be allowed to reign. He then took possession of the Carnatic and added it to the Madras Presidency. Thus all the coast of India, from Bengal to Cape Comorin (except Pondicherry), was now under British rule, and instead of stretching only a mile inland, in the south of the peninsula, British possessions stretched from sea to sea.

When Wellesley wrote home to tell of these triumphs, he said, remembering what had befallen Clive and Hastings, "I expect either to be hanged or rewarded. In either case I shall be satisfied, for an English gallows seems better than an Indian throne."

Wellesley, however, was not hanged. He was thanked and rewarded as the conqueror of the tyrant Tippoo. He was given a large sum of money and was made an Irish marquess. But, far from thinking this honour great, he called it his "gilt potato." Such was the pride of "the glorious little man" as his friends loved to call him.

The Maráthás were now the only great danger to British power in India. But they were a great danger. In the north, indeed, Oudh lay between British India and the land of the Maráthás. But the rule of the Nawab of Oudh had grown weak, and his native army became hardly more than a rabble of wild, mutinous soldiers, which cost him a great deal, and were of little use.

It was plain to Lord Wellesley, that in case of war, Oudh would be no defence. Besides the Maráthás, he feared the Afghans. He knew that often before they had descended from their mountains in conquering hordes. Now, he was afraid that once again they might attack Oudh, and from there sweep over Bengal.

So Lord Wellesley made the Nawab disband his soldiers, and in return for part of Oudh, he promised the Nawab to protect and fight for him. This was called the treaty of Lucknow, and by it, still more of India was added to the possessions of the Company.

But now the Maráthás began to quarrel among themselves, and at last their over-lord, who was called the Peshwá, fled to the British for protection.

Wellesley consented to help and protect him, but he demanded a great deal in return. The Peshwá was a weak young man, he was mad with fear, and was ready to consent to anything. And by the treaty of Bassein, signed on the 31st of December 1802, he became little else than the vassal of the Company.

The Peshwá gave up part of his land to the British; he promised not to go to war without British consent, to make no treaties whatsoever, and to take no Frenchmen or any other European into his service.

Lord Wellesley made much the same kind of treaty with several of the native princes. These treaties were called Subsidiary Alliances. A Subsidiary Alliance means a union for help. It generally means the union of a lesser or weaker power with a greater. The Indian princes paid a "subsidy" or sum of money, in return for which, the British promised them soldiers, help, and protection in time of war.

By making these treaties with native rulers, Wellesley hoped to force them to keep peace with each other, so that there might not only be peace within British India itself, but around its borders. But when the other Marátha chiefs heard of the treaty of Bassein, they were very angry. They would by no means suffer the overlordship of the Company, and they prepared to fight. One of their chief leaders was called Sindhia. He was young, vain, and proud. He had hoped one day to make himself Peshwá, but now his treaty had "taken the turban off his head," he said.

So Sindhia gathered an army and war began. This is called the second Maráthás war, as the first was fought in the time of Hastings.

At first the Maráthás did not seem sure of what to do. They marched back and forth with restless haste, now here, now there. But at last British and Indian forces met in a great battle at Assaye.

On the British side the leader was General Arthur Wellesley. He had only a small army, but, as so often before, the small British force beat a huge Indian army. Yet the fight was fierce, and when the battle was over, many of the British lay dead. But the Maráthás were fleeing from the field and the power of Sindhia was broken. Assaye was fought on the 23rd of September 1803, and is one of the greatest of Indian battles.

Other battles, other victories followed. In the north, in Hindustan, a British army fought against the French sepoy troops. There, too, they gained victory after victory, and at last, in a battle called Láswári the French sepoys, "who fought like demons rather than like heroes," were scattered forever.

The war had begun in September. It was over in December. On the 30th of that month, proud, vain Sindhia signed a treaty by which he owned the Company as over-lord.

Of all the Marátha chieftains, only one now refused to bend to British power. His name was Jeswant Rao Holkar. He had no dreams of Empire, but was a wild, free, raiding horseman like his forefathers, who had been a terror to India. From his capital of Indore he swept out with his robber horsemen, plundering and wasting at will.

Like the freebooting Scots of old, he and his men rode with a bottle of water and a bag of grain at their saddle-bow, caring not through what desolate country they passed. They lurked in the hills, they dashed upon the enemy unawares, slaughtering stragglers, but never meeting them face to face in open battle.

While the Maráthá war lasted, Holkar robbed and plundered at will. Now he was warned to keep within his own land, and cease from hurting the friends of the British.

But Holkar was proud and haughty. The length and breadth of India was his if he chose to claim it, and he threatened to burn towns and villages and slaughter the people by hundreds and thousands, if he were not allowed to take what he thought was his due, and rob and plunder where he pleased.

This was not to be endured, so a campaign against this haughty chieftain began.

At first, things went well. Then came disaster. A small British force under Colonel Monson found itself face to face with the whole of Holkar's army. Monson had food for only two days, and suddenly struck with fear he turned his back upon the enemy, and marched away.

Now came the wild chieftain's chance. His light horsemen followed and harrassed the retreating British, dashing upon them unawares, swooping down upon stragglers, surrounding and slaying those who went in search of food. Hungry and weary the British toiled on. The rains began and the rivers became swollen and impassable torrents. The roads were churned to seas of mud in which the wheels of the gun carriages sank axle deep, so they had to be left behind, and the ammunition destroyed. Wet and weary, covered with mud, stricken with sickness and famine, the men lost heart. The retreat became a rout, and after weeks of toil and suffering, a battered few reached Agra. "I have lost the flower of the army," writes the commander, "and how they are to be replaced at this hour, heaven only knows. I have to lament the loss of some of the finest young men and most promising of the army."

Holkar was now insolently triumphant and he began to besiege Delhi. But although he and his barbarous hosts swarmed around the ten miles of shattered wall and fallen rampart, they were bravely held at bay by the mere handful of determined men within. Then hearing that another British army was coming, he marched away, plundering and destroying as he went, the fires of burning villages and the blood of the slain marking the road by which he passed.

But Holkar's triumph was not for long. He, too, was beaten at last, and was sadly forced to bow the knee before the might of the British.

CHAPTER 16

THE MUTINY OF VELLORE

NOW suddenly there came an end to Wellesley's "forward policy" as it was called.

At first both the directors of the Company and the Parliament of Britain had been dazzled by the way in which he had brought prince after prince under the rule of the British. But the directors soon began to be annoyed and anxious too. It was trade and money that they wanted and not Empire. And instead of bringing in money, Lord Wellesley's wars swallowed it up. Then when the news that a bandit chieftain had destroyed a troop of British soldiers reached home, their patience gave out and their fears increased. They thought that the whole of the Maráthás would again rise. The idea, too, that India could only be ruled and kept in peace by forcing the native princes to bow to British law, was new to them. They did not see the need or the use of all Lord Wellesley's alliances with native rulers. They were tired of wars, so Lord Wellesley was recalled, and Lord Cornwallis sent out again as Governor-General.

Lord Wellesley returned home a sorely disappointed man. But he left his mark on Indian history. He founded the first college for officers of the Company at Calcutta, and he may be said to be the founder of the Indian Civil Service as it is to-day.

Lord Cornwallis came to India the second time with orders to free the princes from their treaties, and not to interfere any more in their quarrels with each other or with their subjects. But Cornwallis was now an old man, and he had not been more than ten weeks in India when he died. So the orders of the directors were not fully carried out, neither were the plans of Wellesley followed, and for two years, India was full of unrest. Holkar, on the eve of being conquered, was not conquered. All his lands were given back to him, and although he was made to promise not to disturb British possessions, he burned, plundered, and slaughtered in Rajputana, which was not under British protection. Holkar became more and more haughty and wild. He fought and drank until he made himself mad, and was at length shut up as a madman, until he died.

Yet within the borders of British India there had been peace for a time. Now suddenly it was broken.

The army officers at Madras began to think that the sepoys would look much better if they were all dressed alike. So the commander forbade them to wear earrings or "caste" marks. They were also ordered to shave their beards and trim their moustaches all alike, and worst of all they were made to give up wearing turbans, and told to wear a round black hat very much like what Europeans wore.

The Madras sepoys hated all these new orders, and to make matters worse, the other natives taunted them and laughed at them. They said that this was only a beginning, and that soon their white masters would force them to give up both caste and religion, and become Christian.

Stories of their discontent and anger were brought to the officers. But they did not believe them, or did not care, and they insisted that the new orders should be obeyed.

At the fortress of Vellore there lived the sons and relatives of Tippoo Sultan who had died, you remember, fighting against the British.

Here there was a garrison of less than four hundred British, and about fifteen thousand sepoys. And it was here that the anger of the sepoys broke out, encouraged, it is thought, by these Indian princes.

In the early dawn of a July morning, the sepoys silently and stealthily surrounded the barracks and the houses of the officers. All was still and quiet, when suddenly the hush of the morning was broken by the loud crack of guns. Through the windows of the barracks the sepoys poured volley after volley upon the sleeping men. Some of the officers, awakened by the noise, ran out of their houses to see what the matter was. They were shot down upon their doorsteps. Others were slaughtered in their beds. Before they could arm or defend themselves, every officer and half of the men were killed. But at last those who remained drove the mutineers back and took refuge in a jutting out part of the fortifications near the gateway. Here they awaited help, for they managed in some way to send news of the mutiny to Arcot.

In the meantime the flag of Tippoo was planted upon the walls, and the rebel sepoys were feasted by the native princes.

Help was not long in coming. Arcot was only eight miles away, and there was a brave and eager officer called Colonel Gillespie. As soon as he heard the news he gathered his men and galloped to Vellore as fast as he could. So eager was he that he outstripped his men and arrived first at the gates. He found them fast shut, and guarded by the mutineers. Alone thus against the enemy he was in great danger. But the British soldiers on the rampart, when they saw him, buckled their sword belts together into a long rope, and, letting it down over the wall, drew the gallant colonel up into safety.

Soon the troopers and two cannon arrived. They burst the gate open, rushed in and charged the mutineers. Everywhere the rebel sepoys gave way. They could not stand before British bayonets. Some fled, others were taken prisoner, and four hundred lay dead among the narrow streets of Vellore.

Colonel Gillespie with his quick action had broken the spirit of the mutiny. There were other riots both near and far, which showed how widespread had been the discontent. But the British were now on their guard, and the worst of the danger was over.

CHAPTER 17

THE GHURKAS

IT was in the year 1813 that a great change took place in the trade with India. As the Company became more and more rulers they became less and less traders. Indeed, instead of making money by their trade, they lost it. Yet they had a monopoly of the trade with India, and no one else was allowed to take part in it. Indeed no European was allowed to live in British India unless he held a post in the Company.

Besides this all the goods from or to India had to pass through the India House and the Port of London, and rising ports, such as Liverpool or Glasgow, had no hope of any profit from it. For not only had all the goods to go to London, but they had all to be carried in ships belonging to the Company.

At last the other merchants and shipowners of Great Britain began to be impatient of the Company's monopoly and wanted to share in the Indian trade. Napoleopn, too, was still trying to ruin British trade by shutting all the ports on the Continent to our goods. And the manufacturers and millowners of Lancashire and Yorkshire saw in India a new outlet for their wares.

So merchants and shipowners sent petitions to Parliament begging that the trade of India might be made free to all. The directors of the Company, although they were now losing money, were bitterly opposed to this. But the people of Britain won the day. In 1813, when the Charter of the Company was renewed, the ports of India were opened to all the merchants of Great Britain, who were free to trade from their own ports, and to carry goods in their own ships and not in those of the Company only. But people who wished to live in India had still to get a license from the Company. It was not until twenty years later that any one who liked was allowed to live there.

For some years after Lord Wellesley left, the plan of not interfering with the native states and their wars was followed in India. In Central India the wild Maráthás and a still wilder tribe called the Pindaris plundered and spoiled at will. Meantime the British were occupied fighting the French both at home and abroad. But that struggle was coming nearly to an end, when in 1813 Lord Hastings went to India as Governor-General and the new trade began. This Lord Hastings has of course nothing whatever to do with Warren Hastings, the first Governor-General.

At home Lord Hastings had been one of those who had found fault with Lord Wellesley's wars and conquests. But he had hardly arrived in

India when he was obliged to change his mind, for he found himself forced into war.

The Maráthás, the Pindaris, and a third people called the Ghurkas had made Central India a waste of misery. The Ghurkas were a warlike race from the mountains of Cashmere. They were small and hardy. From their mountains they had swept down upon the peaceful province of Nepal, which lies along the base of the Himalayas, and completely conquered the people. Having conquered the people of Nepal and taken their lands, the Ghurkas next attacked towns and villages within British borders.

At first, for the sake of peace, and to carry out the orders of the directors about not interfering, no notice was taken. Finding that the British did nothing, the Ghurkas grew bolder and bolder. At last their attacks became so bold, that just before Lord Hastings arrived, the governor sent a message to the Ghurka chief ordering him to give up the British lands of which he had taken possession.

The Ghurka chief, having so long done as he liked, refused. Then war began, for Lord Hastings saw that there would never be peace in India until these bandit chiefs were made to keep the peace even within their own borders.

The Ghurkas were very proud and haughty. They were a brave and fearless race of mountaineers, and they did not fear the British. "What power can fight against us in Nepal?" they asked. "Our hills and fastnesses are the work of God. They cannot be taken by mortal men. As for the British, they cannot even conquer mud fortresses which are the work of men's hands. How then can they take our forts, which are created by the Everlasting One?"

At first it seemed as if the Ghurkas were right. The British in India were not used to mountain warfare. The little Ghurkas were very fierce in battle. Their charge was terrible, like that of our own highlanders. After firing their guns, they rushed upon the foe with fierce yells, attacking them with their little deadly knives. And the sepoys, dismayed by this sudden onrush to which they were not used, gave way before them again and again. Misfortune and disaster followed each other.

Apart from fighting, the difficulties were great. The British army had to pass through almost trackless jungle where wild beasts prowled, and poisonous snakes glided. The toils and hardships of the way were enough to make the bravest falter. And it is told of one officer that he was so terrified that he turned and fled back to camp leaving his soldiers to their fate. But not many were like him.

When the jungle was passed and the mountains reached, troubles and hardships were by no means left behind. Up pathless valleys, along ledges overhanging sheer precipices, the heavy cannon had to be dragged. As they rose higher, icy winds whistled around the men, snow lay deep upon the ground through which they had to struggle.

Every pass was defended by a fortress easily held by a few against the attacking army. General Gillespie, the hero of Vellore, besieged one fort for a month. It was held against him by only six hundred Ghurkas. But both sides fought with so much determination that the garrison was reduced to seventy before the fort yielded, and of the besiegers five hundred lay dead, among them the gallant general.

From all sides came news of failure and disaster. The Ghurkas rejoiced in victory, and seeing the British worsted, all the bandit chiefs in India began to plot together for the overthrow of the British Raj.

But at length the tide of war turned. A gallant general, sir David Ochterlony, carried fort after fort in the face of every difficulty and danger. In spite of their heroic fighting, in spite of their brave defences, the Ghurkas were defeated. They saw at length that their vaunted "Heaven built" forts, and mountain passes were no defences against the British Lion. So they gave in.

By the treaty of Segauli peace was made. A brave enemy became a firm friend, and from that day to this there has been no quarrel between the British and the Ghurkas. Later, the Ghurkas became British soldiers, and the Ghurka regiments are among the best of our Indian army.

CHAPTER 18

THE PINDARIS AND THE LAST MARÁTHÁ WAR

THE trouble with the Ghurkas was over, but the lawlessness of Central India became worse and worse. The Pindaris made life a terror. Rather than fall into the hands of these fierce bandits, whole villages of people were known to burn themselves alive in their huts. Rather than be driven off by them like sheep, so be sold and slaughtered, women drowned themselves in the village wells.

Yet, while horrors unspeakable still raged around, and the Pindaris carried fire and sword among the peaceful, defenceless villages, Lord Hastings could do little, for the directors at home kept telling him not to interfere.

But at length he made up his mind to look on no more, but to crush the power of the Pindaris for ever. To do this, he gathered the largest army ever seen in India. From north and south the soldiers came; from Madras, Bombay and Bengal, until the Governor-General had an army 116,000 strong. It was a far greater force than was needed to crush the Pindaris. But Lord Hastings knew that he had not only to deal with them but with all the Maráthá chiefs, who were weary of their Subsidiary Alliance, and of the peace that it gave them, and who were longing to be free again to fight and plunder as of old. And if the Pindaris were successful ever so little, Lord Hastings knew it would give the Maráthás courage to rise against the British too.

But before there was any fighting, Lord Hastings found means of settling with several of the lawless chieftains. The Pindaris thus found themselves forsaken by many of their friends, and surrounded on all sides by a watchful enemy. In the battles which followed, many of the Pindaris were slain, some yielded themselves prisoners, and many were killed by the villagers whom they had been used to oppress and plunder, and who were now glad of revenge. Some sought refuge in the pathless jungle. For nearly a year the last chief held out, followed by a little band of about two hundred. But he, too, at last sought shelter in the jungle, and there, one day, his dead body was found, torn and mangled by tigers, while beside him, grazing quietly, was his horse, the only friend from whom he had not been forced to part.

So thoroughly were the Pindaris rooted out, that in a few years their terrible deeds were almost forgotten, and those of them who were left became as peaceful farmers and weavers of cotton as the peasants whom they had plundered in days gone by.

The Peshwá, or over-lord of the Maráthás, had, you remember, made an alliance with the British. But for a long time he had been growing restless, and eager to be rid of his alliance. Although he still pretended to be friendly, he was really trying to stir up the other Marátha chiefs against the British, urged on by a favourite called Trimbukji Dainglia, in whose power he was. Already, about two years before the Pindari war, Trimbukji had murdered a man because he would not side against the British.

For this, Trimbukji was put in prison. The prison was not very strong, but so that he might have no chance of escape, he had a guard of British soldiers. But in spite of this, when he had been about a year in prison, he escaped. It was very cleverly managed.

One of the British officers had a groom who was a Marátha. This man used to walk his master's horse up and down outside the prison, passing under Trimbukji's window. And as he passed he used to sing Maráthá songs, which, of course, the guard could not understand. But these songs told Trimbukji that friends were near and were making ready for his escape. This is something like what he sang:

> Behind the bush the bowmen hide
> The horse beneath the tree,
> Where shall I find the knight will ride
> The jungle-paths with me?
>
> There are five-and-fifty coursers there, and
> four-and-fifty men;
> When the fifty-fifth shall mount his steed,
> The Deccan thrives again.

Soon all was arranged. A hole was cut through the wall of Trimbukji's room, into a stable next it, and one dark, wet night, he squeezed himself through. Then in the dress of a common workman, carrying a basked on his head, he boldly marched out of the gate. The four and fifty men were ready waiting for him, and throwing himself on his horse, he was soon galloping with them through the darkness and the rain.

To hunt for him was useless. He had vanished. The Peshwá knew all about it.

It was soon heard that Trimbukji was raising both men and money. The Peshwá, too, began to gather his army. Other Maráthá chiefs joined them, and the last Maráthá war began.

Now again there were many stern fights, brave defences, gallant deeds. Both the Bombay and the Bengal sepoys proved heroes, and faithful to their British masters. In the end the Peshwá was utterly defeated. His land was taken from him, and added to the Bombay Presidency. But he was left with his title and given a pension of £80,000 a year, and so, wealthy and idle, he lived in luxury in Cawnpore till he died, an old man.

The Maráthá power was broken for ever, and Rajputana, which had been torn with war and bloodshed for nearly a hundred years, was at last at peace. Indeed, for the first time in all known history, there was peace in India from the Himalayas to Cape Comorin.

THE FIRST BURMESE WAR

ALTHOUGH Lord Hastings had come out to India with the determination not to fight, he had been obliged to fight in order to win peace and justice for India. His rule will be remembered as great, however, not merely because he added many lands to the Empire, but because he brought peace to these lands.

Lord Hastings was the first Governor-General who took any interest in the teaching of the people. Before his day the Company had been inclined to think that it was just as well that the people should remain ignorant, as they would then be more easily ruled. Lord Hastings did not think so, and he helped to found native schools, and in many ways tried to make the lives of the Indian peoples better and happier.

The change to free trade, which had taken place at the beginning of Lord Hastings' rule, had proved a great success, and the affairs of the Company had never been better than when he gave up his post and went home in 1823.

Lord Hastings left India in peace, and it was hoped by all that the peace would last. But very soon after Lord Amherst, the new Governor-General arrived, he was forced into another war.

Beyond Bengal, and stretching in a long, narrow strip down the bay, lies Burma. The Burmese, about this time, had great wars among themselves, and some of the rebels had fled into Bengal, asking protection from the British. The King of Burma ordered the British to give these fugitives up. But they refused, knowing well that the poor wretches would be put to death with terrible tortures. This made the king angry, and, having conquered Assam, he next began to attack British possessions.

Even then Lord Amherst tried to arrange matters peacefully. But it was in vain. The king mistook the wish for peace for fear. He haughtily commanded one of his generals to drive the British out of Bengal, and to bring the Governor-General back in golden chains, so that he might be put to death.

Lord Amherst saw, at length, that war was not to be avoided, and began to collect ships and men. He meant to send his army across the Bay of Bengal in ships, and attack the Burmese in their own land. But the Calcutta sepoys refused to go, for their caste rules would not allow them to sail upon the "black water," as they called the sea. So Lord Amherst was obliged to send part of his army round the bay by land, where they endured terrible hardships, for the roads were almost impassable. The sepoys of Madras were not so particular, however, and soon a little fleet set sail for Rangoon.

When the Burmese saw the British fleet they were both astonished and frightened. They had never expected that the enemy would come by sea, and they had made no preparations. What frightened them most was a small steamship called the *Diana*. It was the first steamer which had ever been seen in the East, for the power of steam was only being discovered. The Burmese had an old saying that they should never be conquered until a ship came up the Irrawaddy without sails or oars. Now the ship had come, and it struck terror into their hearts.

After firing a volley into the town, the British landed at Rangoon. But when they reached the town they found it empty, silent, and deserted. Men, women, and children had fled. The only human beings were eleven Europeans who were found tied and bound, ready for death. As soon as the fleet had appeared, they had been seized and condemned to death. They were seated upon the ground, and the executioner stood over them sharpening his knife, when a cannon ball burst into their midst. In terror the Burmese fled, leaving their prisoners behind them, to be found and set free again by the British.

The Burmese were cowardly, ignorant, and puffed up with foolish pride. Their army were a mere rabble, without order or courage. They were badly armed and worse drilled. The British ought to have crushed them in a few weeks. But instead of that the war dragged on for two years. From the first to last there seemed only to be mistakes and misfortunes.

In those days Burma was almost an unknown country. The British knew little of the people and less of the land which they had come to conquer. They found it full of impassable forests and deadly swamps. All round Rangoon the land was a desert. It was swept bare of grain or food, and there was not a human being to be seen.

Soon the rains began. The whole country became a reeking marsh from which rose foul mists, bringing sickness and death. Although the rain poured in torrents, the weather was stifling and hot, the men always hungry. In vain the country was scoured for food. There was none to be found. The soldiers had to live on biscuits and tinned meats sent from Calcutta, and these were bad.

The British commander had hoped to sail up the Irrawaddy and attack the king in his capital of Ava. But the rains made the river a rushing torrent, upon which it was impossible for sailing vessels to go. So, for six months the army remained at Rangoon. Man after man was stricken down. The hospitals were quickly filled to overflowing. The men died in hundreds, and when the rains ceased, it was found that every tenth man was dead.

Now Bundula, the great Burmese general, marched against the British with sixty thousand men.

The Burmese had a curious way of fighting. Instead of attacking the enemy in the open, they built high fences of interlaced bamboo. Then they dug holes in the ground behind the fences and burrowed in them like moles or rabbits, and from behind these ramparts they fired upon the enemy.

In this way they now surrounded the British, who watched them curiously as they made their preparations. The Burmese worked so fast that it seemed as if their entrenchments rose by magic, and in a few hours the British were quite surrounded.

Then fighting began and lasted for a fortnight. Bundula, himself, was brave, and his army was twenty times as large as that of the British But at last the British charged the Burmese in their burrows, and they fled in disorder.

The British now marched up the river to Ava. Bundula was killed, and with him died all the courage of the Burmese. The king began to tremble for his throne. He offered his soldiers great rewards to encourage them to fight, for by this time fearful stories were told of the might and cruelty of the "white demons." But the British swept all before them, and the king was ready to make peace.

Then there came to him a boasting warrior called the Lord of the Sun-Set. He begged leave to lead the army, and swore to the king that he would save his capital from the white demons, and scatter them in flight. So the last army which the king could collect was given him to command.

But the Lord of the Sun-Set, too, was defeated, and his army fled. Then the king, in wrath, gave orders that he should be trampled to death by wild elephants, as a reward for his boasting and his failure.

Now peace was made, and, by the treaty of Yandaboo, the King of Burma gave up Assam, Aracan, and Tenasserim to the Company, and promised to pay a large sum of money.

When the news of the war reached home, the directors were, as usual, very angry about it. It had cost thirteen times more than the Pindari and the last Marátha wars. All the money that Lord Hastings had gathered had been used. The Company was once more in debt. They had lost twenty thousand men, and all that they had in return were three swampy, forest-covered provinces.

But these same swampy provinces have turned out to be among the most important of British India. In places, where in 1826, there were only a few bamboo huts, prosperous towns and harbours have sprung up. The foul swamps have been changed into the most fertile of rice-fields. Aracan has become the granary of Bengal. The tea-gardens of Assam are famous the world over. More than half the tea we drink at home comes from Indian tea-gardens, besides which much is sent to the Colonies and to the Continent.

CHAPTER 20

THE SIEGE OF BHURTPORE

MEANWHILE the news of the losses and disasters in Burma had been brought to India. Many of the Indian chiefs and princes, who had not yet quite settled down under the over-lordship of Britain, began to be restless. As the war dragged on month after month they began to believe, and to hope, that the Burmese would overthrow the power of the British. They began to look forward to the time when the Company should no longer be over-lord in India, and when each prince should be free to fill the land with lawlessness and bloodshed as before.

When things were at their worst in Burma the Raja of Bhurtpore died. He was succeeded by his son, a child of seven, with his uncle as regent. But a cousin, who wished the throne for himself, murdered the uncle, and put the little Raja in prison. Thus he defied the British, who had accepted the little boy as Raja.

But Lord Amherst wanted no more fighting, so he made up his mind not to interfere. When the usurper saw this he became very bold and haughty. All the chieftains of Central India openly cheered him on, and men of every conquered tribe gathered to him, until he had an army of twenty-five thousand men.

The fort of Bhurtpore was the strongest in India. The Indians, indeed, believed that it could never be taken by mortal man. It was surrounded with five miles of enormous sun-dried, mud walls sixty feet thick. It had nine gates and thirty-five strong mud towers. Outside the wall was a broad ditch fifty-five feet deep, and one hundred and fifty feet wide. This ditch, in time of war, was filled with water from a lake near the town.

Lord Amherst soon saw that he had made a mistake. He saw that if the usurper of Bhurtpore was not punished there would be war all over Central India. So he sent an army against the fort. Fortunately it arrived in time to stop the bank of the lake being cut, and water let into the moat, and it was still dry.

The siege began. For days the British battered the mud walls with their heaviest guns. The roar and thud of cannon, the shriek of shells, filled the air for weeks, and still the brown walls stood solid and unbroken.

Then it was resolved to blow them up. Three mines were dug, the biggest being filled with ten thousand pounds of gunpowder. The train was lighted, and the army waited ready to rush in the moment there was a breach. In a few minutes the earth seemed to shake, a low rumble as of distant thunder was heard, the great wall trembled. Then huge masses of mud rose in the air carrying with them the shattered bodies of many of the defenders. The sky grew dark with smoke and dust, and lurid with flames. The air was filled with shrieks of pain, yells of triumph, the thud and crash of falling masses, as the British rushed through the yawning breach in the mighty wall.

Yet, before the fort was taken, there was terrible slaughter, six thousand or more of the defenders falling in the fight. But at last it was over, and the British were masters of the place.

Next day the little Raja was brought from prison, and again set upon the throne, and the usurper, in his turn, became a prisoner. The war was at an end and the Rajas or princes, who had been ready to make war, but who had been waiting to see what would happen, settled down in peace again. The famous walls of Bhurtpore were levelled to the ground, and with them the last rampart against British rule in India seemed to vanish.

CHAPTER 21

SATI AND THAGS

NOW at length there came to India a time of peace, and Lord William Bentinck, the next Governor-General, could spend his time in trying to make the lives of the people happier.

One of the first things he did was to forbid Sati or widow-burning.

When a Hindu died, his body was not buried but laid on a great pile of wood and burned. It was the custom for his widow to throw herself upon the burning pile and be burned too. Sometimes she did it willingly, being carried along by a kind of religious madness, and believing that she was doing a great and noble deed. Sometimes the wretched woman had to be forced into the flames with threats and blows, sometimes she was drugged with opium until she knew not what she did.

Now Lord William made this horrible deed a crime, and anyone who helped in it was punished with death. It was thought at the time that the Indians would be very angry with this new law which seemed to interfere with their religion. But there were no riots. Sati soon died out even in provinces not under British rule.

Lord William also put down the Thags. These were stranglers and thieves by trade. They were born thieves. The fathers and mothers were thieves, and they taught their children to be thieves, as naturally as a father who was a tailor, taught his son to be a tailor too.

Dresses as ordinary people they went about the country. They made friends with those they met upon the road. Often they would travel for days in seeming friendliness, making the journey pass pleasantly with talk and laughter. But suddenly, one evening, perhaps, as the whole party was resting under the cool shade of trees or making ready an evening meal by some village well, the chief would give a sign. Quick as lightning each Thag would draw a rope from its hiding-place. Whirling through the air came the noose, and in a moment it was drawn tight round the neck of his victim.

In a few minutes the wretched unsuspecting travellers lay dead. They were robbed of all they possessed, and buried at once. For the Thags always carried a kind of pick-axe with them with which to dig holes for the graves of their victims.

They had many tricks, too, with which to deceive travellers. Sometimes a rich young man would come upon a beautiful lady weeping by the roadside. Full of pity for her, he would stop to ask what was the matter. In a moment the noose would be round his neck. And when he lay dead the beautiful lady, wiping her pretended tears, would be among the first to rob him.

The Thags had a secret language of their own. The children were trained when they were quite young as scouts and spies. The cleverest were chosen to use the lasso, and so skillful did they become that no traveller whom they attacked ever escaped.

It was not easy to put down the Thags, for although they wandered all over Central India, their ways were so secret that it was hard to find them. But Lord William was very determined to root them out, and in various ways two thousand of them were caught in about six years. Some were hanged, some put in prison, and some were pardoned and settled down into peaceable citizens, and at last the Thags quite disappeared.

Lord William Bentinck ruled in India for nearly eight years. He not only fought against evil customs but he tried to bring good into the lives of the people. He was perhaps the first British ruler who saw that India must be ruled for the good of the Indian people, and not just to put money into the pockets of the British.

It was during Lord William's rule in 1833 that another great change in the Company took place. In that year the Company was made to give up all trade, and made to attend only to the ruling of India. The trade of India was made quite free to all, and people of any country were allowed to live there, if they wished, without first asking leave from the Company.

It was while Lord William Bentinck was Governor-General that Lord Macaulay went to India as law member of the Council. And when the people raised a monument in memory of Lord William, it was Lord Macaulay who wrote the words carved upon it. Among many things which a man might be proud to know were said of him were the words. "Who never forgot that the end of government is the happiness of the governed."

THE FIRST AFGHAN WAR

IN 1837 the ruler of Afghanistan was called Dost Muhammad. He was a rough soldier, young and brave, and he had proved himself a good ruler of Afghanistan, although he had no real right to the throne. Afghanistan, like other countries, had been torn with wars and revolts. The real ruler, Shah Shuja, had fled, and was now living in India under British protection.

Ever since the days of Peter the Great, Russia has been spreading her empire southward until; "Russian designs on India" have become a sort of nightmare to Indian rulers, for now only Afghanistan lies between British India and Russia.

But in 1837 the Punjab had not yet become a part of British India, and it also lay between, and its ruler, Ranjit Singh, the Lion of Lahore, was friendly to the British. The British wanted to make sure that Afghanistan was also friendly, and Lord Auckland, who was now Governor-General, sent a messenger to the court of Afghanistan. This messenger was supposed to be going to arrange about trade. But trade had little to do with it. He really went to persuade the Afghans to be friends with the British, and to make war, if need be, with the Russians.

There had been war between the Afghans and Ranjit Singh, and he had taken part of Afghanistan called the Peshawar valley. Dost Muhammad was very anxious to get this back again, and was willing to promise the British anything if they would help him to get it.

But as Ranjit Singh and the British were friends, Lord Auckland refused. It was not the habit of the British, he said, to interfere in quarrels between other states. So his messenger came back from Afghanistan without having been able to arrange anything. And at the same time a Russian messenger was kindly received there.

Lord Auckland then made up his mind, that as Dost Muhammad would not do as he wanted, he would put a king on the throne who would. So he sent an army into Afghanistan to drive Dost Muhammad from the throne, and set foolish old Shah Shuja upon it.

This was surely folly, for the Afghans were well content with their ruler. They hated Shah Shuja, who was proud and haughty, and "neither a soldier nor a gentleman." Years before they had driven him out, and now that he was old and stupid, they certainly did not want him back again.

Ranjit Singh, although he was quite friendly, wanted to have as little to do with the British as possible. Now he refused to allow our army to pass through his lands. So it was obliged to go by Sind, which at this time was not under British rule. But the ruler of Sind was not so strong as Ranjit Singh, and so was unable to prevent the army passing through his land.

It was a long, weary march that now began. At first the roads were good. Then came long tracts of pathless desert where wild hill-men attacked the soldiers. The country was barren, and food grew scarce. Half starved and weary the army at last arrived at Kandahar.

Here the Shah rode in triumph through the town. Crowds of people thronged the streets, but it was curiosity, not love, that brought them. Along a path strewn with roses, with beat of drum and thunder of guns, and the shouts of a half-hearted few in his ears, the Shah rode to the tomb of his forefathers, to give thanks for his restoration.

Thus far there had been little fighting. Now there was a fierce battle, when Ghazni, the strongest fortress in Afghanistan, was taken. When Dost Muhammad heard the news he fled, and a few weeks later Shah Shuja rode in triumph into Kabul.

Seated upon a white horse, gorgeously clad, and sparkling with jewels, surrounded and followed by splendidly dressed servants, the Shah rode towards the palace from which, thirty years before, he had been hunted out. With him rode the British officers in their gayest uniforms. But as the glittering procession passed through the streets there was never a cheer. The sullen, scowling Afghans scarcely turned their heads to look at their returned king, or at the hated white-faced "Feringees" who had brought him.

Lord Auckland had said that as soon as the king was seated again upon his throne the British army would leave Afghanistan. But now that was found to be impossible. The Shah was indeed once more upon his throne, but it was only the glitter of English gold, and the gleam of English bayonets, that kept him there. The people did not want him, and it was easily seen that as soon as the British left, they would drive the Shah away once more.

So ten thousand British soldiers stayed in Afghanistan, and thousands of pounds in good British gold were paid to the wild hill-men to keep them quiet. Months passed, Dost Muhammad yielded himself a prisoner, the people were sunk in a gloomy, sullen quiet. The British believed that they were conquered, that they had accepted the ruler thrust upon them. English ladies came from India to join their husbands and brothers. Soon, in the heart of Afghanistan, the British had settled down to the gay social life of home. In summer they shot, and fished, and rode. In winter they skated and danced. And all the time they were making merry on a volcano, all the time the hatred of the Afghans seethed and boiled in secret.

At last it burst out. Early on the morning of the 2nd of November 1841 the streets of Kabul were filled with angry crowds. As the hours went on, the crowds grew denser and wilder. Thirsting for blood, eager for revenge, they attacked the houses of the British. Men, women, and children were slaughtered. Houses were robbed, wrecked, and burned. The whole town was one seething mass of uproar and riot. Mad with blood, the Afghans became cursing, howling beasts.

Yet the British did little or nothing. They had six thousand troops ready to command. But no orders were given. "We must see what the morning brings, and then think what can be done," said the commander. He waited to think "to-morrow" when he ought to have been acting. So all day the riot raged, and it was only with the falling darkness that the city sank once more to rest.

Next day things grew worse. From every side Afghans poured into the city. Seeing that the British had not crushed the rioters at once, every man took heart again, and did his best to drive the hated foreigners out. Day after day passed, days of horror, filled with fighting, with mistakes, with misfortunes, with commands given and withdrawn, with misery and confusion.

The Afghans commanded the surrounding hills. They were splendid marksmen, and their guns carried farther than the British muskets. Secure upon the heights they aimed at leisure, and the British went down before them like slaughtered sheep.

The fort, in which food for the British army was stored, fell into the hands of the Afghans. Hungry and weary the men lost heart, and discipline was at an end. "Our troops are acting like a pack of cowards and there is no spirit left amongst us. We have only three days" provisions for our men and nothing for our cattle," writes one.

At last even the blindest had to admit that there was nothing left but to get out of Afghanistan as best and as fast as they could.

So the British Ambassador had a meeting with the Afghan chiefs. At this meeting it was agreed that Dost Muhammad should be given back to the Afghans, and, that in return, the British army should be allowed to march out of Afghanistan in safety.

But even now there were delays. The Ambassador began to think that he might make better terms, and that after all he would not need to march back in the disgrace of defeat. He began to plot with some of the Afghan chiefs. But they had only led him in order to destroy him, and when he met with them upon the hill slopes outside the town, he was foully murdered in broad daylight. His body was then cut to pieces, and his head was carried through the town in triumph. And the British were powerless to avenge the insult. Days of humiliation and misery followed, but at last everything was arranged, and the long march homeward began.

Four thousand soldiers and twelve thousand camp followers, many of them women and children—ladies, unused to hardship, children unable to walk—streamed out of the fatal town into the country beyond. They meant to make their way to Jellalabad, where there was a British garrison.

It was a clear and sunny winter's morning, but bitterly cold, and snow lay thick upon the ground. Hardly had the British left their houses when the Afghans swarmed into them seeking plunder. They found little, for the British had carried away or destroyed all that they possessed. So in their disappointment and rage the Afghans wrecked the houses and set them on fire. Then they followed the retreating army.

Soon the white snow was trampled and brown, and stained with blood, and all the ways were strewn with dead and dying. It was a bad beginning to the long march, and as it began, so it went on. While the crowd of men, women, and children, wound through the narrow valleys, the wild hill tribes rushed down upon them from the heights, slaughtering them without mercy. The march became a headlong flight. In the frantic rush, baggage, ammunition, provisions, all were left behind. Without tents, without food or shelter, many lay down to die in the snow. Attacked by their pitiless enemies, they could scarce defend themselves. Muskets dropped from their numbed, frost-bitten fingers, and they were mown down like corn before the reaper.

The son of Dost Muhammad, who had promised that the army should march in safety, was powerless against the wild hill tribes. But he now offered to take care of the ladies and the children, and with heavy hearts the men gave them into his keeping. It was a terrible risk, for how could any one be sure that they would not all be murdered horribly. Yet there was a chance that this wild Afghan would keep his word and bring them to safety, and if they went on with the army, they must all certainly die of the hardships of the way. The Afghan chief did keep his word, and months later all those left in his charge returned home in safety.

Faint with hunger, sick and numb with cold, the men continued the march. But they could not escape from their savage black enemies. Crushed by rolling stones, mowed down by volleys of musket shot, cut to pieces by knives, pierced by bayonets, the men fell by hundreds, and the army grew smaller and smaller.

At last, on the morning of the thirteenth of January, a sentry on the ramparts of Jellalabad looked out along the road from Kabul. There he saw one lone traveller come. He rode a lean and wretched pony, and bent forward, clinging to its mane like one in deadly agony. Soon the wall was thick with anxious men straining eager eyes towards the lonely horseman. As they gazed, their hearts sank within them. It seemed as if he were the messenger of some dark mischance. Then flinging themselves into the saddle, a party rode out to meet him.

Stricken, wan, more dead than alive, they brought him in. And when his white lips could speak, they learned that he alone, of all the sixteen thousand who had set out from Kabul, was alive to tell the tale of that awful journey of a hundred miles through mountain passes, beset with foes.

From first to last the expedition to Afghanistan had been a mistake, and

"Crushed by rolling stones, mown down by
volleys of musket-shot, the men fell in hundreds."

the British had to acknowledge that they had been beaten. But they could not remain beaten. Besides, there were those hundred or more women and children in the hands of the Afghans who must be rescued.

So an army was sent to avenge the defeat. Once again Kabul was taken, once again the British flag was planted upon the ramparts. But meanwhile Shah Shuja had been murdered, so Dost Muhammad came back to his throne, and the British army marched away to India leaving the Afghans to themselves.

CHAPTER 23

THE SIKHS

IN 1839, while the British were fighting in Afghanistan, the brave and wicked old ruler of the Punjab, the Lion of Lahore, died. After his death the Punjab was torn with civil wars. Plots and murders followed fast upon each other, until the whole country was seething with misery and bloodshed.

The people of the Punjab were called Sikhs. They were not a nation like the Maráthás or the Ghurkas, but a religious body. Under Ranjit Singh, however, they had grown into a nation. He had formed an army which he called the Kalsa or "Saved ones." These "saved ones" were fierce, brave men, splendidly armed, perfectly drilled, and so full of a kind of wild, religious zeal that they were ready to fight any one, or do the most desperate deeds, in the name of God.

The Kalsa was now the greatest power in the Punjab and a terror to all. After much fighting among themselves, they suddenly marched across the river Sutlej, and invaded British India.

The British were in a manner prepared, for seeing the unruly state of the Punjab, they knew that war must come sooner or later. But they had not expected it so soon, nor had they expected to have to fight such a great army as now marched into Hindustan. So secure, indeed, did they feel, that the Commander-in-chief was going to give a grand ball, when the news of the invasion arrived. The ball was given up, and soon the army was marching in hot haste towards the frontier.

In a few weeks four great battles had been fought. Never before had the British in India had to fight such stern foes. In each battle the British loss was very great, and if the Sikh leaders had been as wise as the Sikh soldiers were brave, things might have gone ill. But their leaders were cowardly or foolish.

In the last battle of the campaign, which is called the Battle of Sobraon, the Sikhs were utterly defeated and driven back across the Sutlej with great slaughter. Lord Hardinge, the Governor-General, then marched to Lahore, the capital of the Punjab. The country was now quite conquered, and, had he wished, Hardinge might have added it to the possessions of the Company. But he did not wish to do this, and Dhulip Singh, a supposed son of Ranjit Singh, was set upon the throne. He was, however, only a boy of eight, so had not much real power. A great part of the famous Kalsa army was disbanded, a British resident and garrison were left at Lahore, the Sikhs were made to pay all the expenses of the war, and lastly, the famous Koh-i-nur diamond was sent as a present to the Queen Victoria. Koh-i-nur means mountain of light. This famous diamond has had many adventures. It had belonged to the Great Mogul, it had been carried off by the Shah of Persia, and after its many wanderings it came at last to our own little island, and was the largest diamond belonging to the British crown, until the great South African diamond was presented to King Edward.

Having arranged matters in the Punjab, Lord Hardinge marched home to Calcutta in triumph, and it was hoped that the Punjab would soon settle down in peace.

For about two years all was quiet. Then suddenly two Englishmen were treacherously murdered at the town of Multan. It was the first spark. Soon the whole Punjab was ablaze again with war.

"The Sikh nation has asked for war," said Lord Dalhousie, the Governor-General, "and upon my word, they shall have it with a vengeance."

But once again the British found that they had stern work in front of them. The famous Kalsa soldiers gathered again, and fought with all their old courage. Chillianwalla, the great battle of the war, was almost a defeat. It began late in the afternoon. The Sikhs fought furiously, the air was thick with flying bullets, and dark with smoke, and when night put an end to the awful struggle, eighty-nine British officers, and nearly two thousand five hundred men, were among the killed and wounded.

It was a day of disaster. The British had lost both standards and guns, and once at least their horse had fled before the foe. Yet they claimed it as a victory. So did the Sikhs, and that same evening the men rejoiced, and their leader fired a salute in honour of the victory over the British.

But a month later the memory of Chillianwalla was wiped out by the great victory of Gujerat. Upon the battle morning the sun rose clear and bright, and under a cloudless blue sky the fight began. But soon the air was thick and the sun darkened with smoke from the fearful cannonade which thundered and roared from both sides. So tremendous was the firing that the battle was known as the battle of the guns.

The Sikhs fought with all their old fury and courage. The British, too, fought with a fierce determination to win. And win they did. At last the Sikh ranks broke, and fled. For fifteen miles the British chased the fleeing foe. The famous Kalsa army was utterly shattered. Cannon, standards, camp baggage of every sort, fell into the hands of the British. Resistance was at an end. The Punjab was conquered, and this time it was added to the Company's possessions. Maharaja Dhulip Singh, who was now a boy of ten, was given a pension, and his lands passed into the hands of the British. After a little time Dhulip Singh came to England, where he lived for nearly all his life, like an English gentleman, and died in Paris a few years ago.

There was still another war during Lord Dalhousie's rule in India. This was the second Burmese war. The Burmese began to ill-treat the British traders and settlers at Rangoon, so Lord Dalhousie sent an army against them.

As before, the sepoys refused to go over the sea. But this did not matter so much now, for many of the Sikhs, who had quite lately been enemies, had joined our army and were willing to go anywhere. Now they fought for the British with the same fiery courage as they had fought against them. This second Burmese war was very different from the first. It was soon over, and the province of Pegu was added to British Burma.

Lord Dalhousie was one of the great rulers of India. He, like Lord William Bentinck, thought of the good of the people. He has been blamed for adding so much to British possessions, but he did it often to make the people happier. Many of the native princes, who were independent, ruled badly. They tyrannised over their people, and treated them with great cruelty. Lord Dalhousie warned these princes again and again. But as they would not listen, and try to rule better, he took their lands from them. In this way Oudh, Nagpore, and some smaller states were peacefully added to British possessions.

But although Lord Dalhousie enlarged British India very much, he is to be remembered most for the great improvements that he made there. He made good roads, and cut canals. he laid down railways and stretched telegraph wires over thousands of miles. He brought in a halfpenny post over all India. Towns were lit with gas, and steamers plied up and down the rivers. Schools, colleges, and hospitals were built. In fact, Lord Dalhousie found the great peninsula a collection of many states, of many tribes, and he tried to bind them into one great Empire, one great People. And in this work railways and telegraphs were of the greatest help, for they bring distant places near, and bind together those that are far apart.

CHAPTER 24

THE MUTINY—DELHI

AFTER Lord Dalhousie, Lord Canning became Governor General of India. At first, everything seemed quiet. But suddenly there burst over India a most terrible storm.

It was just a hundred years since the Black Hole, just fifty years since the mutiny of Vellore, when a far worse mutiny broke out.

For some time, the sepoys had been restless, and discontented. They had been angry when Oudh was annexed for one thing. Next, Lord Canning wanted some soldiers to send to Burma. Of course, the sepoys would not go. He was so annoyed at what he thought was foolish nonsense that he issued an order, saying that only sepoys, who would agree to go anywhere, would in future be taken into the army. This made them more angry and more afraid, so they again thought that the British were trying to destroy their caste and religion, and thenceforth high caste men would not join the army. All the sepoys even began to be afraid that the new order included them, and that henceforth they would be forced to go across the "black water," and they grew sullen.

They had many other grievances, real or imaginary. Railways and telegraphs frightened them. They thought they were magic and witchcraft, and said that the white people were binding the whole of India in chains. People, who were unfriendly to British rule, tried to make their grievances and fears worse, and tried to stir the sepoys to greater and greater discontent.

About this time a new rifle was sent out to India. The cartridges of his rifle were greased, and the end of the cartridge had to be bitten off before it was used.

One day, in the barracks, a low class workman asked a high caste sepoy for a drink out of his water-bottle. The sepoys refused haughtily, saying that the touch of a low caste lips would make his bottle "unclean." The workman angrily replied that it was no matter, was soon there would be no caste left, as the new cartridges were greased with the fat of cows and pigs, and the sepoys would have to bite them.

This, to a Brahmin, was something horrible, for to him the cow was sacred, while the pig was "unclean." The mere thought that he would have to touch this terrible mixture with his lips was more than he could bear. He ran off with the tale to his fellows, in horror. The story passed from mouth to mouth, till it spread all over India.

The officers told the men that the grease was mutton, fat, and wax, and therefore could not hurt any caste. It was in vain. The tale had taken hold too strongly. And now that one wild story was believed, others followed. It was said that is very flour of which the sepoys' bread was made, was mixed with cows' bones, ground to dust. To eat this, even unknowingly, would be deadly sin. Forever afterwards, they, who did so, would be outcasts. And so bent with the Sahibs on the destruction of all caste that they stooped to such foul and secret means. The story, of course, was not true, but the sepoys believed it.

They grew sullen with anger. They were wild with fear too, such a fear as it is hard for us to understand. The area was full of mutterings and unrest. In regiment after regiment the hated cartridges were refused. In some places the officers called the mean and offer them in the old cartridges which they had used for years. But fear had become unreasoning panic, and even they were refused. At length, at Meerut, near Delhi, the storm burst.

One on Sunday evening in May, when all the white people were on their way to church, there was an unusual stir. Trumpet calls were heard, mixed with the clatter of firearms and the rush of feet. Then flames burst forth in all directions. Soon the truth became known. The sepoys had revolted. They had fired upon their officers, and as the sun went down they rushed forth madly thirsting for the blood of their white masters.

A night of horror followed. The prisoners were burst open; from the dark and secret places of the town thieves, and murderers, and all evildoers crept out and mingled with the maddened sepoys. They attacked the British in their houses, slaying without mercy. They robbed and plundered at will. All night the sky was red with flames from burning houses, and amid the roar and crackle might be heard shrieks and groans, mingled with savage yells, and the wild clash of cymbals and beat of drum. But when the day dawned the streets were silent. Among the blackened, smouldering ruins the dead lay still. But the murderers had fled.

Along the road to Delhi, through the coolness of early dawn, beneath the glimmer of the rising sun spread the frantic sepoys. Mile after mile, from the ribbon of white road, rose a cloud of dust, marking the path by which the dark-faced, turbanned crowd passed.

By eight o'clock the foremost of the rioters burst into the quiet streets of Delhi. There the ancient King, the last descendant of the Great Mogul, still lived in empty splendour. Long ago his empire had passed into the hands of the British, but yet he kept great court and state, and played at grandeur.

Around his pal at the he wild horde raged, crying that they had killed the British at Meerut, that they had come to fight for the faith. "Help, O King," they cried. "We pray thee for help in our fight for the faith."

Into the palace they forced their way, slaying every white-faced man or woman. Soon the streets of Delhi were is terrible as those of Meerut. Every house belonging to the British was attacked, plundered, and set on fire. Every European was slain without mercy.

There were no British soldiers in Delhi, so to resist was hopeless. The British officers of the sepoy troops succeeded in blowing up the powder magazine, so that the ammunition should not fall into the hands of the mutineers. But that was all that they could do. Then they made their escape, as best they could, with their wives and children into the jungle. There, new dangers and sufferings awaited them, and but few found shelter in distant villages. Soon not a Christian was left within the walls of Delhi, and it was entirely in the hand of the mutineers.

All over India the terrible news was flashed, and in town after town the revolt broke out. Everywhere it was the same story—a story of murder and bloodshed, of robbery and plunder and destruction. Then, after finishing their terrible work, many of the rioters flock to Delhi, to arrange themselves under the banner of the "King."

There were very few British soldiers in India, for the Company had begun to trust almost entirely to the sepoys. Now Lord Canning telegraphed in all directions for troops. Some he gathered from Persia where there had been fighting. Some he stopped on their way to China. The Sikhs and Gurkhas, too, had stood firm, and now they loyally fought for their white masters. Soon the siege of Delhi began. The mutineers held out for three months, but at last they yielded to British guns. The old Mogul was taken prisoner and sent to Rangoon where he died. But meanwhile, all over Northern India there was war and bloodshed.

CHAPTER 25

THE MUTINY—CAWNPORE

AT Cawnpore Sir Hugh Wheeler was commander. When he saw the danger coming he sent to Sir Henry Lawrence at Lucknow for help. But Sir Henry himself had few enough soldiers, and could spare only fifty men. Then Sir Hugh asked an Indian prince, called the Nana Sahib, to help him.

The Nana was the adopted son of the last Peshwá of the Maráthás, to whom, you remember, the Company paid a yearly sum of money, after he had given up his kingdom to them. When the Peshwá died, the company thought there was no need to go on paying the money, for the Nana was not really his son, and had not true right to it. This made Nana angry, for he thought that he should have had the money. Still, he pretended to be friends with the British. Now he promised to help Sir Hugh, and he came to Cawnpore with some soldiers. But as soon as the mutiny had fairly broken out, his men joined with the mutineers against the British.

At Cawnpore the sepoys broke open the jail, sacked the treasury and magazine, and burned and plundered everywhere. But they did not attack the white people. Having finished their work of destruction, they started to join the other rebels at Delhi. But this did not please the Nana. He called them back, and the siege of Cawnpore began.

The place where the white people were gathered for refuge was poorly protected. It was an old hospital. Round it was a crumbling mind wall not four feet high. Within it were gathered nearly a thousand people, but scarcely three hundred were soldiers, and nearly four hundred were women and children. Without the wall there swarmed thousand upon thousands of sepoys, well drilled and well armed, for they had all the heavy guns and ammunition of the magazine. It needed only courage for them to overleap the poor weak wall, and put every white man and woman to death.

But courage failed them. They knew of what stern stuff their white masters were made, and they dared not overleap that wall. So they raged and yelled without, and night and day the flash and roar of guns, and the scream and crash of shells, continued with no pause.

Again Sir Hugh sent to Sir Henry Lawrence begging for help. But this time Sir Henry, with a breaking heart, was forced to refuse. He could not spare a man. So without rest, or pause, or shadow of relief, the siege went on. The sepoys aimed with deadly sureness. The low mud wall gave little shelter, and day-by-day the ranks of the defenders grew thinner and thinner. Yet in hunger, thirst, and weariness, they fought on. Food began

"THE BOATS STUCK IN THE MUD WERE AN EASY MARK."

to fail. A handful of flour and a handful of split peas a day was all each man received. Water was more precious still. It could only be had from a well within the fire of the enemy's guns. And many man laid down his life to bring a bucket of water to still the wailing of a child or the groans of a dying comrade.

Three weeks passed, weeks of sleepless horror amid unceasing noise, and constant hail of bullets. The June sun blazed from brazen sky. The air was heavy with smoke, and bitter with the taste and smell of gunpowder, the heat wellnigh unbearable. Women and children drooped and faded. Men set their teeth, and, gaunt and grim, fought on.

At length the Nana Sahib proposed terms. He promised, the do the British would give him, he would send them all in safety down the river to Alláhábád.

There was not a man within the walls who would not rather have fought to the last. But they thought of the sad-eyed women, and the little listless children, and they gave in.

So early one morning, a dreary procession of weary women and children, of hopeless, wounded men, made their way to the river.

There, some native boats awaited them, covered with thatch to keep off the heat of the sun. The wounded were lifted in. Men, women, and children followed. Then suddenly from the banks the sound of a bugle was heard.

Throwing down their oars the native rowers leaped from their places and made for the shore. Almost at the same moment the thatched roofs burst into flames, and from the banks are roar of guns was heard, and a hail of bullets burst upon the boats.

The boats, stuck in the mud, were an easy mark. Leaping into the river the white men tried to push them off, but in vain. One boat alone got free, and of its crew only four lived to tell the tale. The others were murdered where they stood. Not a man escaped, and those of the women and children, who were still alive, were led back to the terrible town from which they had just been set free. There they were shut up in a place called the Savada house. Later they were taken to another called the Bibigarh. Here they were treated as slaves, and made to grind the corn for the Nana. And so in slavery and imprisonment the terrible weeks dragged on.

Meanwhile, through the burning heat of an Indian summer, a British army was toiling on towards Cawnpore. It was led by General Havelock, as brave a soldier and as good a man as ever lived. Like Cromwell, he taught his men both to fight and to pray, and "Havelock's Saints" were as well known as Cromwell's Ironsides had been.

When the Nana Sahib heard that they were coming, he made up his mind to complete his work. So he ordered the sepoys to fire upon the women and children through the windows of the Bibigarh. But even the sepoys turned from such cruel work, and they fired upon the roof and did little or no hurt to the women within the house. But the Nana could always find people cruel enough to do his bidding. In the evening five men went into the house armed with long knives. For a little time terrible screams were heard. Then all was still. The men came out, and the bodies of the poor women and children were thrown into a well.

Outside Cawnpore the British met the Indian troops. After a desperate fight the Nana was defeated. His army was scattered, and he, struck at last with terror, galloped wildly away through the darkness, and was seen no more.

It is supposed that he died miserably in the jungle.

The day after the battle the British marched entrance into Cawnpore but when they saw the ghastly Bibigarh and the still more ghastly grave of those they had come to save, these war-worn men burst into sobs and wept like children.

These things happily are now long past. An angel guards that once awful spot, and a garden blooms where those poor women died.

THE MUTINY—LUCKNOW

THE Union Jack floated once more upon the walls of Cawnpore, but there was still much to do ere Mutiny should be over. "Soldiers," said Havelock, "your general is satisfied, and more than satisfied, with you. But your comrades of Lucknow are in danger." And with the memory of Cawnpore in their hearts, Havelock and his men marched on to Lucknow.

But Havelock had to fight his way there. He lost so many men and used so much ammunition that at last he was not strong enough to take Lucknow. He was obliged to turn back to Cawnpore and wait until Sir James Outram joined him with more troops. Outram was a gallant soldier, "without fear and without reproach," and together these two brave men marched to help their comrades.

At Lucknow the British had taken refuge in the Residency. This was a number of houses and gardens surrounded by a wall. It was not very strong, but it was far better than the old hospital at Cawnpore. Sir Henry Lawrence, the governor, was a wise and careful man. Seeing the storm coming, he did everything he could to meet it. He gathered stores of food and ammunition, and strengthened the defences of the Residency. But alas, at the very beginning of the siege, Sir Henry was killed.

One day a shell burst into the room where he was talking with some of his officers. There was a blinding flash, a fearful roar, and the room was filled with dust and smoke. In the deep silence which followed, someone asked, "Are you hurt, Sir Henry?"

For a moment there was no answer. Then quietly he replied, "I am killed."

So brave Sir Henry died. "If you put anything on my tombstone," he said, "let it be only, 'Here lies Henry Lawrence who tried to do his duty. May the Lord have mercy on his soul.'" Then with his last breath he urged his men never to give in, but to fight to the end.

The terrible summer days dragged on—days spent amid all the noise and din, dust and smoke of war, nights of anxious watchings, broken with sudden alarms. The houses were shattered and riddled with shot, so as to be scarcely any protection from the burning sun or from the enemies' guns. Food was scarce, clothes were in rags. But still the men fought and watched, and the women prayed and waited, and endured. And like an emblem of their dauntless courage, all through the siege the Union Jack floated from the highest tower of the Residency. It was faded and patched, tattered and riddled with holes, the staff was splintered with bullets, it was broken again and again. But a new staff was always found, and up went the gallant flag once more, a defiance to the foe.

"British soldiers were seen fighting their way through the streets."

At last one morning, distant firing was heard. As the hours passed the sound came near and nearer. Then the garrison new that at length help was at hand. The excitement and suspense were awful. But there was nothing to be done but to wait. It was not until it was growing dark that amid the clamour of fighting the sound of the British cheer was heard, and louder still, shrill and piercing, the scream of the bagpipes, and the yell of charging Highlanders. A few minutes more, and British soldiers were seen, fighting their way through the streets to the Residency gates.

Then from the battlements rose a deafening cheer. Such a cry of joy it is not often been man's lot to hear. It was the first cry of returning hope from the hearts that had grown hopeless. It was a sob, and a prayer, and an outburst of thanksgiving, all in one. And as the gates were opened, and the men, weary, dusty, bloodstained, rushed through, women sobbing with joy ran to throw themselves upon them, happy to touch their bronzed hands or war-worn coats. With tears running down their cheeks the rough soldiers lifted the children in their arms. From hand to hand they passed the little ones, kissing them and thanking God that they had come in time to save them. It was a scene of wild, sweet joy and almost unutterable relief.

But after all the siege of Lucknow was not over. Havelock and Outram had not men enough with them to cut their way back through the swarms of sepoys, and bring all the ladies and children to safety. So the siege began again. It was not until two months later that Sir Colin Campbell landed in India, and cutting his way through the rebels, really relieved Lucknow.

Scarcely a week later Sir Henry Havelock died. Greatly sorrowing, his men buried him in a garden near the city, his only monument being a tree marked with the letter H.

Before the relief of Lucknow, Delhi had been taken, and now the mutiny was nearly over. There was still some fighting, but gradually it ceased. Lord Canning made a proclamation, offering pardon to all who had not actually murdered the British. Most of the rebels laid down their arms, and once more the country sank to rest.

It was now decided that India should no longer be ruled by the Company but by the Queen. So the great Company, which had begun in the reign of Queen Elizabeth came to an end in the reign of Queen Victoria. This was proclaimed to all the people of India on the first of the 1st November 1858. Now, instead of Governor-General, the ruler of India was called Viceroy. And Lord Canning, who had been Governor-General throughout the mutiny, became the first Viceroy.

CHAPTER 27

THE EMPRESS OF INDIA

IN 1862 Lord Canning sailed home leaving India at peace. All through the mutiny he had been cool and calm. When it was over he would take no wild revenge, and earned for himself the name of Clemency Canning, a name by which we may be glad to remember him, for clemency means mildness or quickness to forgive.

Since the mutiny many things have happened in India, most of which you will understand better, and find more interesting, later on. There have been wars and famines, there have been mistakes and mischances, troubles and trials, but on the whole, the great Empire has been peace. The native princes have become educated gentlemen, and, in many ways, West and East have been drawn together.

One thing which helped the princes of India and the British crown to become better friends was the visit of the Prince of Wales, now King Edward.

When the native rulers of India heard that our Prince was coming, they prepared to receive him with great honour. When he landed in Calcutta, the whole town blazed with illuminations. Everyone held high holiday. There were balls and parties given both by white and by native people. And all through India, wherever he went, the princes and their subjects flocked to him honour. Native rulers forgot their quarrels with each other, and joined in welcoming the son of their British Padishah. They brought him splendid presents, and he won their hearts by his kindness and his courtesy. He stayed in their palaces, shot and hunted with them, and when he left, many a prince founded schools or hospitals, or built harbours, in memory of his future Emperor's visit.

All this time, although Queen Victoria had been ruler of India for more than eighteen years, she had never been proclaimed, or taken the title. Now, the year after the visit of the Prince of Wales, that is in 1877, she was proclaimed at Delhi, Empress of India.

To Delhi came the Viceroy, and all the native princes and nobles of India. Princes who before had never seen each other, princes whose fore-fathers had fought in deadly hatred, now all met together as friends, eager to show their loyalty to their Empress.

Outside the walls of Delhi, on the very ground upon which the British troops had encamped when they besieged the rebels of the mutiny, there now arose a peaceful tented city, brilliant in red and blue and white, flashing and glittering with golden ornament. Upon the ground that had been red with hate and war, where shells had burst, and cannon roared, and a hail of grape-shot scattered death, gold and silver cannon, drawn by white oxen gaily decorated with silken, embroidered cloths, were paraded in the sunshine, and those who had been foes met and greeted each other as friends and brothers. Gay flags fluttered, bands played, elephants and camels with gorgeous trappings paced the long streets of gaudy tents. Princes and people from every part of the great peninsula met and mingled. It was the gay mass of moving colour, of red, and green, and blue, and everywhere in the sunshine, gold and silver and precious stones gleaned and sparkled. It was such a pageant as could be seen only in an eastern land, under an eastern sky.

On the day of the proclamation the sky was cloudless blue. Upon a grassy plain the tented throne was raised. Its silken draperies were embroidered with the Rose, the Thistle, and the Shamrock, entwined with the Lotus flower of India, and over all fluttered the cross of St. George, and the Union Jack.

Here, surrounded by the glittering throng, the Viceroy took his seat, while the band played "God save the Queen." He too, was splendidly dressed, in the robes, ermine trimmed and gold embroidered, of Grand Master of the Order of the Star of India.

When the Viceroy was seated, twelve gaily dressed heralds sounded their trumpets. Then the chief herald in a loud voice read the proclamation, which told to all the winds of heaven that, "Victoria, by the Grace of God, of the United Kingdom of Great Britain and Ireland, Queen, Defender of the Faith," should henceforth be known also as Empress of India.

The reading done, the Royal standard was raised, cannon thundered a salute, the band struck up "God save the Queen," and a deafening cheer broke upon the quiet air, as the people of India acclaimed Victoria, Kaisar-i-Hind.

Two hundred and seventy-seven years before, a few sober London merchants had gathered to discuss the price of pepper, and had resolved to adventure in a voyage to the East. Little did they foresee that from that resolve would grow a great Empire, which should be gradually pieced together, like the parts of the huge puzzle, until nearly the whole of the vast peninsula, which was to them an unknown land, should be brought under the sway of a Queen, to whose power and greatness that of their own good Queen Bess would be as the pale light of the moon to the golden shining of the sun.

LIST OF KINGS AND GOVENORS

RULERS OF BRITAIN.		RULERS OF INDIA.	
		GOVERNORS-GENERAL.	
George III., . . .	1760	Warren Hastings, . .	1772 to 1785
		Sir John Macpherson (temporary), . . .	1785 ,, 1786
		Marquess Cornwallis, . .	1786 ,, 1793
		Sir John Shore, . . .	1793 ,, 1798
		Sir Alured Clarke (temporary), ...	1798
		Marquess Wellesley, . .	1798 ,, 1805
		Marquess Cornwallis (second time ten weeks only), .	1805
		Sir George Barlow (temporary), ...	1805 ,, 1807
		Earl of Minto, . . .	1807 ,, 1813
George IV., . . .	1820	Marquess of Hastings, . .	1813 ,, 1823
		Mr. John Adam (temporary),	1823
		Earl Amherst, . . .	1823 ,, 1828
		Mr. Butterworth Bayley (temporary), . . .	1828
William IV., . . .	1830	Lord William Bentinck, .	1828 ,, 1835
		Lord Metcalfe, . .	1835 ,, 1836
Victoria, . . .	1837	Earl of Auckland, .	1836 ,, 1842
		Earl of Ellenborough, .	1842 ,, 1844
		Viscount Hardinge, .	1844 ,, 1848
		Marquess of Dalhousie, .	1848 ,, 1856
		Earl Canning, . .	1856 ,, 1858
		VICEROYS.	
		Earl Canning, . . .	1858 ,, 1862
		Earl of Elgin, . . .	1862 ,, 1863
		Lord Napier of Magdala (temporary), ...	1863
		Sir William Denison (temporary), . . .	1863 ,, 1864

Rulers of Britain.	Rulers of India.
	Lord Lawrence, . . . 1864 ,, 1869
	Earl of Mayo, . . . 1869 ,, 1872
	Sir John Strachey (temporary), 1872
	Lord Napier of Merchistoun,
	(temporary), . . . 1872
	Earl of Northbrook, . . 1872 ,, 1876
	Earl of Lytton, . . . 1876 ,, 1880
	Marquess of Ripon, . . 1880 ,, 1884
	Marquess of Dufferin and Ava, 1884 ,, 1888
	Marquess of Lansdowne, . 1888 ,, 1894
	Earl of Elgin, . . . 1894 ,, 1899
Edward VII., . . . 1901	Lord Curzon of Kedleston, . 1899 ,, 1905
	Earl of Minto, . . . 1905

CPSIA information can be obtained
at www.ICGtesting.com
Printed in the USA
BVHW060526240120
570268BV00002B/8

9 781925 729801